The Bible Teaching
Commentary on
Genesis

Books by Paul J. Bucknell

Allowing the Bible to speak to our lives today!

Overcoming Anxiety: Finding Peace, Discovering God

Reaching Beyond Mediocrity: Being an Overcomer

The Life Core: Discovering the Heart of Great Training

The Godly Man: When God Touches a Man's Life

Redemption Through the Scriptures

Godly Beginnings for the Family

Principles and Practices of Biblical Parenting

Building a Great Marriage

Christian Premarital Counseling Manual for Counselors

Relational Discipleship: Cross Training

Running the Race: Overcoming Sexual Lusts

The Bible Teaching Commentary on Genesis

Life Transformation: A Monthly Devotional on Romans 12:9-21

The Bible Teaching Commentary on Romans

Book of Romans: Study Questions

Book of Ephesians: Bible Studies

Abiding in Christ: Walking with Jesus

Inductive Bible Studies in Titus

1 Peter Bible Study Questions: Living in a Fallen World.

Take Your Next Step into Ministry

Training Leaders for Ministry

Satan's Four Stations: The Destroyer is Destroyed

Study Questions for Jonah: Understanding the Heart of God

Our Digital Libraries include these books as well as slides, handouts, audio/videos, and much more at: www.foundationsforfreedom.net

The Bible Teaching Commentary on
Genesis

The Book of Foundations

Paul J. Bucknell

The Bible Teaching Commentary Series

The Bible Teaching Commentary on Genesis: The Book of Foundations
By Paul J. Bucknell.

Copyright © 2016 Paul J. Bucknell

ISBN-10: 1-61993-062-5

ISBN-13: 978-1-61993-062-9

Digital edition
ISBN-10: 1-61993-063-6

ISBN-13: 978-1-61993-063-6

www.foundationsforfreedom.net
Pittsburgh, PA 15212 USA

The NASB version is used unless otherwise stated.
New American Standard Bible ©1960, 1995 used by permission, Lockman
Foundation www.lockman.org.

Dedication

God's wisdom streams through the words of this masterpiece of beginnings, Genesis. As I further study this book, I more deeply understand and appreciate the Lord's magnificence and glory.

What an awesome God to worship and learn from!

Hallelujah forever to Him alone!

Appreciation

One of my greatest joys have been the numerous opportunities to lead and teach through Genesis over more than two decades with different awesome teacher teams.

I am grateful, exceeding grateful, for my daughter's work on editing Genesis. Allison Bucknell has kindly taken time in her early publishing career for me and the readers.

Preface

The concepts that arise from Genesis build a fundamental understanding for life, society, and worship. While secular societies have hammered secular and evolutionary ideas into our minds to forge us into a new kind of society, God's powerful truths revealed in Genesis provide the keys to understanding and building a great society and people.

By standing firm on the foundation of God's Word, one can live a strong godly life. After all, where else but in Genesis can one learn about the beginning of the world, the roots of society, the nature of man, the character and purpose of God, the nature of marriage, the development of a personal relationship with God, sin's entrance into society, the nature of temptation, the ins and outs of decision-making, the plot of the devil, key global events that shape the world, and, of course, Christ the Promised One and His redemption?

The Bible Teaching Commentary on Genesis is not only a commentary that tackles the interpretation of hard passages, but serves as a study that persistently seeks insight into the reasons God has recorded each passage for us. For example, why did God only spend a little more than one chapter on the exciting creation story, while providing more than ten chapters on Joseph? These materials have come from many years of personal study and teaching of Genesis. If one wants to build a strong Christian life, it is necessary to include a clear, foundational understanding of the Book of Genesis. Genesis is where it all began, and is the place where changes begin to take form in our lives!

The Bible Teaching Commentary series acts as a useful teaching expository commentary designed to release the power of God's Word into our lives by strengthening our teaching ministries. This series is committed to the belief that the Word of God must shape the disciple's heart and mind (2 Tim 3:16-17) rather than become only an exchange of ideas. Empowered by the conviction that God's Word is true and relevant for every Christian, no matter where they live, we step into the classroom in order to release God's full intention for each passage to each student in the allotted time. Other complementary Genesis digital resources like handouts, audio/videos, and slides can be found in the BFF Old Testament Digital Library.[1]

Rev. Paul J. Bucknell

February 2016

---

[1] http://www.foundationsforfreedom.net/Help/Store/Intros/DLibrary-BibleOT.html

Table of Contents

GENESIS

An Introduction to Genesis

Genesis is a book of foundations.

World cultures and philosophies have consistently attacked the story of God's foundational work from since the first society had been formed (Gen 4:17, 11:4). Today the number of nations have increased, intensifying the warfare against God's work.

The success of a nation or individual depends on the degree to which he bases himself on God's work. "If the foundations are destroyed, what can the righteous do?" (Psalms 11:3) This is why we must build our lives on the commands and teachings of Jesus Christ, who re-established the model for the making of faithful disciples.

A mature disciple, then, by definition, is one who has been able, like Abraham, to step out of his world-shaped culture and build his life by faith in the revealed Word of God. He has been able to reevaluate how he thinks, what he does, and how he responds. The crippled Christian, the backslider, is absorbed in the world-tainted culture.

If one can't discern the world's ways from God's ways, then we must conclude that that person is worldly and ensnared in Satan's temptation.

The more we distinguish God's ways from the world's way, the faster we will grow.

We hope that this walk through the book of Genesis will show you the glory of God's way over man's ways. Though God and His purposes might seem hidden, He reveals His wisdom throughout the many episodes comprising Genesis, which provides us a great opportunity to learn from Him and join others in their walk of faith.

Objectives of this introduction

• Provide two outlines of the Book of Genesis.

• Provide six visual ways Genesis truths are interweaved into the whole Bible.

• Educate readers on the importance of embedding the truths found in Genesis into their lives in order that they might live strong Christian lives.

Our success in life will depend on how closely we build our lives on God's foundation. Genesis is the foundation of foundations.

> He only is my rock and my salvation, My stronghold; I shall not be shaken. On God my salvation and my glory rest; The rock of my strength, my refuge is in God. Trust in Him at all times, O people; Pour out your heart before Him; God is a refuge for us (Psalms 62:5-8).

The Genius of Genesis

How does Genesis fit into the overall scheme of the Bible?

The genius of Genesis is seen both in the way it introduces its material in strategic and clear segments as well as in the way its numerous themes are interwoven throughout the rest of the Bible. These powerful themes counter the faulty suggestions that suggest that

Genesis is a compilation of different accounts or a composite of heavily edited portions.

Genesis is the most foundational book in the scriptures and is rightly described as the 'The Book of Beginnings.' Genesis is the first book of the Law, also known as the Pentateuch or in Hebrew the Torah: the first five books of the Bible that Moses wrote . See Appendix one: Old Testament Books in Chronological Order. We see this position affirmed at the end of Moses' life, where it was written:

> And it came about, when Moses finished writing the words of this law in a book until they were complete, that Moses commanded the Levites who carried the ark of the covenant of the LORD, saying, "Take this book of the law and place it beside the ark of the covenant of the LORD your God, that it may remain there as a witness against you" (Deut 31:24-26).

The Old Testament Hebrew Canon Book Order

We can see how Genesis fits into the wider Old Testament canon with the help of the following chart. The Jews divided the Hebrew scriptures into three different sections: the Law, Prophets, and Psalms (Luke 24:44), otherwise called the Writings.[2]

The greatest purpose of the Old Testament scriptures is to reveal the Messiah, Jesus Christ. Jesus said, "...which were written in the Law of Moses, and the Prophets, and the Psalms concerning Me" (Luke 24:44). The Messiah is pointed toward and hinted at in many places throughout Genesis.

The promised seed born of a woman to defeat the serpent speaks of Christ, and so does Joseph in the way he saves God's chosen people.

---

[2] This three-part categorization can be seen in its entirety in Appendix 2: Old Testament Books in Hebrew Bible Arrangement.

Noah's ark represents salvation from God's judgment in Christ, while Jesus is the means by which God's promise to Abraham was fulfilled. The whole Old Testament points to the Messiah, which has been manifested in Christ Jesus.

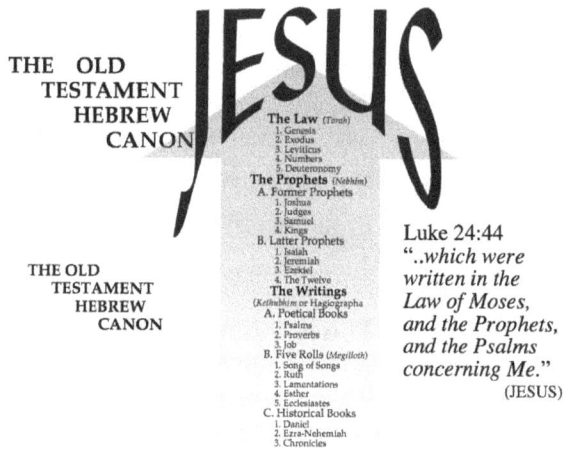

THE OLD TESTAMENT HEBREW CANON

The Law (*Torah*)
1. Genesis
2. Exodus
3. Leviticus
4. Numbers
5. Deuteronomy

The Prophets (*Nebhiim*)
A. Former Prophets
1. Joshua
2. Judges
3. Samuel
4. Kings
B. Latter Prophets
1. Isaiah
2. Jeremiah
3. Ezekiel
4. The Twelve

THE OLD TESTAMENT HEBREW CANON

The Writings
(*Kethubhim* or Hagiographa)
A. Poetical Books
1. Psalms
2. Proverbs
3. Job
B. Five Rolls (*Megilloth*)
1. Song of Songs
2. Ruth
3. Lamentations
4. Esther
5. Ecclesiastes
C. Historical Books
1. Daniel
2. Ezra-Nehemiah
3. Chronicles

Luke 24:44
"*..which were written in the Law of Moses, and the Prophets, and the Psalms concerning Me.*"
(JESUS)

Genesis: Its Reliability and Unity

Demonstration of the Unity of Genesis

Genesis' unity is evident by its clear outlines and interweaving themes. The reliability of the Hebrew Masoretic text (11th century) of Genesis was established with the discovery of the Dead Sea scrolls that were written before the New Testament. Below are two outlines that display the unity of the Book of Genesis.

1. Geographical Outline of Genesis

The three scenes of Genesis help us see the three big stages of God's operations in the early world (see map earlier in the chapter).

Babylonia: Preservation of the Godly Line (chapters 1-11.
    Adam to Noah

Palestine: Provision of God's Promise (chapters 12-36)
>   Abram to Jacob

Egypt: Protection of God's People (chapters 37-50)
>   Joseph and his brothers

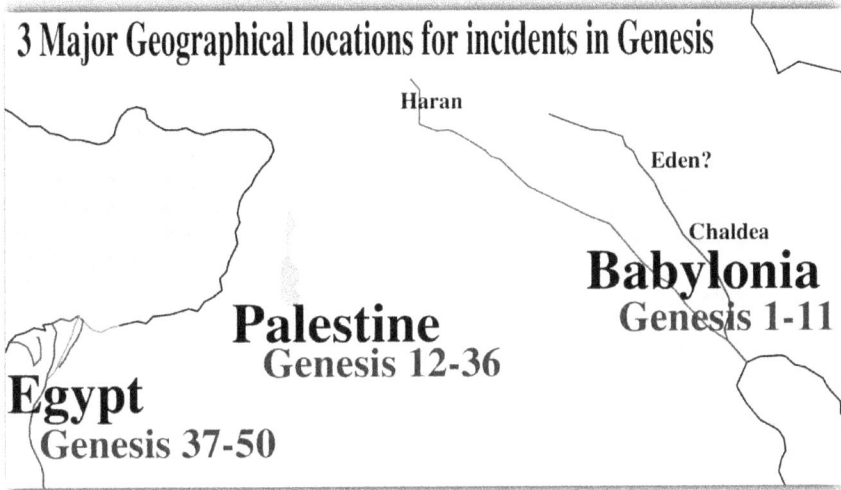

MAP OF GENESIS

2. Genealogical Outline of Genesis

After the prologue where we find the true beginning of all things, we discover ten genealogies, each introduced by the same Hebrew word meaning generation, account, or record (Hebrew - *toledot*).

The most important takeaway from the presentation of these genealogies is the evidence of how God's promise and line of godly seed is passed down. More will be discussed later on when we examine a number of the unifying themes throughout Genesis. When we read different books of the Bible, we will discover the important role that these genealogies have. Most obvious is the way both Matthew and Luke use the genealogical accounts to trace Jesus' descendants. "The book of the genealogy of Jesus Christ, the son of David, the son of Abraham." (Matthew 1:1). "...The son of Enosh, the son of Seth, the son of Adam, the son of God" (Luke 3:38).

Ten Generations

While some will dispute whether the prologue is the first of the records (*toledot* would then end the record), it seems evident that the prologue actually does precede the first record.

#0) Genesis 1:1-2:3 Prologue

In the beginning God created the heavens and the earth (1:1).

#1) Genesis 2:4-4:26 The generations of Heaven and Earth

This is the **account** of the heavens and the earth when they were created, in the day that the LORD God made earth and heaven (2:4).

#2) Genesis 5:1-6:8 The generations of Adam

This is the **book** of the generations of Adam. In the day when God created man, He made him in the likeness of God (5:1).

#3) Genesis 6:9-9:29 The generations of Noah

These are the **records** of the generations of Noah... (6:9).

#4) Genesis 10:1-11:19 The generations of the sons of Noah

Now these are the **records** of the generations of Shem, Ham, and Japheth, the sons of Noah; and sons were born to them after the flood (10:1).

#5) Genesis 11:10-26 The generations of Shem

These are the **records** of the generations of Shem... (11:10).

#6) Genesis 11:27-25:11 The generations of Terah

Now these are the **records** of the generations of Terah... (11:27).

#7) Genesis 25:12-18 The generations of Ishmael

Now these are the **records** of the generations of Ishmael, Abraham's son, whom Hagar the Egyptian, Sarah's maid, bore to Abraham (25:12).

#8) Genesis 25:19-35:29 The generations of Isaac

Now these are the **records** of the generations of Isaac, Abraham's son... (25:19).

#9) Genesis 36:1-37:1 The generations of Esau

Now these are the **records** of the generations of Esau (that is, Edom) (36:1).

#10) Genesis 37:2-50:26 The generations of Jacob

These are the **records** of the generations of Jacob. Joseph... (37:2).

This is an impressive, organized collection of records all with a singular focus: to identify God's redemptive plan through the line of Abraham. God had a message and used Genesis not only to instill crucial knowledge of the past to reveal Himself, but also to plant desires to have His people seek out His greater purposes that stretch beyond the original creation into a new creation.

Themes of Genesis

Genesis can be understood in a variety of ways. Each theme below is common with the others but has different emphases that bring out distinctive aspects of the book of Genesis. Remember, Genesis by definition is 'the beginning.' There is much that follows it. The conclusion of much of the Genesis' imagery introduced here is developed in the Book of Revelation.

Below are only six of many ways the Book of Genesis interweaves itself into both the Holy Bible and into the lives of men and women of the twenty-first century.

GENES

Genesis is coded truth.

Genesis is like the coding of genes, which reveal themselves only after they are fully developed.

In terms of microbiology, Genesis is the gene pool of the truth. It provides the core design into which all other things are shaped. We cannot see the full ramifications of the Garden of Eden, the fall of man, sin, death, birth, Noah's ark, etc. at this point. We can identify the code from Genesis but need time and more revelation in order to reach an understanding of its fully mature state.

PLOT

Genesis carefully introduces characters and situations.

Genesis can be seen as a mystery, in which the plot is incrementally shown. We only get glimpses of it, leaving us with pieces that we can't fully understand; the purpose of this kind of revelation is meant to strike a curiosity within us that will lead us along the path of truth-seeking. We want to read on.

Genesis like a good novel plants subtle plots only to be later disclosed in a climatic and suspenseful way.

Even more interestingly, as we read Genesis, we find that our lives are written in the book itself. We discover that what happens in the book has everything to do with our lives! We must read on.

PROPHECY

With powerful accuracy, Genesis predicts future events.

Genesis is a prophecy. It is the beginning but not the end. We see hints of coming events. We hope for a new garden. We want to see the end of the cursed serpent. We are interested in the 'seed of the woman.' We are interested in Abraham's faith in God's plan and what that would become. We understand that the life of Joseph is a type of the real Savior. Through this, we understand that God has an agenda in history and so it is rightly called "His Story."

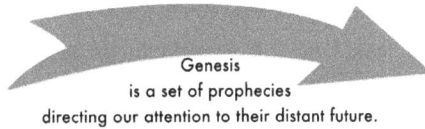

Genesis
is a set of prophecies
directing our attention to their distant future.

HISTORY

Genesis is the key to unlocking ancient and modern history.

Mankind's origins are laid out in Genesis. Blatantly confronting secularism, God says man's roots are founded in God. Man is made for God and by God, and will only find his fulfillment in serving Him.

Genesis is 'His Story' in which He begins to reveal His agenda for man's world in time and space.

Genesis is famous for genealogies. They reveal the history of man with and without God's special grace. Man without God's grace always swerves toward destruction, as is shown in the case of the flood. The only links of hope are found when God reveals His glory and truth to men like Abraham, Isaac, and Jacob. These lives became important threads in the redemptive plan of salvation.

SEEDS

Genesis is the ground on which the seeds of life and truth are scattered.

Just as the nature of a seed later reveals itself as a full-grown plant, so the seeds of truth have been carefully inserted into Genesis so that their fulfillment will be seen in yet another age.

Genesis, like a package of seeds, provides the right start allowing life to fulfill the Lord's purposes.

The garden, river, man's walk with God, the creation of Eve, the uniting of man and woman, the exposure to evil, etc. all powerfully reveal themselves in their full grown up manifestations.[3]

FOUNDATIONS

Genesis provides a theological and moral framework that we can build our lives upon.

Genesis is like the foundation of a tall tower of wisdom upon which to safely build our lives.

Genesis guides us into asking foundational questions regarding life for which we can find in the scriptures satisfactory answers. We might not get a full understanding of life in Genesis alone, but we will get the foundation we need in order to build a solid understanding of life. This is true of all the major truths of scripture.

Consequently, without the truths of Genesis instilled in us, we will develop poor foundations that will not stand the test of hardship. Genesis speaks of origins, marriage, relationships, good, evil, etc., and creates the right categories in our mind so that the truth can be easily sought, assembled, and established.

"If the foundations are destroyed, what can the righteous do?" (Psalms 11:3). The hope of becoming a strong people led by God depends on how actively we discipline the shaping of our concepts, worldview, expectations, and values from the words found in Genesis.

The Success of Our Lives

The success of our lives depends upon the foundation on which we build our lives. The decisions we frame our lives around greatly influence

---

[3] *Redemption Through the Scriptures* powerfully presents the biblical development of these and many more themes wrapped up in God's redemptive plan.
www.foundationsforfreedom.net/Help/Store/Intros/Redemption-RTS.html

what happens in our lives, whether it be regarding our person, family, society, or job.

Most people on earth do not have this insight into the way of life. They think man should just live the way he wants to, that is, according to his lusts or desires. Societies would fall apart in no time if there were no societal rules, but no one wants things to get so bad that they can't enjoy their own sin.

Genesis presents an enlightening aspect when it states that man was good when created. We observe this from just a few words in the text. Human beings did not ascend from dumb apes but quickly declined into moral lapse.

As the Christian culture withers away in various places, society is rightly questioning what they believe, and is searching for what it should believe. Genesis gives us a place to start this search.

The name 'Genesis' literally means beginning. It is the beginning of understanding. Looking at it in another way, Genesis helps us by asking the right questions so that we look for the right answers. We should not try to find a fulfilled life separate from God (e.g. divorce) but should live in the presence of God (finding His love great enough to care for our spouse). Many questions are unhelpful because they are not rightly framed. They are not right because they are based on false assumptions.

Practical Exercise: A Survey of the Book of Genesis

Your Foundations

- Think through the foundations laid in your life. Who shaped your thinking? Were these people convinced of scriptural teaching? Have you gone back and examined these areas of your life and rebuilt them on scriptural principles? Explain.

Rebuilding Your Life

- Pick out the weakest aspect of your life, perhaps the one you have the most difficulty handling. These points uncover the cracks in your life foundation.

- After writing down your thoughts or attitudes about the previously chosen weakness, write down the Genesis passages that address that particular topic.

- Lastly, describe a way that you can build a better foundation for that area of your life.

Themes of the Bible

- Pick out one of the images used in Genesis and trace the flow of it through the Bible. You can use one that has or has not been discussed here. An example might be the river of life, city, promised child, etc.

GENESIS

Genesis 1:1-31
The Worship of God the Creator

> • Is all of mankind obligated to worship God? Why or why not?
>
> • Is the non-Christian who never heard of God liable for his knowledge of God? Explain.

Man's perspective of God, the world, and mankind is largely formed from the truths found in Genesis 1-2:3. By studying these major concepts in light of the great works of God, our worship of God will deepen and inspire greater obedience and personal evangelism.

Objectives

· Understand what the scriptures say about the creation of the world.

· Explain why every person is responsible to worship God.

· Give evidence for how a healthy Christian consciously leans upon God for both physical and spiritual needs.

· Recognize God's freedom to use creation to serve His own purposes.

Worship of the Creator

Many attributes of God are clearly embedded in the Genesis creation account: God's power and eternal nature; His love, beauty, and goodness; His order and purposes. No doctrinal statement is as powerful as the record of God's mighty works in Genesis 1. Let's note three special reasons we should worship Him with our whole heart, mind, and soul.

God is our Maker, Designer, and Provider

God is interested in our lives. He desires the increase of blessing in our lives and has created a world to provide for that goal (though it should be noted that this is not God's sole goal). As our Maker, God brought us into existence.

- As our Designer, He has seen through all the details of our lives.

- As our Provider, He provides for all our genuine needs.

Secularism in all its forms of evolution, Marxism, and humanism have no room for God and thus encourage free living without accountability under the eye of a Judge. Genesis 1 shows that, as Maker, the Lord is also Judge. The concepts of accountability, judgment, obedience, design, worship, ownership, and purpose all stem from the concept of a Creator, and is thus highly disputed. What we do with our body and soul determines our eternal state. "The eight works of creation are prompted by ten divine commands and executed on six different days."[4]

Day #1	Created light. Separated light from darkness (4).
Day #2	Created an atmosphere. Waters below separated from waters above. Separated waters from waters (6). Define: Expanse above heaven.

---

[4] Wenham, Gordon J. Genesis. Waco, TX: Word, 1987, p.6.

Day #3	Creation of continent(s) (dry land). Define: Waters called seas; Dry land is earth. Separated waters from land (10). Earth sprouts vegetation/trees with seeds.
Day #4	Created great light (sun) and lesser light (moon). Created stars. Purpose: to give light on earth; to rule (govern) the day and night. to separate light from darkness.
Day #5	Created sea creatures including monsters. God created sky creatures: every winged bird.
Day #6	Created land creatures, walking and crawling. Created man in God's image. Created male and female. Charged them to rule over the sky, seas, and land. God's provision for man and animal alike.
Day #7	God completed the heavens and earth (form) and all their hosts (fill). God rested on 7th day from His work. God blessed and sanctified the 7th day.

God is our Purpose

Man is expected, like the rest of creation, to willingly and completely live in accordance with God's plan. Genesis 1 breaks down the barriers man has put up in efforts to excuse his disobedience in the presentation of how intimately He is involved in our lives. God is not just an abstract thought. He is deeply involved in our lives, which is evidenced by the way He equips us for His mission and then calls us to fulfill His purpose.

Our life's purpose is to conform to His purpose. God's intimate relationship with man is extended much further because of the special way man was made able to communicate with God (more in Genesis 2). God designed man to live according to His will, not against it.

God is our Deliverer

The problem of man's discontent with God's will does not appear until Genesis 3 when man fell and was cast from God's presence. Everything good seemed to have been stripped from him. One would think that being chased from the Garden of Eden and having death hang over their heads would end everything. After all, God did say that man would die.

Instead, we find God providing clothes for man, and we see God making a promise of deliverance. God continued to patiently work with man throughout early history–all to our complete amazement. God's continued forbearance and design to help man in his need comprises the rest of the Genesis records, indeed, even the whole of scriptures.

- Man's greatest knowledge will come from understanding his life in relationship with God's purpose for him.
- Man's greatest peace will come from living in harmony with God's purpose for his life.

The Meaning of Creation

The glorious creation account is a record of God's works. All of it was and remains to be good. "The LORD is good to all, And His mercies are over all His works" (Psalms 145:9).

Wherever we turn, we see the awesome power and design of God. Only in more recent years, thanks to powerful telescopes, satellites, and precise computer-enhanced microscopes, are we beginning to see the true magnificence of His works. All these marvelous designs swirl about our lives, providing more and more evidence of the glory of God.

Five theories that have to do with creation.

(1) Gap Theory

The Gap Theory was a popular teaching back in the 19th Century in Great Britain and America. It proposed that there was a gap between Genesis 1:1 and 1:2. No support has been found for this.

With a little bit of investigation we discover that Genesis 1:1 starts a whole section that carries on through 2:3. Every verse up to 2:3 begins with the same popular Hebrew conjunction (*waw*- see on side) which can mean 'and,' 'but,' then,' 'so,' etc.. Genesis 2:4 starts a new section without that conjunction.

The English versions don't necessarily show this unity because they use different English words for the same Hebrew word. The NASB insists on a more literal translation by starting each segment with a conjunction (e.g. "**And** God called" (1:8), but the NIV departs and does not always start with a conjunction (examples 1:12, 16,17). The KJV alone faithfully repeats the 'And' at the beginning of every verse. We see one unity, one creation. No gaps.

(2) Literal Days

One wonders why so much time is spent in discussion on whether the days in Genesis are true, 24-hour days as we know them or not. There are many today who still deny a literal day. The basic reason these people deny literal days is to escort modern scientific knowledge under the umbrella of Christian teaching. With good motives, they fear that, if that which they discover is not in agreement with the scriptures, they would need to give up their faith. Their faith, however, is weak and inconsistent; their arguments have done much harm to the faith of many believers.

The proponents of non-literal days assert that a day could mean any time period, and in stating this, they are really just trying to fit it into the evolutionary timeframe (even though they do not agree on any other time frame!). During the days of the early 20th Century, evolutionary proponents seemed to have an edge on facts that went contrary to the scriptures, but with further research, we are seeing that truth always supports truth. We should trust God's Word and wait for answers on things that seem incompatible with what God's Word reveals about its awesome Creator.

For example, at one time evolutionists had many believing that man evolved through the clever misuse of different 'link' fossils. Now several of their studies has been proven untrue. The books don't mention those particular transitional fossils like Piltdown man anymore, though they might attempt to use others.[5,6]

About Time

The early church father, Saint Augustine, said about whether there was time before creation, "I know well enough what it is, provided that nobody asks me; but if I am asked what it is and try to explain, I am baffled!"

–St. Augustine

As discoveries have deepened, we have discovered how cells work. The complicated chemical gene structure could not have evolved on its own, unguided. Even evolutionary scientists like Stephen Jay Gould are abandoning the idea of gradual evolution. The cell functions as a wonderful and highly complex, yet efficient, factory that could not have existed by chance.

Others are caught on the geological strata. They are convinced that the aging of the rocks deny God's Word, so they change God's Word. We just don't know enough. Interesting scientific research by Steven Austin shows that the supposed time needed to lay such strata could be done

---

[5] https://evolutionisntscience.wordpress.com/evolution-frauds/

[6] "The fossil record with its abrupt transitions offers no support for gradual change ... All paleontologists know that the fossil record contains precious little in the way of intermediate forms; transitions between major groups are characteristically abrupt." Stephen Jay Gould, The Return of Hopeful Monsters, Natural History 86, 1977, p.22. (http://www.miraclesormagic.com/the-fossil-record-evolution-evidence-creation-science.html)

rather rapidly, and they use Mount St. Helen's volcanic eruption as an example of such a process.[7] His repeatable experiment demonstrates just what we see in our strata today. We simply need more time to understand God's ways; we must not depart from God's Word.[8]

Others are scared or unsure because they think that the scriptures can be taken either way. Let us note the most basic arguments for literal days of creation. The literal days theory is what is presented face value with a normal reading of Genesis. Several defenses of this theory are below:

Usage of the Word Day

The word 'day' most often means a day as we now know it, a short amount of time of daylight with an intervening short period of darkness. A "fifth day" (1:23) or "seventh day" (Ex 20:10,11) are both ordinal numbers. Whenever the ordinal number (i.e., third in contrast to three) is used with day in biblical Hebrew, it always refers to the 24-hour day.

Morning Follows Evening

By regularly mentioning the night and day, the word 'day' is being unarguably and repeatedly described and defined. The Hebrews' day started from the evening to the beginning of the next evening.

> "And there was evening and there was morning, one day" (1:5).
> "And there was evening and there was morning, a second day" (1:8).
> "And there was evening and there was morning, a third day" (1:13).
> "And there was evening and there was morning, a fourth day" (1:19).
> "And there was evening and there was morning, a fifth day" (1:23).
> "And there was evening and there was morning, the sixth day" (1:31).

Some are concerned about the term 'day' being applied before the sun and moon were made. This inconsistency can be easily understood once we allow for the fact that God established the day (time) before the sun

---

[7] http://www.icr.org/article/mt-st-helens-catastrophism/

[8] Oil can be produced from organic material in 20 minutes. Many thin strata layers are now interpreted to have taken days rather than thousand of years.

and moon. He made the sun and moon to govern the day. This concept of light is not a totally foreign scriptural idea.

> And there shall no longer be any night; and they shall not have need of the light of a lamp nor the light of the sun, because the Lord God shall illumine them; and they shall reign forever and ever (Rev 22:5).

The Sabbath Command (Ex 20:8-11)

The first time the Ten Commandments are given in Exodus 20:8-11, they form part of the sanctity covenant where God authoritatively commands His people to keep the sabbath. The pattern is based upon the creation as the following scripture shows us, and makes perfect sense only if there was a literal week of creation. The six days of man's labor is to imitate God's six days: "Remember the sabbath day, to keep it holy. Six days you shall labor and do all your work, but the seventh day is a sabbath of the LORD your God; in it you shall not do any work."

(3) Framework Hypothesis

The Framework Hypothesis interprets the Old Testament scriptures and asserts that the days are not literal days or even time periods but literary markers for assumed poetic and organizational reasons. The markers then form a framework from which we are to understand the whole creation passage. Unfortunately, many of the conclusions drawn from this theory differ from the ones Jesus and others taught. If these words are not presenting what God said and did, then they are not espousing the truth, and instead are leaving traces of falsehood. People misuse such 'intellectual' arguments to counter the scriptures own teaching.

The word family of 'create' (i.e., creation) is preserved for us throughout the whole of God's scriptures, affirming the earth as a genuine creation by God (119 times - search 'creat*'). Jesus didn't suggest that these first chapters were myth inducing vagueness, but clear truth upon which we can base doctrine. For example, Jesus described the nature of marriage in Mark 10:6, "But from the beginning of creation, God made them male and female."

If we deny the Genesis account, we not only have to deny Jesus' words but also the words of other prophets like Isaiah, "Thus says God the LORD, Who created the heavens and stretched them out, Who spread out the earth and its offspring, Who gives breath to the people on it, And spirit to those who walk in it" (Isaiah 42:5). God created the heavens and earth. He actively participated in its creation. These other theories dishonor the Creator and the creation by suggesting they come by chance, and both discredit God's glory and shamefully propel man's wisdom above God's.

(4) Documentary Hypothesis

Although this theory does not directly deny the creation account, it certainly attempts to shape our thoughts of it. This mother of liberalism proposes that the Pentateuch, instead of being God's divine word for man, is a collection of documents written by man and enhanced by redactors (i.e. editors). It is sometimes called JEDP after the four main contributors who have made significant contributions to the Pentateuch. 'J' represents the sections of the Law that use the word Jehovah (Yahweh); "E" for Elohim (God); 'D' for Deuteronomist and 'P' for priests;[9] but summed up they wholly reject Moses' authorship and divine inspiration. This theory has destroyed many people's confidence in God's Word and, to this day, their unbelief in the original place and purpose of God's word can be seen represented in numerous commentaries by the way they approach the books of the Bible.

(5) Modern Science

Modern science is based upon three principles. Interestingly, all three have their origin in, and are consistent with, Christian teachings.

---

[9] This JEDP order originated by Julius Wellhausen.

1. The world is real and the human mind is capable of knowing real nature.

2. The structure of science is based upon cause and effect.

3. Nature is unified.

Important early scientists like Isaac Newton, Robert Boyle, Lord Kelvin, and Michael Faraday depended on these biblical principles to make key advances in science. Today, unbelieving scientists still assume these principles, which originated from the Intelligent Creator, to further their work and make discoveries. Though they do not believe in God, they are not embarrassed to use Biblical concepts in their studies. If only they knew! They are living by faith in God's creation but with ignorance to its Creator. If we have so much confidence in the world God made, maybe we ought to put more trust in the God who made and sustains the universe!

Creation Lessons about God

Our understanding of God, the world, and man largely comes through the Genesis creation account. We are not saying there are no other teachings–there are many, but when we think of the overall picture, Genesis 1:1-2:3 is invaluable to understanding our picture of God. We will look at six lessons:

1. God's Name

Although nothing is directly said of God, we are able to gain an immense understanding through what He did and said. The word 'God' is used 34 times alone in Genesis 1:1-2:3. Some suggest this plural Hebrew word 'Elohim' is used to indicate the Trinity (plurality in unity). Others suggest it is a plural of majesty. The shortened form 'el' is often seen on the end of

Elohim (a transliteration)

אלהים

God, god

אלה

God, mighty one

אל

names such as Joel. No one seriously suggests that one should translate Elohim as gods because every time it appears it takes a singular verb form.[10]

Starting in 2:4, God's personal name, 'LORD' (Yahweh) is used in scripture when speaking of God's personal relationship and fellowship with man.

2. God's Word

God is separate from nature; He is not creation. The universe, the heavens (almost always in plural form) and earth, is something He created. The creation came into existence from God's Word. God spoke, and it came into being. The phrase "Then God said, 'Let…'" occurs eight times; the phrase "God said" occurs ten times.

God spoke and His purpose, design, and provision was made. Although God existed in eternity, God created the universe–everything there is–with a beginning. A whole series of commands uttered from God created matter, time, spiritual entities, order, and change (e.g. moving stars and planets). Pantheism must be rejected; God is not the sum of what exists because He exists beyond it.

Notice how He spoke to man His words of blessing in verses 1:28-29. Psalm 19 takes the same pattern, dividing how God reveals His glory through His works with the specific words of revelation He spoke to man. God warns us of the consequences of disobedience, emphasizing the importance of following God's Words.

Here is a sample of God's Word in action:

Gen 1:3 Then God said, "Let there be light"; and there was light.
Gen 1:6 Then God said, "Let there be an expanse in the midst of the waters, and let it separate the waters from the waters."
Gen 1:9 Then God said, "Let the waters below the heavens be gathered into one place, and let the dry land appear"; and it was so.

---

[10] For example, let's examine the phrase: "they are…" The verb 'are' is not 'is' because of the plural subject. Although Elohim is plural, the subject, unusually takes a single verb form.

Gen 1:11 Then God said, "Let the earth sprout vegetation, plants yielding seed, and fruit trees bearing fruit after their kind, with seed in them, on the earth"; and it was so.

Gen 1:14 Then God said, "Let there be lights in the expanse of the heavens to separate the day from the night, and let them be for signs, and for seasons, and for days and years;

Gen 1:20 Then God said, "Let the waters teem with swarms of living creatures, and let birds fly above the earth in the open expanse of the heavens."

Gen 1:24 Then God said, "Let the earth bring forth living creatures after their kind: cattle and creeping things and beasts of the earth after their kind"; and it was so.

Gen 1:26 Then God said, "Let Us make man in Our image, according to Our likeness; and let them rule over the fish of the sea and over the birds of the sky and over the cattle and over all the earth, and over every creeping thing that creeps on the earth."

Gen 1:28 And God blessed them; and God said to them, "Be fruitful and multiply, and fill the earth, and subdue it; and rule over the fish of the sea and over the birds of the sky, and over every living thing that moves on the earth."

Gen 1:29 Then God said, "Behold, I have given you every plant yielding seed that is on the surface of all the earth, and every tree which has fruit yielding seed; it shall be food for you.

3. God's Thoughts

Five times we see the phrase "God called." He provided a way for us to understand certain things He had made. Once He names something, man is obligated to use His understanding to think of those objects:

Gen 1:5 And God called the light day
Gen 1:5 And the darkness He called night.
Gen 1:8 And God called the expanse heaven.
Gen 1:10 And God called the dry land earth, and the gathering of the waters He called seas.
Gen 1:10 And the gathering of the waters He called seas.

As we believe God's Word, His thoughts become our thoughts. Man is called to shape his thoughts after God's. When we do this, our thoughts, guided by God's word, will guide our actions. We need to note, though, that in 2:19 and 2:23, God gave man the authority and privilege to 'call' the animals their own names. In 2:23, man actually names 'woman.' This granting of authority to name people and objects should caution us to the power and influence of words.

4. God's Power

Nothing should awe us so much as God's ability to do what He says. This is real authority and power. Two words stand out in this Genesis 1:1-2:3 passage: created (*barah*) and made (*'asah*). The first word 'create' gives us the sense of 'out of nothing' while the second, 'made', speaks of form and shaping. This is not so evident until we look at the actual word usage. The more creative-demanding works such as sea monsters and man utilizes the word 'create.' Note the following chart:

Ge 1:1 In the beginning God **created** the heavens and the earth. Ge 1:21 And God **created** the great sea monsters, and every living creature that moves, with which the waters swarmed after their kind, and every winged bird after its kind; and God saw that it was good. Ge 1:27 And God **created** man in His own image, in the image of God He created him; male and female He created them.	Ge 1:7 And God **made** the expanse, and separated the waters which were below the expanse from the waters which were above the expanse; and it was so. Ge 1:16 And God **made** the two great lights, the greater light to govern the day, and the lesser light to govern the night; He made the stars also. Ge 1:25 And God **made** the beasts of the earth after their kind, and the cattle after their kind, and everything that creeps on the ground after its kind... Ge 1:31 And God saw all that He had **made**, and behold, it was very good. ...
Ge 2:3 Then God blessed the seventh day and sanctified it, because in it He rested from all His work which God had **created** and **made**.	

When we begin to understand our mighty God, we should find ourselves humbled that this powerful God would deal so graciously and kindly with His creatures, "The Lord is not slow about His promise, as some count slowness, but is patient toward you, not wishing for any to perish but for all to come to repentance" (2 Pet 3:9).

5. God's Goodness

Seven times the phrase, "God saw that it was good" is used to describe what God thought of His work (Gen 1:4, 10, 12, 18, 21, 25, 31). If what a person produces characterizes his inner self, then we can say with confidence that God is good. God is good because He does good things. He sees His work as that which is absolutely wonderful. Non-Christians confirm this by saying that the only problem with this world is man (the fallen and sinful man). The term 'Mother Nature' for creation insults God's design because it assumes an 'accidental becoming' rather than asserting God's goodness made manifest in its many marvelous and diverse forms, which is why a proper understanding of the creation of the world remains so crucial. If people can see God's goodness in what they see around them, they then might seek Him. Despite the evidence of God's goodness all around us though, we find that this world lies under a curse so that God's goodness is partially hidden from its full glory.

> For the anxious longing of the creation waits eagerly for the revealing of the sons of God for the creation was subjected to futility, not of its own will, but because of Him who subjected it, in hope that the creation itself also will be set free from its slavery to corruption into the freedom of the glory of the children of God (Romans 8:19-21).

Asceticism is the rejection of God's good gifts. Some ascetics have rejected marriage, sex, and certain foods. Instead of thinking that abstinence from things is necessary to be spiritual, God shares this account with us so that we can, in moderation, enjoy His provisions and remember in that enjoyment that God loves to be good to us.

6. God's Wisdom

We must note that God was perfectly satisfied with the whole creation. Everyone has a list of projects for their house or yard in an effort to make it better, but God used the seventh day to rest, not strategize about how He could make the world a better place. The idea of taking a day off because everything is done to its completion is beyond our comprehension. God knew everything was complete. Nothing was lacking. The world and His redemptive plan were set in motion.

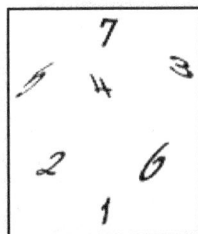

> And by the seventh day God completed His work which He had done; and He rested on the seventh day from all His work which He had done. Then God blessed the seventh day and sanctified it, because in it He rested from all His work which God had created and made (Gen 2:1-3).

God has established a pattern for us, which reminds us that though there is always things to do, we can enjoy the pauses of life. Don't live life in a rush, unwilling to pause and enjoy it, and never operate just as a cog in a machine; we were designed to reflect, enjoy, and worship. We dare not move through a series of seven days without resting for one, for then we violate God's pattern and insist on our work over God's mandated rest.

> Genesis 1, the most amazing composition in all the world's literature, using only 76 different word forms fundamental to all mankind, arranged in a wonderful poetical pattern yet free from any highly colored figures of speech. It provides the perfect opening to God's book and establishes all men really need to know of the facts of creation. No man could have invented it: it is as great a marvel as a plant or a bird. It is God's handwork, sufficient for Hebrew children or Greek thinkers or Latin Christians; for medieval knights or modern scientists or little

children …rich or poor, simple or learned … sufficient for all! Only God could write such a chapter … and He did. (Frederick Filby, professor of Chemistry in England)[11]

This brief study on God, the world, and mankind ought to amaze us, but now we must take what we have learned and apply it to our understanding of religions and philosophies.

---

[11] F. A. Filby in in Creation Revealed.

GENESIS

Genesis 1
Reflections on World's Religions

We have discussed the purpose of the Genesis creation account in our own worship. As a person mixes with people of different religions and persuasions, however, he or she will find that people think differently of God. Let's focus on two issues regarding creation.

Creation: A Polemical Account – A God above gods

First, we want to think through what the ancients might have thought about Genesis. It is proposed that Genesis was written as a defensive treatise for God. In other words, the Genesis creation account was specifically designed to show God's power over the gods of the ancient world. For example, Moses understood the Egyptian's tendency to turn virtually everything created into a god to be revered.

Let's go through the creation account and draw some comparisons. Were they purposed and deliberate or just incidental? The contrasts are fascinating.

One God

In the ancient times before Judaism–aside from God's people, we do not know of monotheism, the acknowledgment of only one God. The ancient cultures were dominated by polytheism (many gods). The introduction of only one God would astound those in the big cities of the ancient world. Today, with Christianity, Islam, and Judaism, we take monotheism for granted, but back then it was a startling suggestion. The creation account is remarkable.

As we read on through the creation account, we can imagine that the objects that are listed as created or made by God were worshiped by people in those times. They worshiped fish, people, the sun, moon, revers, and all kinds of animals. God made every one of those things, however. The creation account in one blow cripples the case for polytheism. The names of the luminaries are perhaps not mentioned because they were names for gods that were then worshipped.

God Unrivaled

God's origin is never mentioned. Everything is said to have come from Him, and thus there are no rivals to His power or authority. The Greeks, for example, believed that the gods came into existence the same time as the world. Genesis teaches that time and matter all come into being at His supreme command and that they, like servants or tools, do whatever He desires.

God is not dependent upon the world, but the world and everything in it, including man, is totally dependent upon Him. He is the self-existing one. Matter is different from God. God is a personal God; He has a will and thus is not some mere encompassing power or force.

God and Man Differences

In the Chaldean myth, we find that after Bel cuts the woman and makes heaven and earth by the two halves, he then cuts his hand and from the drops of blood man is made. Genesis tells us that God creates man from the dust. He is not made from God, but from matter.

In many ancient accounts, man is said to be the slaves of God, whereas in the Biblical account, men are seen as stewards or viceroys of God's world.

> *That they may know that Thou alone, whose name is the LORD, art the Most High over all the earth (Ps 83:18).*

The human being is radically different from any animal because he is made in God's image, which provides:

1. Self-awareness

2. A moral awareness and guide, the conscience

3. Inherent ability (Spirit compatibility) to commune with God

4. Eternal awareness and existence

These were soon lost in their perfect sense, but their functions still continue to distinguish mankind from animals.

Creation, Religions, and Philosophies

How are we to understand God in relation to the many religions and philosophies in the world? When thinking of the major religions of the world, we should remember that there are many variations within every religion. We find several major groupings of belief dependent upon one's view of God/power.

1. Personal God
   (a) Monotheism: God is above the world as Creator.
   (b) Polytheism: Many gods live around the world (idols, animistic).
2. Impersonal god
   (a) Pantheism: god is the world
   (b) A Force: god is the spirit force in the world
   (c) World Soul: god is spirit force - no real world
3) No God (atheists, secularist, certain religious philosophers)

1. God is Above the World

When we try to categorize the different religions of the world, we could begin by discerning whether they acknowledge a Creator or not.

Those that do will mostly be called monotheistic religions, which affirm one true transcendental God who is separate from and in control over the world and man. This includes Judaism, Christianity, and Islam. They all grew from the Hebrew scriptures.

Their worldview generates worship toward this God due to His esteemed greatness, but because God is holy, man must seek reconciliation because of his sin. Compromise is not tolerated; only obedience is accepted. They see the world as God's gift. Unfortunately, many seek a way of reconciliation with God through their own efforts rather than through God's provision in Christ Jesus.

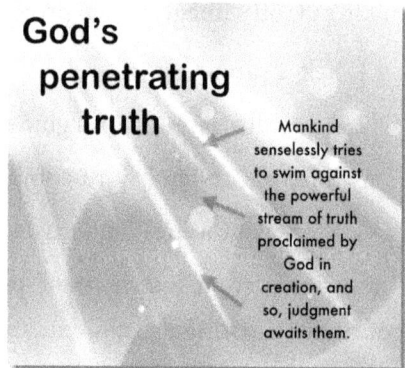

God's penetrating truth

Mankind senselessly tries to swim against the powerful stream of truth proclaimed by God in creation, and so, judgment awaits them.

2. Many Gods

Polytheism associates special godlike spirits with different parts of the world. Sometimes the object is equivocated with the god, or hovers about it. There might be the sun god or tree god. The creation account scoffs at such an image of god as incomprehensible. This idolistic worldview generates fear and suspicion of the world. They are busy trying to appease whatever god that might cause them trouble. Worse yet, they operate in darkness and can only guess at what the problem really is.

Another form of this polytheism is humanism, where man exalts himself as the sole determiner in what he does in life. Again, the God of creation would laugh at a man who dares to claim self-determination. "He it is who reduces rulers to nothing, Who makes the judges of the earth meaningless" (Isaiah 40:23).

3. Impersonal God

Religions such as proper Hinduism or Christian Scientists understand the power of the universe as impersonal, having no nature or will. Man's job is to align himself with this impersonal force.

Many see matter as evil and spirit as good. They want to link their immaterial part (soul) with the Great impersonal Spirit or Force (Hindu *Atman*). Their worldview asks them to reject the world as evil and tends toward asceticism or philosophical religion.

4. No God

A growing group of people deny the very existence of God or gods. Secularism flagrantly denies the supernatural world and instead comes up with the solution of man's problems by political means (e.g. Marxism, communism, socialism), scientific means (science and evolution), or other means (e.g., ecology).

These people live by the religion called humanism, in which man is exalted as the chief. They worship themselves and treat themselves as a god. Psalm 53:1 says, "The fool said in his heart there is no god."

Summary of Man's Responsibility

The world is a stage where man has the opportunity to understand God, which in turn will dictate man's place in the future world. Each person is personally accountable for what he or she does, and it will impact their future. As Maker, God holds man accountable. God is responsible to 'right' all situations as Judge. Man must discern God's purpose for his life and is responsible to follow that purpose.

The Apostle Paul explains in Romans 1:18-21 that the creation provides such a powerful display of God that man is inexcusable for His supposed ignorance of God. God reveals Himself in creation (Romans 1) and man's conscience (Romans 2). Although man tries to prove his irresponsibility toward God's presence and commands, everything fights against him. He suppresses the truth, but it springs up, accusing man for his unwillingness to follow God.

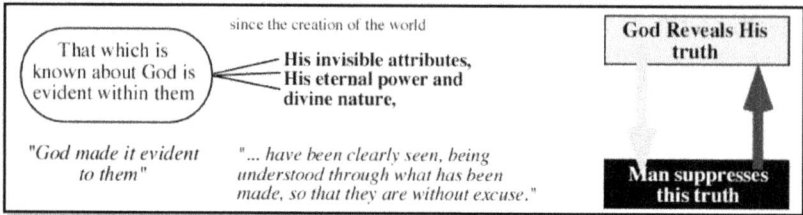

Many people think that if a person does not hear the Gospel of Jesus Christ, then they will not be judged. This is not what Paul taught in Romans. All men, even the ones that never heard the Gospel, are accountable for right behavior before their Maker. Creation constantly echoes its singular call to acknowledge and worship God, making man accountable to God.

Worship at Ground Zero (Gen 1:1-2:3)

God is the Maker of all things and therefore deserves our worship. Real worship is dictated by God's terms and purposes. Worship is doing what God wishes with what He has given to you.

Today, we find man boasting in the ungodly, "Let it all hang out" transparent mentality. They boast in their identification with reality, and sometimes God, by expressing their hearts–the 'real me.' Instead of showing all that we think and feel, it is much wiser to consider what God expects from our lives. He is our Wise Overseer who examines our thoughts and activities. As we seek Him, He will graciously help us live for Him according to His ways.

GENESIS

Genesis 1:27
"Male and Female He Created Them"

> "And God created man in His own image, in the image of God He created him; male and female He created them" (Gen 1:27).

When Satan begins to tamper with a foundational doctrine such as gender, marriage, and family, we should not be surprised when societies start to shake. This chapter on the family is both an attack on common and accepted falsehoods in society today as well as a reinforcement of the right and pure words of God. It is the laying aside of the old self and the renewal of the spirit of our minds (Eph 4:20-24).

If we are really going to understand man as an individual, and accept the family as a basic unit of society regardless of your location, we have to hear God's voice. We must allow God, our designer, to speak.

This argument is simple. I believe in Adam and Eve because Jesus Christ, the Son of God, believed them to be true. The only other real option is a denial of Adam and Eve's existence. Throw out so-called scholarship and interpretations that deny their existence. Those who say such things are using their heart's persuasion to guide them rather than their minds and logic. Mark 10 provides two clear statements from Jesus' mouth:

"But from the beginning of creation, God made them male and female. For this cause a man shall leave his father and mother, and the two shall become one flesh; consequently they are no longer two, but one flesh. What therefore God has joined together, let no man separate" (Mark 10:6-9).

1. Moses wrote this section of Genesis scripture (Mark 10:3), and more equally importantly,

2. This instruction is God's teaching, worthy to base our lives upon.

At one point in our society, many basic truths of God permeated the culture. Families were obedient to God without knowing or recognizing it. Parents were obeyed; teachers respected. Today, however, the society is not supporting God's truth but opposing it. Like Joshua, we all need to affirm within our families that we will consciously live by God's Word for God's glory.

Many people today don't think that there is an essential difference between male and female. They might say our person is in a male or female body, but that's where the differences end. Society now accepts that people can define their own gender by what they feel they are. The scripture, however, teaches us that there is an essential difference between the male and female. This difference directly relates to the roles He has given us. As an evolutionist we should be surprised to find a real difference, but as a creationist we should expect clear differences.

Male and female are unique, and our sexuality is part of our personhood (eg. men and women differ in every cell of their bodies). Simply stated, many people are crying out for fulfillment and self-esteem because they have stripped themselves of the special distinction that God has robed individuals in, in direct association with their sex. Women are told not to be content with womanhood in the traditional sense; men are called oppressors because they are the providers. God instead wants men and women to rejoice in how specially He formed them; this is part of the way He has gifted people for service in their families and the world.

Our inherent male and female sexualities prepare us for the different roles of male or female God gave to us. Both genders were said to have been created in God's image. Each is valuable because they were each endowed with the likeness of God. Each is blessed today as they obey God. Let's observe God's order.

The Uniqueness of Man the Male

What do we observe about man from Genesis 1-3?

Bible's teaching

- God made man first (2:18-22)
  Man is the responsible leader.

- God made man from the soil (2:7 Adam: red).
  Man has an inherent connection with the world.

- God spoke to man (2:16, 18)
  Man is the spiritual leader.

- Man was not complete without the woman (2:18).
  Man is not complete in himself.

- Man's duty was to name the creatures (2:19-20).
  Man is physically responsible and able to rule over world.

- Man named Eve (2:23; 3:20).
  Man is the head of the wife in the marriage relationship.

- Man was to work in the soil (3:17-18).
  One of man's primary roles is in making provisions.

Physical and psychological differences

- "Verbal and spatial abilities in boys tend to be 'packaged' into different hemispheres: the right hemisphere for non-verbal tasks, the left for verbal tasks. But in girls nonverbal and verbal skills are likely to be found on both sides of the brain." Boys are better at manipulating three-dimensional space. They can mentally rotate or fold an object better.

- Boys show early visual superiority.

- Boys have better total body coordination but are poorer at detailed hand activity.

- Different "attentional mechanisms" and react as quickly to inanimate objects as to a person.

- Boys are more curious about exploring their environment.

- Of eleven subtests for psychological measurements in "...the most widely used general intelligence test, only two (digit picture arrangement) reveal similar mean scans for males and females. There are six differences so consistent that the standard battery of this intelligence test now contains a masculinity-femininity index to offset sex-related proficiencies and deficiencies."[12]

- He commits almost all violent crime. This is not only because in brute strength, men are 50% above women, but that men are consistently more aggressive.

- Differing attitude toward the world.

- The man has a closer relationship with the world of things, whereas the woman has a closer link with the world of persons.

- The man's body is equipped for the practical remodeling of the environment (cf. his bone structure and his muscles). His greater ability in abstract and spatial thinking compared with the woman's also allows him to master mentally the world of things, and this provides the intellectual foundation for its practical reordering. While the woman's body is in large measure built for bearing and bringing up children, the man's, as far as bearing and bringing up children are concerned, is equipped simply to enable the all-important but brief moment of generation. The man's

---

[12] Data gathered by Dr. Richard Restak, Neurologist at Georgeton Un. School of Medicine.

existence is obviously not centered on the personal duty of bringing up children.[13]

Application

How desperately we need our men to be men, faithful and loyal. We need men who have been taught of God and are willing to assume leadership in the home, church, and in society. We need men who will responsibly provide for their loved ones, but also to know their responsibility doesn't stop with material goods. A great problem today is that man has retreated from his roles. Men run away from providing for their families physically. Abandonment and divorce. Men run away from leadership by giving no concern to the family needs.

The Uniqueness of Woman the Female

Bible's teaching

What do we observe about woman from Genesis 1-3?

- God made woman second (2:22. 1 Cor 11:8, 12). Women are to follow their husbands rather than lead.

- Eve was made from Adam rather than soil. Women are relationship oriented.

- Woman was made purposely to be a helper for man (2:18). Women are service-oriented.

- Eve was a helper (2:20; 3:16). Wives are to submit to their husband.

- Satan approached and deceived the woman (3:1-6; 1 Tim 2:14). Women are more prone to deceit.

- Eve would bear children (3:15-16). A woman is to help her husband have children.

---

[13] Werner Neuer, Man & Woman in Christian Perspective (Wheaton: Crossway Books), p. 49.

Physical and psychological differences. Nature confirms this.

From Readers Digest, "Is There a Superior Sex?", Jo Durden-Smith and Diane De Simone say:

- In women the left hemisphere of the brain is better developed. Therefore she has better verbal and communication skills and is more sensitive and context-oriented.

- "...From shortly after birth, females are more sensitive to certain types of sounds, particularly to a mother's voice," but also to loud noises.

- Girls have "...more skin sensitivity, particularly in the fingertips, and are more proficient at fine motor performance."

- Girls are more attentive to social contexts–faces, speech patterns, and subtle vocal cues.

- Girls speak sooner, have larger vocabularies, rarely demonstrate speech defects, exceed boys in language abilities, and learn foreign languages more easily.

Men and women are physically different

- The sexes differ in their basal metabolism– that of a woman being normally lower than that of a man.

- They differ in skeletal structure, women having a shorter head, broader face, chin less protruding, shorter legs, and longer trunk.

- A woman has a larger stomach, kidneys, liver, and appendix, and has smaller lungs.

- In functions, women have several very important ones totally lacking in men– menstruation, pregnancy, lactation. All of these influence behavior and feelings. Women have a wider variety of hormones than men. The same gland behaves differently in the two sexes; it also contributes to emotional instability– she laughs and cries more easily.

- Women's blood contains more water (20% fewer red cells). Since these supply oxygen to the body cells, she tires more easily and is more prone to faint. Her constitutional viability is therefore strictly a long-range matter (eg. when the working day in British factories under wartime conditions was increased from 10 to 12 hours, accidents of women increased 150%, of men not at all).

- A woman's heart beats more rapidly (80, vs. 72 for men); blood pressure (10 points lower than man) varies from minute to minute, but she has much less tendency to high blood pressure– at least until after menopause.

- Her vital capacity for breathing power is lower in the 7:10 ratio.

- Holds a differing attitude toward the world.

- "Her body is less fitted for remodeling the environment than for protectively and lovingly arranging her surroundings, which is vital for the well-being and security of mankind. Her body is also well-equipped for motherhood, for carrying, giving birth to, caring for and bringing up children."[14]

- The greater sensitivity of women gives a special degree of empathy with other people's character and needs. The woman has therefore with some justice been called 'Nature's psychologist'. Even young girls show 'a much more refined and developed identification with the situation of others' than young boys do....[15]

Still have doubts? Differences go far beyond conditioning from family influence.

The American Steven Goldberg has demonstrated in a thorough study (described as convincing by the famous anthropologist Margaret Mead) that throughout the world, past and present, there has never existed a society in which the overwhelming majority of key positions in state, industry and society were not

---

[14] Ibid, Werner Neuer, pp. 49-50. (Several from this page).

[15] Ibid, Werner Neuer, pp.49.

occupied by men... Goldberg demonstrates further that in societies past and present the generally dominant conviction is that the man should lead and have authority in marriage, family and society. In fact men, as Margaret Mead, says, 'have always been leaders in public affairs and the final authorities in the home.[16]

Application

Can a woman be a full person apart from her female sexuality? Women need to stop fearing their female nature. While feminists shout that it is not their nature to fit into the traditional roles, they have not only refused to listen to God but also have denied scientific analysis of men and women in the world. We are not talking about capability but design, purpose, and joy. God has spoken clearly. Women were designed primarily for their husbands. They were designed for bearing and raising children (I Tim 2:15 and Tit 2:3-5).

Their Complementary Natures

The couple: Man and woman (*Ish* and *Ishah* –Hebrew).

- Females are chemically and biologically more adapted to child-bearing and raising.

- Males are more chemically and biologically adapted to hunting and providing.

- The great fault of Adam in the fall was his denial of responsibility for spiritual leadership, and instead of submitting to God's command submitting to his wife's leadership. So God begins his sentence 'Because you have listened to the voice of your wife' (Gen 3:17). The sin of Adam therefore consists not just of disobeying god, which is of course decisive, but in the perversion of his created situation vis-à-vis Eve.[17]

---

[16] Ibid, pp. 53-55.

[17] Ibid, Werner Neuer, pp. 38.

- Women - receptivity. Greater ability and willingness to imitate, greater adaptability and suggestibility, greater linguistic aptitude, and her superior capacity to sympathize, which rests on her greater sensitivity to people's expression of feeling.

- Men - spontaneity (self-initiated activity). Greater drive, aggressiveness, creative achievement.

By breaking down sexual differences, the family that incorporates the strongest of relationships is undermined. Only in complementary differences do we find the role of marriage very significant.[18]

Conclusion

The redefining of sexes has hurt us. The more people attempt to redefine the sexes to be two varieties of one rather than two unique sexes, the more our children will be confused as to their own sexuality, responsibility before God, and be willing to accept the notion of homosexuality. Marriage's design will not be able to be understood by them and instead purse self-fulfillment which can never be found.

Reflection

• Do you think birth control has enabled us to redefine man and woman along with their roles and interrelationship?

• Do you think there is a design for the two sexes, male and female along with their associated roles?

---

[18] Ibid.

Genesis 1:28
God's Greater Plan

> And God blessed them; and God said to them, "Be fruitful and multiply, and fill the earth, and subdue it; and rule over the fish of the sea and over the birds of the sky, and over every living thing that moves on the earth" (Gen 1:28).

When Jesus said, "The truth shall set you free," He meant it. The bars that imprison us are lies. For non-Christians, these bars have authority because they live under the evil one's power, but for Christians truth dissolves any lies binding us to sin.

We need to be very careful to uncover lies in our lives and replace them with truth. This step-by-step process frees us to live abundant lives without the bars restraining us. We instead strengthen our lives by surrounding them with beams of truth. The truth becomes our guard. The wise person, Proverbs says, is the one who seeks wisdom, God's truth. Paul calls this process the "renewing of our minds." What one might call it is not as important as that you actually become free from lies.

Realizing this truth has been one of my major objectives in speaking about the family. We have accepted too many lies into our lives, and those lies have affected our society and families:

It is the high duty and privilege of the scientifically trained sex educators, as representatives of society's "best minds", to provide children and their parents with whatever up-to-date information they need to adjust their standards and values. A smooth transition in logic leads to the ordination of the sex educators as the new high priests of the new orthodoxy. No appeal to a higher law is possible for the masses; for there is no higher law than the most up-to-date facts announced by science.[19]

Satan uses some of his best lies to counter the purpose God has given us on earth. Let's look at one main purpose God has given us that is found in Genesis 1:28. It cannot be accomplished by man alone, and neither can they be accomplished by woman alone.

The Truth

- Command: "Be fruitful and multiply, and fill the earth."
  Result: An earth filled with people, friends, company, and families that are capable of sharing, giving, and joy.
- Counterfeit: The fewer the people, the better.
  Result: Lonely, isolated, selfish people with many others murdered.

This is a hot topic. I don't know of anyone who has ever countered the modern thinking that it is better to have fewer than more. Modern thinking quickly answers God's mindset with, "The earth is already filled!" I think we have done very poorly in dealing honestly with this biblical truth. One of the foremost commands is to be fruitful and multiply and to fill the earth, and we are convinced that we are honoring God by thinking how unselfish we are by having a few children, if any. Our mindset for the most part is backwards. Here are some invalid excuses:

• We can't afford children

Did you ever see such a lousy excuse? We are dripping with $100,000 $300,000, or $500,000 homes that are just begging to be filled with

---

[19] Jacqueline R Kasun, The War Against Population, pp.107-108.

children. Your excuse might rotate around the poor but it doesn't for they tend to have more children. What about us, the rich? Do we dare use the excuse of others! Moreover, the facts about the third world culture prove that argument false:

> Output has remarkably outstripped population growth where we have data (from 1960 to 1982 only 12 countries had population growth exceed output growth). 2 have highest per capita incomes in world. The other 10 all had extreme external or civic unrest and pressures.[20] Or why does Taiwan have fives times as dense a population as the mainland and yet have a greater GNP many times. Or S. Korea, Japan, W. Germany, UK, Switzerland or Pennsylvania have higher density of population but increased GNP? Facts don't figure.[21]

Lastly, isn't this argument about putting our trust in money rather than in God, especially when He has so clearly commanded us?

• Too many people

If anyone should be talking, it shouldn't be Americans. We have a good deal of space. It is true we might not always use it wisely, but that doesn't negate the fact that we do have space. I once was talking about the 1.6 million babies murdered each year in this free country and my daughter said, "Daddy, why do they kill them? There is plenty of room all around us." Taiwan has one of the highest density populations (1,393/mile). When we returned to the States in 1990, we were amazed by how much land wasn't being used. But even in Taiwan, there was lots of room.

> We could put the entire world population in the state of Texas and each man, woman and child could be allotted 2,000 square feet (the average home ranges between 1,400 and 1,800 square feet) and the whole rest of the world would be empty.[22]

---

[20] Kasun, p. 64.

[21] Ibid, p. 72.

[22] Mary Pride, *The Way Home: Beyond Feminism, Back to Reality*, p. 62.

• Not enough resources

We don't realize how much garbage we have been fed:

> The much–reported Global 2000 computer model, developed
> under the Carter administration, achieved its gloomy forecast by
> simply assuming, without any basis in fact, that the earth is rapidly
> running out of essential resources....It incorporates the
> assumptions that economic growth depends on the rate of
> investment and the investment cannot keep up with population
> growth.[23]

> The idea of "limits to growth" or the "carrying capacity" of an
> earth with "finite" resources is hardly anything new but dates back
> "to Thomas Malthus' Essay on the Principle of Population (1798),
> which held that the growth of population must inevitably outrun
> the growth of food supply.... though Malthus' forecast has proved
> mistaken–that, in fact, the living standards of the average person
> have reached a level probably unsurpassed in history....[24]

• Negative Effects on the Economy

Now you and I know we do not live for the economy, but let's look
at the facts. Mark Perlman of University of Pittsburgh says, "If we use
anti-natalist programs, we do so for reasons other than those simply
offered by what we as economists now know."[25]

> The well–known development economist P.T. Bauer has
> trenchantly criticized the view that population growth retards
> economic growth. Finding that "rapid population growth has not
> been an obstacle to sustained economic advance either in the
> Third World or in the West", he documents his conclusion with a
> wealth of case studies and statistical evidence gathered from all
> continents.[26]

---

[23] Ibid, p. 54.

[24] Ibid, p. 26.

[25] Ibid, p.55.

[26] Ibid.

The facts are that economies do better with more people. You become more creative, more resourceful, and more economical. A greater number of people would create a greater marketplace. With more people buying products and houses, we would need more jobs. Now, with a decreasing amount of children, many societies are being crushed by a lack of young people to support the society. Dying civilizations no longer need to be proven as they surround us.

Refocusing

But all of these questions and problems are covering up the real problem. We have been convinced that it is better to raise our standards of living than to have children. In other words, it is better to be worldly than to obey God. You probably feel very restless with this whole issue– I hope so! Once we have become self-focused rather than family-focused, we have brought sin into our lives. We have been trying to fulfill God's so-called will our way and not His way. We achieve a distorted perspective as we live in disobedience and believe in lies. Notice how the world has swayed the common person's beliefs:

• Children are a blessing, but we think they are a detriment to our happy lives. So when you get children, if you are ever so blessed, you are sad and live in depression. Instead, you should wake up to God's unique blessing upon your marriage and rejoice!

• Many have so idolized their materialistic lives that they have utilized this overpopulation thinking to sanction abortion, genetic screening, and all sorts of sex education.

Even believers identify what they consider valid reasons for not following God's command to have many children.

- Not wealthy enough: Were not your parents' circumstances growing up more difficult than yours?

- Not capable enough: Can't cope? What about God's grace? Will not God provide grace and strength to care for His children?[27]

God's goal is to create life. Why didn't He just create everyone at the same time or in large groups? He evidently wants to work through us to bring in our own will and distinctive qualities. It would be fair to say that God is pro-life, whereas Satan is pro-death. God wants to fill the world, whereas Satan wants to empty it. God says, children are a blessing, and Satan says children are a bother and burden. Some people wonder whether this command is still in effect today.

The Blessings of the Truth

We have no reason to believe that this command has become any less mandatory than from the beginning. If God at anytime would have thought to modify it, it would have been right after the flood. Man was doing a lot of multiplying but so was evil. God wiped out everyone and everything except that which was on the ark. But when Noah came out, God said to him in Gen 9:6-7, "And as for you, be fruitful and multiply; Populate the earth abundantly and multiply in it."

This Genesis 9 command shoots down the argument that says our society is so evil so that we don't dare bring anyone else into it. That is Satan's voice that instills fear within us. I do acknowledge that at times it will be very difficult for parents, but fear should not rule our lives. Was it not hard for Moses and Jesus' parents? It certainly was.

I wonder why we have so quickly accepted a view of life that differs so radically to Christian morals of the first two millenniums. Birth control became a tool to change the structure of the world to fit their models.

---

[27] In *Principles and Practices of Biblical Parenting* I provide ways to raise a godly family. www.foundationsforfreedom.net/Help/Store/Intros/Biblical_Parenting_Intro.html

Application

- I am concerned about young women today who are not only taught to prepare for a full-time profession but have not been given any training or hope of motherhood. How many cherish the idea of motherhood?

- What about men? We must prepare ourselves for being responsible, hard-working, and caring men. We should see boys becoming men by their early teens. We should see maturity. We should be able to see an understanding of the world, of politics, of religion, of mechanics, of science, and especially of relationships.

- Should we or can we wait? Is birth control wrong? We should think of it like this: If God has given you a gift of speaking or knowledge, is it not wrong to develop it and use it? Marriage gives us the gift of making life (we understand some couples can't have children).

- The greatest means of evangelism and missions is through our families. We should be multiplying, not just adding. Jesus said that life revolves around obedience and love.

Summary

We are on the freedom trail. God has made us free. We are God's children and free to obey Him. It might take faith; yet the state of our faith should be considered if it can't stand up to the challenges the world gives. May we all have the spirit Mary, the mother of Jesus, had when she was notified of a very inconvenient and socially embarrassing pregnancy (Luke 1:36-38). May God grant that we be fruitful and multiply, and fill the earth!

We cannot escape from birth control. Either we are going to try our hand at limiting God's blessings or we are going to open our lives in complete obedience to Him.

Notice how verse 1:28 began, "The Lord blessed them…". We are fools to think that God is trying to keep the best from us when we obey Him. His blessing is a command! When we find ourselves locked in a prison of lies and sin, we should be able to recognize that those bars can no longer hold us back. They didn't hold God back when the Israelites were in Egypt and they must not hold us, those who hear the propaganda machine working day and night, back from God's purpose and vision for the world He created. God means for us to live in hope and obedience.

GENESIS

Genesis 1:28-30
"Subdue it and Rule Over..."

And God blessed them; and God said to them, "Be fruitful and multiply, and fill the earth, and subdue it; and rule over the fish of the sea and over the birds of the sky, and over every living thing that moves on the earth." 29 Then God said, "Behold, I have given you every plant yielding seed that is on the surface of all the earth, and every tree which has fruit yielding seed; it shall be food for you; 30 and to every beast of the earth and to every bird of the sky and to every thing that moves on the earth which has life, I have given every green plant for food"; and it was so (Gen 1:28-30).

Here we find a few of the top reasons for man's existence on earth. The first is to multiply, that is, to have many children. The second command, to subdue the earth, necessitates the first. One cannot subdue the earth without first filling it. Remember, if God desires order and purpose, Satan's goal is to confuse our roles and functions. God has already signed your name up for a job. Let's look at this important command:

- Truth: "…Subdue it; and rule over the fish of the sea and over the birds of the sky, and over every living thing that moves on the earth…."
  - Result: A cared for world. Food. Prosperity. Hard work. Creativity. Order among man. A green world. Research. Hope. Management control.

- Counterfeit: Be subject to the world; be constrained by her (e.g. extreme environmentalists, naturalists).

  - Result: Chaos. Ignorance. Strained relationships. Empty stomachs. War. Government waste. Pollution. Being passive and constrained. Earth worship. Anti-tech.

I would first like to share with you some ways mankind is expected to think about God, and then follow that with a discussion of the actual command and its application for today.

The Commander (Gen 1:26-28)

It is interesting how a person can read these first chapters of Genesis and not really think about the implications for their own lives.

Sensitive to His Wishes

We must first discuss God who gave the command. God handed the keys over to us, but we are responsible to God to subdue and rule in the way He would have us. The earth is not ours; we are His stewards and overseers, not the rulers of this earth. As His managers we must use the resources wisely to produce that which is consistent with His character and purpose. Our rule over animals is the same. We ourselves are to subdue and rule, and yet we are here to do the owner's wishes. He even gave us permission to eat and consume His resources. However, whatever we do must be done with respect to the purpose and intent of His will.

For example, consider how foolish the notion is that a leader's morals have nothing to do with his leadership. Don't trust those who say such things; either they are deluded or protecting their selfish expression. Theodore Morris–the great merchant, lawyer, and planter from Pennsylvania who drafted the final version of the Constitution said:

Liberty and justice simply cannot be had apart from the gracious influences of a righteous people. A righteous people simply cannot exist apart from the aspiration to liberty and justice. The Christian religion and its incumbent morality is tied to the cause of freedom with a Gordian knot; loose one from the other and both are sent asunder.[28]

Able to Provide

Another point that sets the context of our responsibility is the fact that God has given us all that we need. Provision is expected. God is not like the CEO of a manufacturing company who demands we produce without supplying the resources necessary to create those productions. We expect to find what we need in order to live, and we live in hope because God has provided well for us, which is contrary to how the world lives or thinks today. These ideas can be summarized into two points:

1. God has provided all that we need, and

2. God has given creativity and understanding to use what He has given to us to respond to our needs and provide for them.

The earth is a tool to be used, resources to be carved up, material to be fashioned. We must not treat the earth as though it were divine or part of God or part of ourselves. People have begun to describe humans as leeches sucking life from the earth. People are hurting "Mother Gaius." Read this PBS religious ad and consider what it has to say about the earth:

Since life began, Earth and the creatures upon it have shared an intricate relationship.... In a controversial hypothesis, James Lovelock and Lynn Margulis have extended this understanding to include the proposition that Earth can best be understood as a living being, actively regulating her chemical cycles to maintain conditions suitable for life. Lovelock, a British chemist, named his

---

[28] The Blood, Grant, p. 109.

hypothesis Gaia in honor of Ge, a Greek Earth goddess also commemorated by the words geography and geology.[29]

False • Too many people?   Not enough resources?

When we begin to think of our lives as dependent on the earth, we will not think of ourselves as dependent upon the Lord. I understand the necessity of a friendly environment for us to live in. We know our bodies have been made from the earth and that to the earth they will return (Gen 3:19). The cell consists of matter; it is chiefly composed of carbon with hydrogen, nitrogen, and sulfur. We are not denying our dependence upon the earth, but we must be sure that this dependency does not have a final say about how we live our lives.

1. Our lives should not be wholly centered in the maintenance of our bodies. To say that our lives are completely wrapped up in this body is wrong. Life and death are descriptive states of the relationship man has or hasn't with God, the Creator. There is a heaven; there is a hell. Life goes on beyond this world.

2. Our bodily lives are not 100% dependent upon Gaia's breath, as one would often hear. In the scriptures, we find that God can somehow modify circumstances: a bush that has flames but does not burn; Shadrach, Meshach, and Abednego are thrown into a fire, but were not harmed; Enoch suddenly was not; a basketful of bread and fish feed five thousand. Also, consider how the Israelites' shoes didn't wear out in the desert over the forty years they wandered.

3. Our bodies will be transformed. This earth is unsuitable for them, and in them we cannot accomplish God's full will here and now. God raised Jesus, and will likewise raise us all (Jn 5:29).

4. We are dependent primarily upon God for life rather than the mothership earth. God is the giver and sustainer of life. If we acknowledge that this power belongs to our environment, we are

---

[29] The Miracle Planet, PBS, p. 99.

committing blatant idolatry as well as denying the divinity of God, the author of life.

We must choose by which philosophy or religion we will live. Those who confess the Lord live in faith and hope that He has provided well for us. We believe, "Seek first the kingdom of God and all these things shall be added unto you" (Matt 6:33). Those who live in idolatry will live in fear and deprivation. They will grab and hurt to protect their lives. This is the motivation behind the birth control and death control propaganda. They are very clearly linked to two teachings.

The first is centered on the belief that there is a scarcity of sufficient resources for everyone. They must make sure that their quality of life is not threatened by the number of other lives.

The second teaching is very close to the first one. It is sometimes found in particular philosophies such as genocide, but more generally, it is simply the assumption that your life is more important than any other life. It is pride's most ugly face. It expresses itself in hatred. They say, "We tolerate you just so you believe what I believe and affirm my pride."

We are finding that these prejudices and fears controlling more and more people. It might be the neo-Nazis in Germany who feared the foreigners, especially the Jews who encroached on their jobs and economy. (In fact, typical low income immigrants have by a large proportion only taken the jobs the natives don't want.) Or it might be the Americans who panic every time they hear of Japanese imports. Or of the whites fearing the blacks, or blacks the whites who are clearly distinguished by insecurity, selfishness, laziness, and, most problematic, excessiveness due to fear.

- God wants us to be convinced about the sanctity of life.
- God wants us to love sharing our resources.
- God wants us to hope and trust Him.
- God wants us to have children, love children.

When a person or nation abandons the worship of God, they become restless. Peace and order no longer rule their lives. Selfishness grows and giving decreases. Instead of peace, war increases because people are living off of lies. People become self-focused, more concerned with killing off children and older people than working hard to provide for them. Laws built on lies are passed. Dangers of abortions to mothers, the use of the RU pill, or the use of the most detestable 'experiments' and the Kinsey reports on sex, which have been proven false, are utilized to convince and manipulate.

Application

- How foolish it is to think that man can eat food and have the needed clothes without being thankful to God (1 Tim 4:4-5). We claim it is our hard work that got us the food on our tables, but that is a ridiculous and ignorant statement about God's provision of the resources it takes to care for one's life.

- The truth is, "There is no peace for the wicked" (Is 48:22). When we reject God, we are no long able to live confidently that there are sufficient resources to do His will. Instead, we become preoccupied with watching out for number one: ourself. The true environmentalist is one who worships God and respects His commands.

The Command (Gen 1:28-30)

It's best to look at this command as having two essential components: subdue and rule.

Subdue the earth

Subdue the earth, don't be subject to it. By carefully utilizing the earth's resources, we can express God's glory. The word 'subdue' means to "bring into bondage, keep under, force."

> "The verb and its derivative occur fifteen times in the OT. ... In the OT it means 'to make to serve, by force if necessary.' Despite recent interpretations of Gen 1:28 that have tried to make

"subdue" mean a responsibility or building up, it is obvious from an overall study of the word's usage that this is not so. *kābash* assumes that the party being subdued is hostile to the subduer, necessitating some sort of coercion if the subduing is to take place.... Therefore "subdue" in Gen 1:28 implies that creation will not do man's bidding gladly or easily and that man must now bring creation into submission by main strength. It is not to rule man." [30]

We must actually subdue the earth.

The earth is the setting. Man and woman's duty is to make sure that God's will is implemented on the earth. The resources are ours; the animals can be used though not abused. Whether the resources be plants or coal mines, they have been given to us to utilize to glorify our God.

We must go and subdue the earth in a positive way. It is not easy; anyone who has tackled the job of farmer to make corn, cucumbers, or flowers knows this. The potential is there, but it takes hard work.

Application

The world places fear into our lives, but we need the Lord to cleanse it from us to go forth in faith, fighting all sorts of challenges. We are content with living our lives, but the truly godly man must begin to see that his duty goes beyond his four walls, into society.

Rule over the living creature

Rule over the living, don't let them rule you. Don't live in fear of them. There is a clear purpose for the animals that God has given us. They have been provided so that we are able to shape the earth and its environment so that we can fully utilize it. A free pony is not necessarily the best pony. The Lord prepared the earth for us, and He wants to see us make a good impact upon it.

---

[30] Theological Wordbook of the Old Testament, Vol 1, p. 430.

Rule: a specialized meaning is "to tread." However, the second meaning "to rule" is used some 22 times in the OT. Generally *rädä* is limited to human rather than divine dominion (Ps 110:2). It is used to refer to the rule of Israel over its enemies (Is 14:2), and of the Gentile nations' rule over subject peoples (Is 14:6).[31]

Many of us do not understand the importance of the animal world. We merely think of a zoo or aquarium or pets. However, for thousands of years, the world depended upon animals for their livelihood whether it be because of their strength, edibility, endurance, or transportation potential. They could do things or provide things for man that man couldn't accomplish himself. God gave us a charge to rule over them.

It is by ruling that we state our belief in God. By ruling we understand that we are implementing God's rule on earth. God wants us to be fascinated by what He has for us. Ruling over the creatures does not mean abuse, but a proper respect for them. Our profit margin should not give us room to waste, whether it be an animal or a tree. We need to be careful how we use their bodies in experiments or even in eating. Gen 9:3 clearly states that after the flood, man could then also eat animals.

You might ask, "What about man ruling man?" This is not discussed in this verse, but even if man is to rule over man, and it certainly is valid regarding governments (Rom 13:1), it must be in deference to the real King. If God is at any point stripped from man's government, it becomes profane and has become an idol.

Solutions to the environmental crisis are not going to come through idolizing the earth or by recognizing the planet as our mother. This is abominable and believers must defy these attempts to cause us to live by fear and falsehood. Whenever man puts God out of the picture, we will no longer live to the glory of God, but only for our own comfort and ease.

---

[31] Theological Wordbook of the Old Testament, Vol 2, p.833.

Man doesn't want to work

In contrast to this "subdue and rule" idea, we have seen an evil philosophy come among us. This 'all-nature' philosophy adapted from the 60s, and earlier from Rousseau, is most easily seen in the way man treats his work. He lives today for rest rather than for work. Entertainment is escape rather than reordering the universe as God has called us. The virtues of discipline, hard work, and fun for the sake of learning are largely lost in the sea of humanism.

> Work did not bring dignity to the individual, but the individual brought dignity to the work. Along with the work ethic went the principle of discipline and responsibility practiced by the family.[32]

Why, then, should we work? Let's look at Colson's summary:

- Because work gives expression to our creative gifts and thus fulfills our need for meaning and purpose.

- Because work is intrinsically good when done with the proper attitude and motive.

- Because we are commanded to exercise stewardship over the earth, participating in the work of Creation in a way that glorifies God.

- Because we are citizens of this earth and have certain responsibilities to our fellow citizens. If we don't live according to God's way, then we will live our way.[33]

Application

Our society is wrongly rewarding the lazy, undisciplined, and criminals. But reward perhaps is the wrong word; we are torturing them. We are giving them things they have not earned. Let the homeless work, and let us provide for mothers who care for their children. But our

---

[32] Why America, p. 152 by Ken Wessner.

[33] Charles Colson, (Random House Press, 1991. p. 178.

economical set up is creating problems seemingly unparalleled in the past. The crown of cities have become garbage dumps of human beings.

Summary

Notice how verse 1:28 began, "the Lord blessed them … ." We are fools to think that God is trying to keep the best from us when we obey Him. His blessing is a command! "Why doesn't America work? Because for too long too many of us have waited for someone else to do something. Change starts with us."[34]

The Christian has every reason to continue researching the world and tapping its resources beyond the command to do so. The Christian believes that it is perfectly sufficient for man's livelihood. We can send packets of information at terrific speeds. We have machines that imitate man's bodily actions. If anything, we must confess that we have explored far too little; we have not subdued the earth.

The Great Commission is just an extension of the great command to subdue and rule the earth. It recognizes that evil has dominated the world, but also that Christ has broken the spell. Those who believe in Christ are developing His kingdom on earth. God intended for the Israelites to implement His rule on earth, but now this is being done through the church as God's people live by His Word.

---

[34] Ibid, p. 179.

GENESIS

Genesis 2:1-17
Between God and Man

Genesis 2:4-17 defines how man's relationship with God should function. In it, we see God's desire to maintain an intimate relationship with man, which in turn becomes man's supreme purpose in life. Meaning in life comes from fulfilling the design God has for us.

Why not make robots instead?

Or just all animals?

Wouldn't life be easier or better without man?

Robots and People and Design

Now that robots have become popular, we can more clearly see why God made people instead of robots. After all, He could have made perfect robots that didn't have their own opinions or the ability to reject His. They would always do what He told them to! But God chose to create humans.

Robots are interesting because they help us understand what God did when He made human beings. Not all robots are mechanical, at least in my thinking. A program is a robot of sorts. It is more like a programmed cell that is dependent on a host. Animals are a kind of robot; they are furry robots! They run on a program that we call instinct. Place them in a certain environment, and they do their thing.

Man is quite different. In fact, with the way that man has messed up the world, we hardly can think why God didn't make robots instead of mankind! When we step from chapter one of creation to chapter two of fellowship, we are forced to step back in unbelief. Why would such a great God associate with man at all, especially on the levels that He does?

When God chose to make man, it was because robots would not do the job. If He wanted man to be loving or creative, then man would have to be given a will. If He created the robot to have a will of its own, then it would no longer be a robot. What would happen if the robot decided to do something on its own that differed from what God wanted? Even worse, what if God gave man the authority and power to this thing called man, and he chose to regularly do something different from what God wanted and serve some other purpose or being?

Intimacy with God brought the greatest happiness to man. The loss of this closeness became the greatest curse.

Let us go through Genesis 2:4-17 and see what the scriptures say about man and his relationship with God, and man's meaning and purpose in life.

Genesis 2:4-17 defines how man's relationship with God should function. We see God's great desire to hold an intimate relationship with man, which in turn becomes man's ultimate purpose in life. This relationship is fortified by our complete obedience. Here are four objectives:

- Show the importance of our relationship with God.
- Describe how the relationship between God and man works.
- Encourage each person to have a personal relationship with God through Christ.

- Convince our heart and mind that to maintain a good relationship with God is the most important thing in life and requires repentance as well as obedience and acceptance of His gestures of love.

Genesis 2:4-17 gives us the inside scoop, which we will illustration from the earliest Chinese characters. Don't worry. You will not need to understand Chinese to understand these illustrations!

Let's start with blessing as God does! The Chinese character for blessing (*fu* below), we see that God with man in the garden becomes the standard for blessing (notice the meaning of parts of the character). Our purpose after the fall, then, is to recover the greatest of all blessing.

福

The Chinese character (fu) for happiness and blessing. God and man in the garden together is blessing!

礻　一　口　田　福

| God | One | Person | Garden, field | Blessing |

God creates the kingdom before He forms man. Environmentalists might wonder whether it is moral to say that the world was made for man; they fear man's abuse because of his sin. God, however, charged man to watch over His creation.

The Preparation of the Earth (Gen 2:1-4)

1 Thus the heavens and the earth were completed, and all their hosts. 2 And by the seventh day God completed His work which He had done; and He rested on the seventh day from all His work which He had done. 3 Then God blessed the seventh day and sanctified it, because in it He rested from all His work which God had created and made. This is the account of the heavens and the earth when they were created, in the day that the LORD God made earth and heaven. (Gen 2:1-4).

Genesis 2:1-3

Genesis 2:4 initiates the first of a series of <u>ten genealogical units that unify the Book of Genesis</u> by use of a common introduction. Most of them are marked by the words, "These are the records of...." The NASB version is confusing because it does not consistently use the same translation of the same Hebrew word (*toledot*) as the NIV does.

God first prepared the universe (heavens and earth) (Gen 2:4), then readied man's habitat (Gen 2:5-6). Just as in chapter 1, chapter 2 points to the creation of man. Everything is made for man. Man, however, is made for God. Man is dependent upon God because he is part of creation, just as a child is dependent upon his parents. These ten sections provide a continuum of life and purpose, each depending on the previous one. This second section establishes man's dependence upon God as stated in Genesis 1:26.

> This is the book of the generations of Adam. In the day when God created man, He made him in the likeness of God. He created them male and female, and He blessed them and named them Man in the day when they were created (Gen 5:1, 2).

> The son of Enosh, the son of Seth, the son of Adam, the son of God (Luke 3:38).

The 'heavens and earth' refers the whole creation, the huge framework in which man lives. Today, in the western world, we call this the universe. One can debate this interpretation and instead claim that the heavens to mean merely the atmosphere, but this would limit its meaning. The earth and heaven used later in the verse show that these concepts, the universe and atmosphere, merge together to mean all that exists.[35]

---

[35] The 'heavens and the earth' necessarily includes the visible and invisible. For example, dark matter is invisible to us and yet it comprises a great part of the universe (68%).

God's Name

God's name is first used in
Genesis 2 in conjunction with His
title 'God.' Genesis 2:4 says, "LORD
God" (lit. Yahweh Elohim). Genesis

> *And God said to Moses, 'I AM WHO I AM'; and He said, "Thus you shall say to the sons of Israel, 'I AM has sent me to you.'" (Exodus 3:14).*

1 only used 'God' (lit. Elohim). When we look at Genesis 2, we discover
that the name for God is used over and over. God is intimately
acquainted with the details of what He was doing. He surely is not a
faraway or 'hands off' God.

The two terms are at first put together in this account (2:4) to make sure
there was no confusion that they were not two different identities.
'LORD' is the poor English translation for God's Name, Yahweh. Some
people out of respect add vowels to His Name and form the word
Jehovah. This Name is never to be said irreverently or even casually (Ex
20:7). As we continue on in this section, we will discover that God uses
His Name when He speaks of fellowship with man. This was not needed
in chapter 1 where He was presented as the Creator.

Documentary Hypothesis - really?

Some teachers have wrongly interpreted the varying usage of the
terms 'God' and 'Lord God' in Genesis 1 and 2. Higher critics used this
observation to misdirect a whole generation of Bible students by
convincing them that Genesis was written by different authors (and
editors), a fact that was detectable by the terms they used for God.

More credibly, the use of God's personal name in chapter two highlights
the change of focus. God is no longer acting as a great Creator, but as
the developer of man with whom He will relate. When relating with
others, we use names. We should expect the introduction of God's
personal name in chapter two. The genealogical outline in chapter 1
reveals the unity of Genesis. There was only one author of the Torah,

which is otherwise known as the Pentateuch or the Law of Moses (see Joshua 1:7; John 7:23). That author was Moses.

Day discussions

The use of the word 'day' here is interesting. It seems to mean a period of time rather than a literal 24 hours. Though perhaps, if the account started on the first day, then it could refer to the first literal day. The Hebrew word 'day' (*yom*) can mean a period of time, but it is always used with a limited perspective. The usage is important to some because they derive their argument for a literal six day creation from the word itself.[36] I interpret this meaning from the numbering of days and the reference to 'morning and evening' in its context rather than to press the word to exclusively mean a 24-hour period of time. Importantly, when the word 'day' is used as an ordinate (first day, second day, etc.) it always refers to a 24 hour period.

God's Creation

Of utmost important is the foundational statement that God has made earth and heaven. He has made all things. This observation is important though often overlooked. Everything owes its existence to God.

Nature has been made by God for His own purposes. This is later shown in the scriptures in the way God blesses his people through good weather or causes storms to bring correction or judgment, as can be seen in Noah or Jonah's case.

Man has been made by God for His own purposes. Man is not a ruler to himself. He should not make laws without reference to God. He dare not do anything without first observing what God wants. His roots are in God Himself:

---

[36] To use the NT phrase '1000 years is as a day with the Lord' to redefine the meaning of day is meaningless. This phrase means that time is no hindrance to the accomplishment of God's will, not that 1,000 years is equivalent to one day!

Then God said, "Let Us make man in Our image, according to Our likeness; and let them rule over the fish of the sea and over the birds of the sky and over the cattle and over all the earth, and over every creeping thing that creeps on the earth" (Gen 1:26).

This is will be later reinforced in Genesis 5 and Luke's genealogy[37] where we see Adam is named as the son of God.

The Preparation of the Habitat (Gen 2:5-6)

Now no shrub of the field was yet in the earth, and no plant of the field had yet sprouted, for the LORD God had not sent rain upon the earth; and there was no man to cultivate the ground. But a mist used to rise from the earth and water the whole surface of the ground (Gen 2:5-6).

Every detail the Lord provides about the first habitat is intriguing. Because so little is said, every mentioned detail is significant. God was getting everything ready, but the garden was not 'planted' (verse 8). Genesis 2:5 mentions three things that did not yet exist, even though the earth was prepared for them.

- No shrubs (inedible fruit) on earth yet.
- No plants (grains) had yet sprouted.
- No man to cultivate the ground.

This seems contradictory to what we see in everyday life, so the Lord tells us two good reasons for it!

1. The Lord had not yet sent rain.
2. There was no man (literally 'Adam') to cultivate the ground.

Seeds were provided for the decorative (fruitless) bushes and grains, but were prevented from growing. Some suggest that this is perhaps a precursor to the fall. If man fell from grace, then these plants would be

---

[37] In Luke's Gospel, though, we see Christ as a descendant of Adam and God where the lordship originated. As true man, Christ could obtain the original blessing of rulership or kingship from God. This was Christ's legal right and authority.

needed. For example, because of sin, man would need more substantial grains, but he would have to work hard for it. The male has the strength to care for the fields. "There was no man to cultivate the ground."

Verse 2:6 serves as a pause to allow readers to catch up with what is being said. The readers of Genesis would be familiar with rain. In order not to confuse the readers, the Lord told us how at that time a mist used to rise from the earth and water the ground. Mist, not rain, was used by God to water the ground. Some conclude from this that there was no separation in the cloud cover as of yet. One solid cloud mass protected man and earth and allowed mankind and beasts to live longer as they were better shielded from the dangerous rays of the sun. This state of the earth would change with the flood; after the flood, the age of man suddenly declined.

Summary

This is the world God readied for mankind because He had a purpose for all of this creation. Before introducing the game, He introduced the pieces. Moving forward, He will give a more detailed introduction of man and how He made him. This will help us understand how mankind functions and how he should relate to God in those functions. If we are going to find the meaning of life, we need to understand more about him. This is why the following passages play an important part in the process.

Creation of Man (Gen 2:7, 1:26-27)

> Then the LORD God formed man of dust from the ground, and breathed into his nostrils the breath of life; and man became a living being (Gen 2:7).

Here in Genesis 2:7 we actually gain insight into how Adam was formed. Let's note some particular facts.

Yahweh God made man

Man did not make or 'invent' God. God invented man, from dust. Man did not have an existence outside of God's creative purposes. Man did not exist before the time when God made him. Man and creation are totally and constantly reliant upon God's grace. Man's life should focus on what God's purposes are for him. Only here will man find true happiness.

Genesis 1:1-2:3 does not use this Name because God's almighty power in creation was displayed. The covenantal Name is used when we see God interacting closely with man, like in 2:4 , starting with the discussion of the Garden of Eden.

Breath of life

Man was made a living soul from the ground. The Chinese character for 'first' comes from a description of the first person made from dust. It is composed of a stroke symbolizing life and combined with the characters for ground and person. Adam then is the first ANCESTOR (lit. first to have life–*syan sheng*), made from the ground into a living soul in God's image.[38]

God breathed into man's nostrils the breath of life. Life is from God; He has the right to give and take. Life is the animation of the body. In 1:20-21 there are living creatures. Breath is life. Because of the advances in science, we know how our breath brings oxygen into our bodies and how important a part it plays in the proper function of all the cells. But is there more significance to this breathing? Does it set man apart from the other creations in the garden? Is it through this breathing that man was made in God's image? We are not sure. We only can conclude that God, through the formation of and breath He gave, made man what he is today.

---

[38] The idea for many of these Chinese characters came from the book "The Discovery of Genesis" by C.H. Kang and Ethel Nelson (Concordia).

The whole air-dependent system provides a good challenge for evolutionists to consider. God says He first made man and then breathed life into Him. This is much more credible than the idea of chance having developed the respiratory system, once we understand the unbelievable complexity of man's body.

God 'formed' man

The verb 'form' (2:7,8,19) is different from 'create' and speaks of a special aspect of God's shaping of man. Creation speaks of the general process while forming the specific details. God carefully formed man using existing substances (chemicals in the soil).

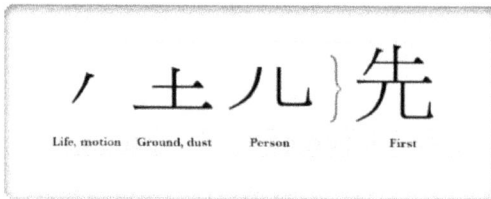

ノ　土　ノㄥ ｝先

Life, motion　Ground, dust　Person　　First

Man did not arrive on the scene by accident, but by design. Contrary to what evolutionists believed, the more advanced scientific research wonderfully pronounces the perfect design of the creation. The cell was formerly thought to be a mysterious compound of material called protoplasm. The cell, we now know, is an intensely complex manufacturing plant that could not have come about by accident–even the most simple cell. Today's evolutionary theory is evolving to accommodate 'sudden' and radical development closer to the creation model.

Those considering to adopt the evolution of man run into a host of unsolvable questions, especially if they profess to hold to the integrity of God's Word. Was Adam a real man? Did God lie about how He made him? Who was God talking to in the garden? Who fell? Who was the son of God (i.e. Adam) and how was man made in the image of God?

If there was no Adam, then there could be no woman; how else can one explain woman's creation? They couldn't evolve together. Humankind would have died out in one generation if they had not been made simultaneously. God clearly says man was made from dust, which leaves no room for belief in evolutionary descent from a humanoid. Not one of those earlier questions can be answered by evolution. The only question is whether one believes God's word or the myths of evolution. We should not be scared of evolution, even when its advocates appear to speak with such authority. The discovery of the design of living things is shaking evolutionary theories, but because it is embedded into the religion of materialism, it is held in belief without evidence to support it.

Man came from the dust

Even though Adam was created in the image of God, man is a fragile creature wholly depending on his environment creature. God's origins are not spoken of because He is eternal. He was before and after time; time exists outside Him.

Man's roots, however, are from the ground. The Hebrew word for man is almost the same word as ground. They both come from the common root of 'red' (red-colored earth). 'Adam' is simply a transliteration (i.e. pronunciation) of the Hebrew word. Below are Chinese characters that connect God's word with the creation of man, as well as his roots from the ground. The Chinese character below for 'speak' joins the character representing the breath that God gave man and the ground from which he was made.

God made both a walking and speaking creature!

Because of sin, our earthly natures must remain here (die). From dust to dust. We should not be surprised to see that the chemicals in man and other animals are similar. Our humble frame leaves no room for pride.

田　力　} 男

Field　　Strength　　Male

The Image of God

> Then the LORD God formed man of dust from the ground, and breathed into his nostrils the breath of life; and man became a living being (Gen 2:7).

Life is not equivalent to our physical lives. God breathed into man's nostrils the breath of life and so the first life came forth. Life is the animation of the body (Genesis 1:20-21 speaks of living creatures).

Life comes from spirit, the same Hebrew and Greek word for breath and air. The soul is the real person; the body is the needed 'shell' through which it can live. Man is a combination of the physical and spiritual. Although man can exist without his human body for a short time (after death before judgment), without a soul there is no existence. Man's soul is a direct result of being made in the image of God.

There are many very long discussions as to what the image of God means. The phrase comes from chapter 1.

> Then God said, "Let Us make man **in Our image, according to Our likeness**; and let them rule over the fish of the sea and over the birds of the sky and over the cattle and over all the earth, and over every creeping thing that creeps on the earth." And God created man in His own image, in the image of God He created him; male and female He created them (Gen 1:26,27).

The word 'image' is repeated several times for emphasis. Furthermore,

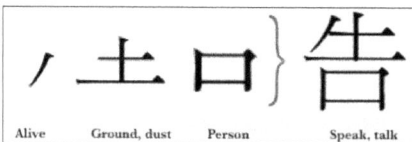

ノ	土	口	} 告
Alive	Ground, dust	Person	Speak, talk

the scripture clearly states that both male and female were made in God's image (27). Man and woman were both made in God's likeness, and it is evident that this likeness enables him to rule over the earth with his reason and will.

Outward Image

God is a spirit and does not have a body like man. The similarity to God, then, seems to refer to man's inner makeup. It is possible that an outward likeness of God was seen in the cloak of light, God's glory, that surrounded man. After man fell, he recognized his nakedness. His glory was taken from him. It seems then, that before the fall man was clothed with light, in the same way that God makes Himself manifest.

The following verses make a special connection between the glory (light) of God and the image of man.

> For a man ought not to have his head covered, since he is the image and glory of God; but the woman is the glory of man (1 Corinthians 11:7).

> O LORD my God, Thou art very great; Thou art clothed with splendor and majesty, Covering Thyself with light as with a cloak (Psalms 104:1,2).

God's glory shone upon Moses after he met with God on Mt. Sinai. Moses had to cover his face to hide that glory. We saw the same thing with Jesus, Moses, and Elijah during the transfiguration. Note the Chinese characters that seem to indicate man's original 'clothing' to be God's glorious light.

Notice how fire-light comes from man. Man inherently had this glory. Nakedness is the flame thrown down from the body. Could it be that man wore light before he fell, and that this marked God's image on man? Nakedness was only felt

人 火 榮 赤
Man   Fire   Glory   Naked

丷丨丿 一 丿乚 光
Flames   One   Person   Light

after the fall, and therefore the need for clothing. People argue that naked is natural, but something happened to man when he fell that made him feel naked, or incomplete. If his covering was not the light of God's glory, then it needs to be something else. But God is light, and because man was made in God's image, he must, at one time, have been covered with that light.[39]

Inward Image

Man's nature and person sets him apart from other creatures. It is interesting that those who state that man evolved are often the ones that deny an immaterial part (the soul) of man. But it is precisely this immaterial part that sets him apart from animals. This immaterial part is partially what enables man to have a relationship with God. He can listen, observe and obey God. Man is conscious of God's values because he was made in His image. The two main purposes God had in making man in His own image was to relate to Him and work with Him in caring for the world. Here are a few special characteristics that set man apart from animals:

- A sense of a higher being (worship and God-consciousness).
- Self-awareness (connected with memory).
- Concern for moral values (sense of justice connected with conscience).
- Possesses a will (associated with abstract reasoning).
- Creative (makes tools, art, etc.).
- Concern about the future (aware and concerned about life after death).

Because mankind is made in the image of God, they are accountable to God for the way they respond to Him. When man disobeys, there are consequences that influence his ability to relate to God. Man is called to exercise his will to complete what God sets before him. Man's sense of fulfillment is based on finding what God has for him and doing it.

---

[39] The scriptures do not state that man had a covering of light before the fall. It does seem to make a lot of sense as we draw clues from the scriptures. The Chinese characters are used for illustration rather than proof.

> *Thy kingdom come. Thy will be done,*
> *On earth as it is in heaven (Mat 6:10).*

Those that deny the existence of God need to realize that being able to understand the difference between right and wrong, and to comprehend the notion of a greater being has huge implications on their choices. This is the reason many modern philosophies so virulently argue against biblical christianity.

✦ **Ethical Questions: When does life start and end?**

There are different suggestions as to when a person's life starts, but the Christian community reasonably seems to have reached the conclusion that life begins at or near conception. Life comes with creation, the fertilized egg. We know in fact that embryos obtain their breath through their mothers for the first nine months until birth, where they are finally released to the world to breathe on their own.

Adam and Eve's life started differently than ours. All but these two came from a mother's womb, including Jesus Christ. But man is more than a body. He has that immaterial part of him, a soul. Adam became a living creature after God formed him from the dust and breathed air into his nostrils.

Our hearts are sad to think of the millions of children in America and across the globe who have been killed because of the incongruous argument that life only begins outside the womb. This is doubly true when we consider how each child should have begun his or her life by being embraced in the context of love. Life is cheaply valued because human beings are, by many, no longer considered to be made in God's image.

✦ **Ethical Questions: What about cloning?**

Cloning is the duplication of life through the replication of cells rather than through the creation of a cell through the normal means of sex, pregnancy, and birth.

The attempt to produce life outside of normal marriages is clearly wrong and immoral because man is countering God's design. Cloning parts of the DNA should not be a problem, but it is wrong when it comes to the creation of new life.[40] Instead of focusing on what kind of child we are trying to form, we should understand what God instructed us to do and why.

There is a reason God made man and woman to be born from parents. Whenever we step away from God's instructions, we step into immorality. We don't have to understand why it is wrong. If God told us to do it one way, then we can assume doing it any other way is wrong unless a special provision is given.

Creating people through fornication is wrong because it is not within the confines of marriage. Adultery breaks the bondage of marriage. In either case, the couple is not committed to each other for life and therefore do not truly love one other. If a person has a child because of passionate desires, then one can be sure that the child will not gain the love it needs.

By contemplating the cloning of life, our society is stepping into very treacherous waters. God did not tell us to multiply this way. If fornicators have children through unprincipled desires, then what is the motivation for cloning human beings? Is it mere curiosity, or do people want a supply of medical parts or sex partners? Or are we looking for alternate cheap labor? Or cheap soldiers? After all, they would belong to the owner. We are purposely running back into the days of slavery. Those who foster such immoral plans, should be locked up and their labs destroyed.

---

[40] The replication of any cell parts should clearly be debated, but for space sake and focus, I largely focus on the duplication of life as a whole unit rather than the individual tiny parts for it counters God's means of giving life and should by all means be avoided.

Everyone thinks about their own needs. No one thinks of the children.

Having children should only be thought of in the context of a normal marriage. There the child is born in love and will receive all the love, protection, and instruction that he or she needs for life.

The Purpose for Creating Man (Gen 2:8-17)

> And the LORD God planted a garden toward the east, in Eden; and there He placed the man whom He had formed. And out of the ground the LORD God caused to grow every tree that is pleasing to the sight and good for food; the tree of life also in the midst of the garden, and the tree of the knowledge of good and evil (Gen 2:8-9).

> Now a river flowed out of Eden to water the garden; and from there it divided and became four rivers. The name of the first is Pishon; it flows around the whole land of Havilah, where there is gold. And the gold of that land is good; the bdellium and the onyx stone are there. And the name of the second river is Gihon; it flows around the whole land of Cush. And the name of the third river is Tigris; it flows east of Assyria. And the fourth river is the Euphrates (Gen 2:10-14).

The Garden of Eden (Gen 2:8-14)

God did not create a garden, but 'planted' one. Note, however, that the garden is not Eden. The garden was in the eastern section of Eden (toward the rising sun). Eden was not itself a garden, but a fairly large district. The Hebrew word '*Eden*' means pleasure or delicacy. If Eden was pleasurable, the garden must have been exquisite. From the creation of this special garden, we can discover the intensity with which God our Father wants us to enjoy what He has made.

I have always been surprised at the time that is taken to describe the rivers. Only one verse is used to describe man's creation (2:7), but five are used to describe the rivers. Is there a hidden message here?

One river flowed out from Eden. Either it was a spring that came from the ground within the garden or a tall mountain stream that flowed down through the garden. Once the river reached the center of the garden, it divided itself into what became four huge rivers, which would necessitate a huge garden. A few of the names given for the rivers are familiar to us, others are not. We suspect, due to their size, that they are the same. The other rivers must have been changed due to the flood.

- River #1 was Pishon: flows around Havilah where there is gold, bedllium, and onyx stone.

- River #2 was Gihon: flows around Cush (Ethiopia)[41]

- River #3 was Tigris: flows east of Assyria

- River #4 was Euphrates.

There are two Chinese characters for garden. One describes the garden above with its four rivers. The other describes the garden's occupants.

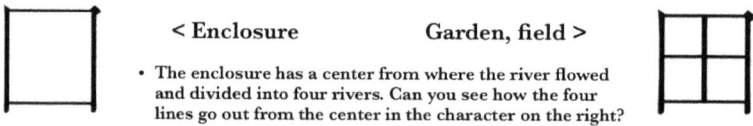

< Enclosure   Garden, field >

- The enclosure has a center from where the river flowed and divided into four rivers. Can you see how the four lines go out from the center in the character on the right?

A second Chinese word for garden describes those who lived there: only two people. God spoke and formed man from the ground. Eve, the second person, came from the side.

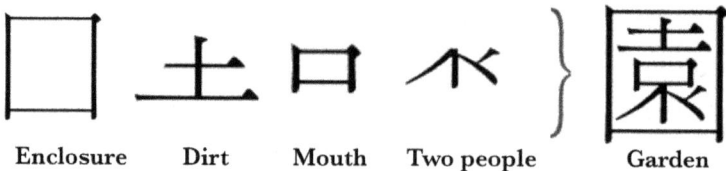

| Enclosure | Dirt | Mouth | Two people | Garden |

So perhaps the whole of Eden was in a lofty place, but the garden was at a lower plateau where the rivers would gain more momentum as they flowed on out of Eden to the other parts of the world. Because of the location of the Tigris and Euphrates Rivers, we assume this land was

41 Perhaps the Abay River that surrounded old Ethiopia.

near the present day rivers. The whole land of Eden seemed central; all the known world was centered around it–perhaps it was the location of Jerusalem.

This one initial river flowing from God's new paradise stands for the blessing that came from God and would bring enriching provisions to the world. One can see how the Garden could seem like the throne of the world subjected to a higher throne in heaven reflected in Revelation 21-22. This thought of God's divine blessing flowing to earth from His throne above is very common in scripture (see Psalm 65:9-13). "And he showed me a river of the water of life, clear as crystal, coming from the throne of God and of the Lamb" (Revelation 22:1).

Adam's Calling (2:15)

> Then the LORD God took the man and put him into the garden of Eden to cultivate it and keep it (Gen 2:15).

Man was not originally in the garden. God made man and then the garden. After the garden was made, God placed man there. We can't live in the new home until it is finished!

- Man was charged to do two things:
  1. Cultivate the garden: implies the growing of crops.
  2. Keep the garden: manage so that it stays ordered.

Adam was charged to keep the garden because God wanted him to. There is no other ifs or buts about it. In the end, we are to serve God faithfully. We should always keep in mind that the point of our work is to serve God and not base our faithfulness on whether our boss is kind, gives good bonuses, or fringe benefits.

Adam was God's steward. He was charged to manage God's resources. We likewise are to be duty conscious. In the end, we only work on what God has given us to do. Whether in a high-rise office or on a farm, an owner or hired hand, the situation remains the same: We are always working for God.

Adam's Command (2:16-17)

> And the LORD God commanded the man, saying, "From any tree of the garden you may eat freely; but from the tree of the knowledge of good and evil you shall not eat, for in the day that you eat from it you shall surely die" (Gen 2:16-17).

Ownership

All trees are God's trees. How gracious He is to welcome us to eat from them. The trees in 'our yards', however, still belong to him. We are stewards. Man wants to claim things as his own when in fact those things belong to God. Perhaps our greed for property would change if we knew we were creating more responsibility for ourselves to keep God's big yard.

The Lord is generous to us. This is God's goodness, and we ought to be good to others in response. God does not ask man to first earn his reward by obedience and service but provides more than he needs, as is evident in the number of trees Adam could have eaten from. Clearly, the image of God here is not a boss but a father. We are part of His family.

Accountable

God had already commissioned Adam to cultivate the garden; he was not created to laze around. Heaven will not be an eternity of doing nothing! Sometimes we think we are not doing many significant things, but what we don't realize is that we are getting trained for something important, bigger. This is the case here. A small area was given to Adam to test him.

> He who is faithful in a very little thing is faithful also in much; and he who is unrighteous in a very little thing is unrighteous also in much. If therefore you have not been faithful in the use of unrighteous mammon, who will entrust the true riches to you? And if you have not been faithful in the use of that which is another's, who will give you that which is your own? (Luke 16:10-12)

Choice

God gave man a lot of choices. Adam had many kinds of fruit to eat from. In verse 2:16, God clearly points out the vastness of Adam's choices. "From any tree of the garden you may eat freely." Diversity brings extra satisfaction and knowledge that God really has thought about man's needs and wants, because He loves him.

木木
Two Trees

'Any tree' is also symbolic of the choices we have in life. Let's pause here to think of the great abundance of things that God gives to us. He made this world to provide these good things. Man was not required to first do this or that to show his worthiness to receive such things; they were his to enjoy! We can even see how the task to cultivate and keep (before the hard labor came in) was designed to enable man to further enjoy the good things God has given him. We need not only be thankful; we should cultivate a faithful and thankful heart.

Boundaries

God gave man a responsibility to refrain from eating from the "tree of the knowledge of good and evil." As much as modern man detests boundaries and limitations, God made them an essential part of Adam's life from the start. Man must trust the wisdom of God's commandments.

The commands in 2:16-17 are very different from the instructions in keeping the garden. This command includes both general guidelines as well as a prohibition. This was the test of their faithfulness and compliance.

There is also a prohibition. After creating many trees, God forbade man from only one thing: to not eat from one tree. "But from the tree of the knowledge of good and evil you shall not eat, for in the day that you eat from it you shall surely die" (Gen 2:17). God did not try to trick man. The tree was clearly placed so that man would not accidentally eat from it. Along with the prohibition came a warning of the dire consequences if he were to eat from that tree. God spoke clearly: if man ate from the tree, he would surely die. The Chinese word for 'forbid' below derives from two trees on top and the character for 'decide' underneath them. What a remarkable connection to God's first prohibition!

Modern man cannot tolerate the thought that man should be restrained from any one decision. They pride themselves in being able to discern good and evil, and to make the best choices through that discernment. We think we know how to rightly evaluate decisions. We can't understand why God would forbid us to eat from this tree or force us in our decisions. We tend to put more confidence on our decisions than the ones God makes for us. Do we really need to know and experience things to make the best decisions?

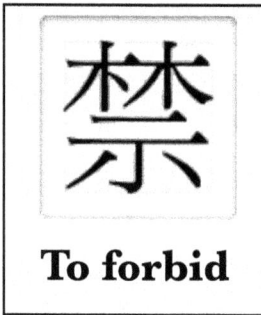

禁

To forbid

Ethics of Two Trees

People ask a number of tough questions regarding God's purpose in placing the tree of knowledge of good and evil in the garden. God could have chosen to put the tree somewhere else, but instead He deliberately put the tree in the garden in tandem with His prohibition.

- Could the garden still be perfect with the tree's existence?
- Could man be content without eating from this tree?
- Why did God put that tree there?

What was man's knowledge like when God formed him?

Adam did not know good and evil as God did (Gen 3:22). God desired to keep Adam innocent of this knowledge, at least for a period of time, and perhaps forever. He, however, knew the consequence of eating from that one tree ("you shall surely die"). That was sufficient knowledge to direct Adam and Eve's choices.

How did eating the forbidden fruit change man?

When Adam sinned, he not only found out the difference between good and evil, but also became acquainted with evil. His world fell apart. His judgment became skewed. Knowledge became tainted with corrupt desires, which corrupted his future choices and life.

The prohibition was a window of opportunity. Man had a chance to show himself faithful; he was not tempted beyond what he could handle. In fact, if anything, everything was geared in such a way to help man choose to be faithful. God created many, many trees, all of which were good. Only one, not fifty percent, was off limits.

We, likewise, need to practice this kind of choice each day, many times. We have opportunities to follow or not follow Christ. We can obey God in those choices or disobey Him. Some things have become so ingrained in our lives, like reading and meditating on God's Word, that we no longer think of the issue of obedience. But it is. It is also the important link to doing more.

When a Christian faces temptation, he is much more like Adam than an unbeliever compelled by the old nature. We have overcome the evil one through Christ, and we have the Spirit of God through which we can obey. Satan tries to fool us and make us defeated, to believe that God's plan is not the best.

- List a time when you encountered a situation where you faced a test. How did you do? What could have alternately happened? How did it affect your relationship with God?
- Are Christians like Adam before he sinned, that is, morally free? Read Colossians 3:10 and Ephesians 5:8-9.

Reflection on Death

Death is not natural, but a consequence of disobedience. God could have cut man off immediately, but instead He chose to delay judgment. Man chose to serve the serpent and disobey God. The decision on whether to eat, then, is much more than a simple decision of the kind of food to eat, but an immoral one fuly deserving death.

Death does not mean reincarnation. After death comes judgment, and then the afterlife. There is no second chance to determine our future. I suppose we have thousands of chances while we live, but many choose to walk in the dark. This theme is amplified in chapter 3. God used the word 'death' to cultivate a healthy fear of the tree, the fear of God. No religion or philosophy can give a good explanation for death.

Conclusion

Meaning in life comes when we seek to please and glorify God. This is the reason we were made. Happiness in life comes through doing what God wants, not what we want. This is where the world gets it wrong. Meaning in life comes about as we recognize that God made us as humans, not robots, who can grow in their relationship with God. The Lord reached out to mankind when He sent His Son to die for His people so that they could have a close relationship with Him through Jesus' death on the tree.

Joy, contentment, and fulfillment all come from such a relationship. God didn't make man a robot programmed to obey because He wanted to have a close relationship with his creation. He wanted to share His joy in mankind. In chapter 3 we will see what that relationship looked like more clearly.

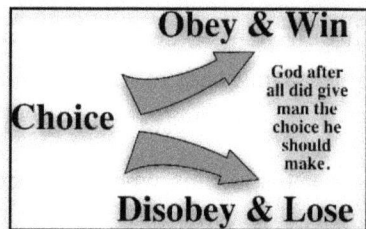

Obey & Win

Choice

God after all did give man the choice he should make.

Disobey & Lose

One legend says that god made man as an afterthought to help care for his own needs, but Genesis is totally different. Unlike the notions of the gods of ancient people, God lived above and beyond the creation. He was before it ever came into being, existing without the earth or the things on the earth. Without effort, He spoke and the universe came into being. Man was deliberately and carefully crafted not to 'help God out', but so that man could reign and work with Him.

God invested so much in man (creation, time, and energy). Anything else would have been much easier (from man's perspective). God, however, wanted man to choose to serve Him of his own free will. God did a lot of things to help man, but man needed to love God from his own heart.

GENESIS

Genesis 2:18
"Not good... to be alone"

Being alone and feeling alone are two different things. If you feel alone, you can have many people around you. You might even be at a party or a big worship service, but as far as you are concerned, you are alone: isolated, no meaningful communication, and no one who can understand you. This is what a person perceives, whether or not it is true. Some people feel like no one loves them, but there are people there who care for them. However, the one who feels alone doesn't perceive that love and shuts themselves off. However, being physically alone certainly does makes one alone. There is no one else there. That person might not have the feelings of a lonely person–left out, no one to share his or her life, no one to talk to, but the fact is that there still remains the isolation and the intangible feelings of loneliness.

- Is this isolation good, bad, or neutral?
- Can being alone be preferable?
- Should I feel guilty about feeling alone?
- What should I pray when I feel alone?

Being Alone in the Beginning

Then the LORD God said, "It is not good for the man to be alone; I will make him a helper suitable for him" (Gen 2:18).

There is no better place to understand what God wants for us than in His Word. Go to the garden. It was God who noticed the loneliness of Adam, and He wanted to point it out to us. He wanted us to know that the creation of more than one person was not accidental, but had to do with His purpose in this universe. I shared several passages on how God Himself had a fellowship built in to His existence. Three persons and yet one Being. When Jesus was on earth, we could see the importance of this communion. And yet, being man, we see that Jesus enjoyed being with people. He had close friends and could easily relate to others.

In the Garden

- Perfect man (Gen 2:7-8;1:31)

- Perfect environment (Gen 2:8-9)

- No sin (Gen 3)

- God's presence (Gen 3:8; 2:16)

We must note that the relationship between God and man was insufficient for Adam. He could have talked with God for eternity, yet his loneliness was considered "not good" (different from not good enough). But Adam's person was not complete (Gen 2:18a)

- To be, exist. Used 3540 times in Biblical Hebrew but very rarely used as a stative verb. But here in its clear description of truth, uses it to affirm how being alone is not good.

- Alone, by itself, apart, besides (*badad*). The core concept is "to be separate and isolated."[42]

Adam perhaps didn't know better, but God saw the aloneness and isolation. Adam had everything, one would think, but it was not good. We read that it was only when God had made male and female that it was declared good.

---

[42] Theological Wordbook of the Old Testament, Vol 1, p. 90.

Man is a social creature. He longs for companionship so deeply that he can say, "I hate you" to someone and yet still want to be with that person. When man is isolated from others, whether physically or emotionally, trouble begins to develop. Man was made for companionship.

> For the first time we encounter something that is not good: man's lack of a corresponding companion. The skies without the luminaries and birds are incomplete. The seas without the fish are incomplete. Without mankind and land animals the earth is incomplete. As a matter of fact, every phenomenon in Gen 1-2, God excepted, is in need of something else to complete it and to enable it to function.[43]

Solitariness of God

One might think it strange that God was the one who noticed this loneliness. But we need to remember that God made us in His image, so our sense of fellowship is something that also has to come from God. We can see indications of this in God's person. God's fellowship is resolved in having three persons. Notice in Genesis 1:26 the "Let us" or in Genesis 2:18 "Elohim". Even if God never made man or any other creature, He would never have been lonely or alone. He is self-contained perfection. He needs nothing. Man does not make Him any more perfect or complete. We might not understand how it all works out in the scriptural teaching regarding God's fellowship in the Trinity, but it is there, and human beings, made in His image, are proof of this.

> II. 2. God hath all life, glory, goodness, blessedness, in and of himself; and is alone in and unto himself all-sufficient, not standing in need of any creatures which he hath made, not deriving any glory from them, but only manifesting his own glory, in, by, unto, and upon them: he is the alone fountain of all being, of whom, through whom, and to whom, are all things; and hath

---

[43] Victor P. Hamilton, *The Book of Genesis, Chapters 1-17*: [NICOT], p. 175.

most sovereign dominion over them, to do by them, for them, or upon them, whatsoever himself pleaseth....[44]

II. 3. In the unity of the Godhead there be three persons, of one substance, power and eternity; God the Father, God the Son, and God the Holy Ghost. The Father is of none, neither begotten nor proceeding; the Son is eternally begotten of the Father; the Holy Ghost eternally proceeding from the Father and the Son.[45]

Two Human Persons

1. Do not have the same substance

2. Exist separate from each other

3. Can exist without each other

Two Divine Persons

1. Have the same substance

2. Exist inseparably

3. Cannot exist without each other

God is full of glory and yet His image can be seen in us in our need for fellowship. The word 'alone' is used of the "Lord's incomparability and uniqueness in his exclusive claim to deity as seen in his extraordinary works (Dt 4:35; 32:12; Job 9:8; Is 44:24; Neh 9:6), or in his splendid exaltation (Ps 72:18; 148:13; Is 2:11, 17)."[46] The Lord alone can be praised and be perfect in Himself. He deserves all praise and honor. Man on the other hand derives from God; all He has is from God. What great things we do or aim to do must be from Him and unto Him.

Application

- Man must not celebrate individualism or selfishness, but instead see them as forms of idolatry. By focusing on ourselves apart from God, we enter the arena of idolatry.

---

[44] G. I. Williamson, The Westminster Confession of Faith: For Study Classes, p. 23.

[45] The Westminster, p. 26.

[46] Theological Wordbook of the Old Testament, Vol 1, p. 90.

- We must resist that type of Christian who finds fellowship with God to be enough, concluding he doesn't need to go to church or meet with other Christians.

Society's Plan to Utilize Loneliness

Aloneness has resulted from the breaking up of the family, the networks of religion, and of society. You can be sure that when God says something is not good, it is not good. Satan wants what God does not want: unholiness. He is so deceived that he thinks his ways are superior to God's. God says it is not good to be alone while man says, "It's okay to be alone," or "It's better to be alone."

- That way you don't have people bothering you.

- That way you don't get hurt when people let you down.

- That way you get richer.

- That way you lessen your obligations to others and become more independent, etc.

Aloneness is not just a result of our poor secular theories but is a means of making us more dependent on others or things. Satan is devising ways for man to be alone to make people dependent on him. Satan delights most in a generation that only listens to his voice rather than the voice of reason and truth.

General Plans

The breakup of the family is deliberate rather than accidental or coincidental in the modern age. This is a great part of Satan's strategy in controlling people and bringing about rebellion against the creator. I'd like to share three examples of his strategy.

The youth culture is his major means of breaking up the family, and is being accomplished through pornography, drugs, and cult worship through video-music. Satan accomplishes his purposes primarily in two ways: 1) Destroying family relationships, and 2) Isolating individuals.

The United Nations wants a brotherhood built on toleration. This is stated and an oft repeated fact. Toleration is superficial, self-oriented, and totally unsatisfactory.

On the other hand, God is building a family nation on love. A family with genuine motives, who are committed and generous. Close relationships foster commitment, and commitment causes deeper relationships and encourages good values. Christ's work was love itself and preached a ministry of reconciliation. He was building bridges and bringing people together (Eph 4:3-7; 11-16; 6:1-9). This focus on family relationships in the Confucian ethic is the reason the Chinese empire stuck together throughout the centuries. A person with Christ's love can genuinely live next to someone who differs from him. If God's love has changed him, then he must put aside racialism, sexism, and nationalism. Christ came to break down the barriers with love.

The world is propagating a cold world. The world is selling substitutes, and unfortunately many of us are buying them. We know how good our families and our church fellowships are, but it's not uncommon that believers remain aloof and uncommitted. We are too easily distracted by the unholy, leaving no contentment to be with God.

God's Intention to Eliminate Loneliness

Someone recently came up to me and mentioned how special it is to know how close God is to us. I was encouraged by this but also scared. God should be your closest 'friend'. A close relationship with God, however, is only a partial answer for our troubled relationships. A good relationship with God can help us find and restore good relationships with others.

In our world of death and trouble we must be realistic; we do not always have this companion—a mate. God will help us through those extra tough times, and there are those necessary substitutes where God becomes the husband of the widow, and the team worker for the single missionary. These, though sufficient, should be considered secondary, not primary, provisions. For example, the single missionary being adopted by some nearby missionary or native family as a member. Marriage is part of God's will for most of us; it is an important part of life. The problem is that many have put off marriage and its concept for the sake of furthering education and job opportunities.

1. Society's leaders are fostering pornography, fornication, and immorality to lessen the acknowledged need for marriage. Society increases the opportunities for people to experience sex without love. The young are made to think sex is marriage's greatest benefit, and if they can have sexual relations without marriage, then all the better. College campuses have become the greatest whore houses the world has ever known.

2. Marriage is being taught as an out-lived and unwanted institution. They compare crummy marriages to glittery immoral relationships on TV, reinforcing the idea that these immoral relationships are fun, while marriages are always breaking up because of trouble. They poke fun at marriage, and they make divorce a morally positive decision. Marriage should instead be held in honor as God's great means of providing the close companion that you need.

3. Society believes and conveys that finding a successful career is more important than finding your life partner. The government is interested in your contribution to society by means of taxes, and being the materialists we are, we must have everything before we get married. Again, we dangerously postpone thoughts of marriage, raising the age of marriage far from where it was.

4. The world's concept of marriage is so secular that it stinks. The world teaches that marriage eventually becomes a mere toleration of each other where loneliness still reigns. However, God designed man to have companionship and so has instituted marriage. The world says 1+1=2; God says 1+1=1.

GENESIS

Genesis 2:18-25
"They shall become one flesh"

Biblical Marriage Raises Godly Children

It might surprise some of you that God would use marriage to typify the glories of heaven and the intimacy Christ would have with His bride, the church. It seems that even Christians have believed the world and blindly accepted the notion that marriage is of human origin, something man devised (follows belief in evolution). Marriage, however, is God-created, not man-created. Marriage stands as a symbol of lifelong satisfaction, security, and intimacy. Order, peace, joy, and love were to characterize that relationship because it reflected the relationship man originally had with God.

After the fall, marriage became a pointer to what God was preparing for man in terms of his relationship with God (Rev 21). Marriage did not come after sin nor as a result of sin wherein man legitimized his control over the woman. That is a lie of the world. Marriage was to be the perfect symbol of intimacy.

Unfortunately, our dreams of marriage have been raped through pornographic flicks. Adolescents' plans for finding a spouse have been replaced with a masturbation. Parents, neighbors, and friends are 'good' only to the point of how it profits their own lives. They worship themselves. We should not be surprised that the speed they enter marriage with self-fulfilling notions is matched only with how fast they exit their marriages. One should not get married to make oneself happy, but to fulfill God's awesome plan for life. In obeying Him, you will receive joy, but that pursuit of joy must not be the ultimate purpose of obedience.

Here are four principles that are needed to make a good marriage as seen in Genesis 2:18-25. God is teaching us the foundation of marriage, simply 1+1=1. Since it is a mystery, God gives us a little of the background in which He hopes we accept its divine character.

The Need For Marriage (Gen 2:18-20)

> 18 Then the LORD God said, "It is not good for the man to be alone; I will make him a helper suitable for him." 19 And out of the ground the LORD God formed every beast of the field and every bird of the sky, and brought them to the man to see what he would call them; and whatever the man called a living creature, that was its name. 20 And the man gave names to all the cattle, and to the birds of the sky, and to every beast of the field, but for Adam there was not found a helper suitable for him. (Gen 2:18-20)

We are born unmarried so that we, like Adam, can realize our need for a mate. Life would have been made so much easier if we were from the start paired off. Even the big mean and tough Gaston in *Beauty and the Beast*, who is selfish and rude, wanted a wife. We can identify with this deep longings for companionship. We accept his desire of gaining one and are aware of this inherent need.

1. God noticed man shouldn't be alone. "It is not good for man to be alone."

2. God made the animals come by in pairs to emphasize the need for a partner.

3. God left him single long enough for him to recognize his need.

Application

- "Is marriage worth it?" some ask. They do not see the need for a helper. If one is single for God's kingdom or because of hard circumstances, that is fine (I Cor 7:6-7). But some think they live beyond the touch of other people. They no longer believe that anyone can bring something special into their lives. This recognition of "I need you" sets the stage for the giving and receiving of love.

- God also wants to come close to you. God wants us to recognize our need for Him. He is so patient, but this does not make Him undesirable of our commitment to Him. Maybe this is why he hates it when we flirt with the world (Jam 4:4). He desires our total love and life.

The Design of Marriage Partners (Gen 2:21-22)

21 So the LORD God caused a deep sleep to fall upon the man, and he slept; then He took one of his ribs, and closed up the flesh at that place. 22 And the LORD God fashioned into a woman the rib which He had taken from the man, and brought her to the man. (Gen 2:21-22)

"You were made for me." The husband is not complete without her. Only together could they multiply and fill the earth.

The feminists are destroying women's lives by encouraging them to prioritize their own rights over their call to serve their husbands, children, and others. They think they are liberating women but instead they are enabling women to be used by man without any legal recourse (e.g. the guy wants the girl to murder their child through abortion). God is the guarantor of freedoms; He makes the life of a human being important, no matter how old one is. In these verses, God has shown what great dignity He has given to the woman in her role.

1. He made woman from man (similar but not alike); she could share and talk with him.

Eve was not taken out of Adam's head to top him, neither out of his feet to be trampled on by him, but out of his side to be equal with him, under his arm to be protected by him, and near his heart to be loved by him.[47]

2. The Lord fashioned both man and woman, but He especially fashioned woman for man (2:20).

3) God brought her to Adam. God designed marriage!

It is through the making of woman, the designing of woman, the order in which He made woman, in the way He brought the woman to man, and finally in the declaration of the marriage in verse 24 that God instituted marriage.

Two important truths:

1. The man is not complete without the woman.

2. The woman was made for the man.

Application

- Problem: Our focus is on ourselves. The world teaches us to see ourselves as individuals and demand our rights within marriage. Marriage, however, holds a mysterious interdependence rather than the independence of two individuals. Even today the adage stands: Behind every good man is a great woman. The purpose is to complement not to compete; to support, not to tear down.

- The church is Christ's bride. How foolish and silly it would be for her to run about doing her own will, thinking that doing this or that will help out. A wise church does exactly as Christ the head has directed, and in this service finds great satisfaction.

Appreciation of Marriage (Gen 2:23)

And the man said, "This is now bone of my bones, And flesh of my flesh; She shall be called Woman, Because she was taken out of Man." (Gen 2:23)

---

[47] Matthew Henry, p.

This is Adam's big, "Thank you!"

1. Recognition: He knew she was the suitable helper he so desperately looked for. The woman is the glory of man (I Cor 11:7b-8). The church is the glory of Christ. As the woman serves man, she brings glory to man; when the church serves Christ, it brings glory to Him.

2. Appreciation: He was happy and appreciated it. The wife complements her husband through her service. The husband should obviously be appreciative of her and thank her!

Application

- God is the source of our solutions. Just as He provided Eve for Adam, He knows our basic needs and cares for them. He knows our aching hearts. The times of transition are the hardest, before marriage, and when one has lost his or her partner. But thankfulness and trust must still ring in our hearts.

- If we don't appreciate what God has done for us in providing a spouse, we will take that one for granted and often abuse him/her. If we don't appreciate the special partner we have, then we will look elsewhere and terribly frustrate the present one. It is interesting to note that Adam does so well what husbands often forget to do: show appreciation to their wives.[48]

The Permanency of Marriage (Gen 2:24-25)

24 For this cause a man shall leave his father and his mother, and shall cleave to his wife; and they shall become one flesh. 25 And the man and his wife were both naked and were not ashamed. (Gen 2:24-25)

Genuine: "And they shall become one flesh" (Gen 2:24).

Result: Harmony, peace, understood role, life loyalty, stable and loved children. "I am part of you." 1+1=1.

---

[48] בנה God <u>built</u> woman from the Adam's rib.
הרטם: (Literally,) <u>This time</u> bone of my bones. rzj: Means help, support; helper.
(Cf. Ps.121:1-2)

Counterfeit: They remain two at heart, keeping their distance.

* Result: Disharmony, fighting, arguing, divorce, loneliness, and unhappiness.

God speaks in Genesis 1:24

1. Marriage is a sacred ritual and will continue on in society. It is a pronouncement, an official statement for which marriage was intended. It is permanent in nature.

2. The two form one unit. The man and woman leave their parents' authority and jurisdiction. The individual marriage continues, "till death do us part." 'Becoming one' steers the couple to work problems out together. The survival of marriage depends on staying as one. The union of bodies speak of an intimate sharing of self called 'oneness'. The sharing of one's body is only the beginning step of a long series of personal revelations. One's intimate life of feelings, emotions, struggles, physical self and victories are all to be shared. Marriage speaks of an official oneness, but it is something that needs to develop and grow if it is to be special and rewarding.

Though we might see the family only as a unit within society, God the creator-designer has challenged us to see it as his intentionally designed unit. It is foundational and considered a norm all across the world only because God has built it into mankind. Several governments have tried to do away with marriage by encouraging divorce, but only found they must come back to stricter standards.[49] Breaking down the family creates chaos and nothing less than chaos, which should be expected if indeed marriage and family are functional units that were built into us, rather than something that is merely convenient in different circumstances. The first stage of attack against marriage, then, worked

---

[49] Earle Cairns says, "Even the Russian Communists, who at first permitted easy divorce, had to tighten laws to protect the family." Earle Cairns, *Christianity Through the Centuries* (USA, Zondervan Press, 1967) p. 496.

on having people accept the identification of two entities within a marriage instead of one, such as in divorce.

• "I belong to you." "I am part of you."

God's math is 1 +1 = 1. Husband and wife are equally important. Each is an essential unit. They complement each other. Without each other they are alone. By looking at man and woman both physically and emotionally, we can see how the puzzle fits together. Put two men or two women together, and you don't have a complement, but a most hated sight in God's eyes. They never have and never will form "one." Remember, "This mystery is great" (Eph 5:32). This kind of math goes beyond what we learn in our schools and yet it is so common that society, culture, and state breakdown when it is violated.

This unity patterned in the Godhead is the fellowship intended for man. The closeness between husband and wife has been specifically designed for intimacy of the greatest kind. The church is to be so caught up in Christ's person, that her will is only to obey Christ.

Challenging Questions for Marriage

What happens when sin hits? Only in the context of a God-designed marriage can we answer the following questions rightly.

• Can a person get a divorce? Is divorce an option?

Jesus said man shall not separate what God has joined together (Matt 19:5-8). The oneness God speaks of obviously should not be broken apart. God has declared them as one through the marriage vows. Only death should break that covenant. They are not two to be broken apart.

• What about trial marriages?

If we see marriage as a manmade custom, then our marriages will fold, along with the strength to meet the challenges that come with marriage. The idea of 'trial marriages' originates with man and lust and ends with a curse. Avoiding the responsibilities of marriage through certain convenient relationships is a poor, unsatisfying choice. Instead of making the commitment to serve each other, they use each other as long as they see fit. They are not living in intimacy because one day the other might say goodbye. They are living as two individuals, best described as 1+1=2. If the trial marriage can never have the experience of a true marriage, then it cannot at all be a true trial marriage, but only an adulterous and wicked affair. God says that all immoral and impure persons will face the wrath of God (Eph 5:3-6).

- What about homosexual marriages?

1 male + 1 male = 2 males; is obviously not one and definitely not marriage. The physical incompatibility reveals this flagrantly contrary to design. But what if I have a homosexual roommate? Transfer out. No one should have to literally live under the tension of sexual attraction.

- What about your marriage?

How determined are you to maintain it? Are you willing to salvage it? You must open your heart to God. God has to be at the top of your list to live out your role properly. Deputy Chief policeman, Bob Vernon, wrote LA Justice, listing five root causes of the riot as they relate to the family:

1. Abandonment of our children. Parents have chosen to gather material wealth over and above the interests of their children. Money cannot substitute for parenting.

2. Hedonism. Pleasure at all costs. Experiences, pursuit of feeling good, and thrills have substituted for loyalty and responsibility. They prefer an affair over their parental responsibilities.

3) Loss of conscience. The real difference in the last 10 years is that the USA is no longer ashamed of wicked behavior. They speak out their perversions. Expressing their lusts fulfills them, in some shallow way, though at the same time that expression destroys marriages and children and society overall.

4) Neglecting principles. Call good, evil and evil, good. We have a complete moral reversal.

5) Arrogant elitism. Politicians aren't interested in the public, in the people, but in themselves and their own interests.

Each of these root causes greatly affects marriages because, though it may not be obvious, each root is breaking down the very foundation of what marriage is.[50] We must be determined to preserve our marriages, but to do this we must do the following:

Be devoted to God. God is the bridegroom and he sets the terms for marriage. He is the authority. We will not allow our hearts to chase after our self-esteem, sexual thrills, money fantasies, or image-worship. We worship God resulting in husbands loving their wives, wives pleasantly submitting to their husbands, and parents consistently disciplining their children in love. Instead of projecting despair, death, divorce, and darkness, our lives will radiate forgiveness, love, hope, and trust. Home will be our haven from the world, a place where we and our children can meet God.

- Order in the home (God-man-woman-children)
- Building up the other (support)
- Appreciate others (kindness)
- Affirm His purpose (have children, display God as people in his likeness, rule over earth through our work)
- Accept differences (gender, habits, skills, etc.)

We must do everything in our effort to preserve our marriages. They are special! Listen to one prisoner speak of his marriage even when he was wrongly separated from his wife and put in jail.

---

[50] Behind the Badge, An interview with Bob Vernon, Assistant police chief in L.A) Focus on the Family, Feb 1993, pp. 2-4.

When pastors were arrested, I sometimes used to think that it must be easiest for those of them who were unmarried. But I did not know then what warmth that radiates from the love of a wife and family can mean in the cold air of imprisonment, and how in just such times of separation, the feeling of belonging together through thick and thin actually grows stronger.[51]

Conclusion

Marriage creates the foundational unit of our society: family, not the individual. We might have hundreds of excuses for neglecting your duties and chasing after your selfish dreams, but God has one call. This call keeps echoing around the world, offering wisdom for its listeners.

- We need each other.
- We were designed to complement each other and so we support each other.
- We need to appreciate each other.

1+1=1, not 2. God through our vows takes a man and woman and makes them one. They are no longer two. As much as they observe God's standards, they will find a beautiful life together.[52]

---

[51] Dietrich Bonhoeffer, *Letters and Papers from Prison*, p. 70.)

[52] My book, "*Building a Great Marriage*" provides many insights for couples to reach that intimacy no matter what troubles a couple may now be facing.
www.foundationsforfreedom.net/Help/Store/Intros/BGMarriage.html

GENESIS

Genesis 3:1-13
The Fall of Man: Temptation and Sin

The importance of this section of scripture is critical to properly understanding the rest of the scriptures. Without knowing about this tragedy that took place in the Garden of Eden, we would have no understanding of temptation, sin, or the redemptive process.

Observations of the Beginning

Everything in the Garden of Eden was perfect–everything that the Lord created was good (Gen 1:31). Here was the world without trouble. Everything was well cared for, and it was a utopia that we all long for. No one would expect that a rebellion or a revolution could be started in a place like the garden of Eden.

Special Relationships

After creating man and woman, God authored and ushered in marriage between one man and one woman (Gen 2:18, 23-25). God established the first and the most intimate of all relationships between Himself and man. God, the creator of the universe and maker of man, set him up as His vice regent over the rest of creation and commanded him to be fruitful and multiply (Gen 1: 28-29). His relationship with man was very personal (Gen 2:4 onwards). God involved man in His own plans and work. We note the presence of three kinds of relationships.

- Unique personal relationship of God with man

- Relationship of man to His wife precede all other human relationships

- Relationship of man to other parts of God's creation under His sovereignty

Man is entirely dependent on God and is called to involve himself in the assignments that God has given to him. Man, however, is not a robot that merely takes and carries out the Lord's instructions. Man's free will requires him to carefully exercise his will through God's loving guidance and strength to accomplish His assigned work. A specific example of God's guidance/word is seen in Genesis 2:16-17.

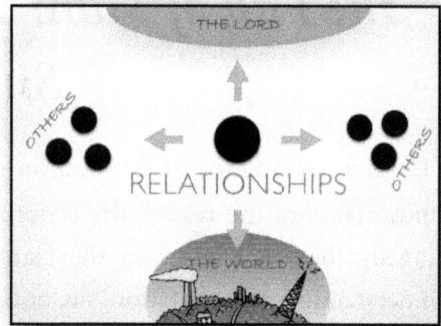

> Of every tree in the garden you may freely eat; but of the tree of knowledge of good and evil you shall not eat, for on the day that you eat of it you shall surely die (Gen 2:16-17).

Observe the expanse of freedom in this area: everything but the one tree he could eat from. "From any tree of the garden you may eat freely" (Gen 2:16). We must never think that man was placed in a place of limited choice. Even the presence of the tree of eternal life indicated God's intention for man. God carefully guided them by informing them of the negative consequences of eating from that one forbidden tree.[53]

---

[53] Many similar questions arise: why did the Lord put that one forbidden tree there in the first place, knowing its potential danger? Is he a good parent to put a hot stove in a room and warn a child not to touch it? Is he not testing them? See Genesis 2:1-17 for discussion on this.

Man's Trust in the Lord

How much should we trust God? From the beginning, man's welfare depended upon his trust in God. The depth of our relationships with God are dependent upon this growing trust. "The righteous man shall live by faith" (Romans 1:17).

There is much more to the universe than our limited minds can observe. God, on the other hand, sees and knows the whole picture. He is God overall. If He is not the utmost/supreme/highest in the entire existent universe, then we have serious cause to be shaky in our trust or commitment to Him, but He is the great Creator we read about in Genesis 1 and the founder of relationships as seen in Genesis 2. Crime, hatred, and evil invaded this lovely world. This God who identifies himself here is the same who revealed Himself through Jesus the Messiah (i.e., Christ) many ages later, the only pillar on whom we should stake our entire being and future. He is worthy of all our trust.

God's Deep Love for Mankind

It is from this perspective that God gives us His word and boundaries. He means not to destroy us but to happily involve us in His work. This can be easily seen through the way God has cared for His creation. He is not mean-spirited but generous, kind, and finds delight in pleasing His creatures.

Adam received everything from God; his position and his mandate were from God. He knew God and he knew what God's word meant to him. He did not know guilt or shame, but had complete fellowship with God. "And they heard the sound of the Lord God walking in the garden in the cool of the day...." (Gen 3:8).

The God of the Bible has revealed to us what He has determined that we need to know. We need to know what he has revealed, treasure it, and wisely use it in worship, making decisions, carrying out our life activities, and in responding to Him.

Some people say that when a person believes in Jesus, he needs to 'check your brains out!' In saying this, they are suggesting that God makes all the decisions for man. But this is not what we find here at all. God has given us the necessary knowledge, strength, and wisdom to carry out His commands, but we are responsible for making the right decisions. It seems that man, on the one hand, protests how God brings all into existence to accomplish His purposes but gets upset with God for leaving one tree in the Garden so man could freely choose (and choose not to choose).

Conclusion

Yahweh God, in His delight, has created and equipped man with what he needs to carry out the activities that He has assigned him. Even though man fails to complete God's will here, we will find later that this same God who designed Him work out a backup plan through Jesus Christ to get mankind back on track in his service to God. We still, however, are not robots. We must exercise our will to fill our minds with God's word and precepts so that we might accomplish the responsibilities that God has set before each one of us.

B) The Test and the Serpent (Gen 3:1-6)

1 Now the serpent was more crafty than any beast of the field which the LORD God had made. And he said to the woman, "Indeed, has God said, 'You shall not eat from any tree of the garden'?" 2 And the woman said to the serpent, "From the fruit of the trees of the garden we may eat; 3 but from the fruit of the tree which is in the middle of the garden, God has said, 'You shall not eat from it or touch it, lest you die.'" 4 And the serpent said to the woman, "You surely shall not die! 5 For God knows that in the day you eat from

it your eyes will be opened, and you will be like God, knowing good and evil." 6 When the woman saw that the tree was good for food, and that it was a delight to the eyes, and that the tree was desirable to make one wise, she took from its fruit and ate; and she gave also to her husband with her, and he ate (Gen 3:1-6).

Genesis 3:1 introduces a third player in the form of one of the creatures–the serpent. Strange that a serpent should talk to man! It is here in Genesis 3:1-6 that we begin to understand why there are so many problems in the world.

The Identity of the Serpent

The scriptures here states one thing about the serpent.[54] The serpent was very crafty, "The serpent was more crafty than any beast of the field" (Gen 3:1). Every other characteristic of the serpent are kept form the reader at this point.

Instead, we are introduced to the serpent through what he does. "You shall know them by their fruits" (Matthew 7:16, 20). The Lord wants us to understand that it is more important to discern false words than to know the source of them. Unfortunately, we spend more time learning about false sources and thought (e.g., religions and philosophies) than on how they deceive and convince us of their thoughts. Knowledge does not equal discernment!

The scriptures later inform us more about the serpent (2 Cor 11:3; Rev 12:9, 14,15; 20:2). This last verse more clearly identifies him as Satan and the devil.[55]

---

[54] I was originally going to say two things, the second being that God had made him. With a closer look, though, it does not here say that God made him but only that He had made the beasts of the field. It is not straightforward whether the serpent was intended to be included in that grouping of beasts.

[55] This study can be expanded as we search for terms like 'Satan,' 'devil,' and 'accuser.' Isaiah 14, Ezekiel 28 and passages like Jude are also very helpful passages to further our understanding Satan and his works. Check out my, "*Satan's Four Stations*": www.foundationsforfreedom.net/Help/Store/Intros/Satan4-Stations.html

And he laid hold of the dragon, the serpent of old, who is the devil and Satan, and bound him for a thousand years (Rev 20:2).

Evidently, the Lord does want us to know more about the evil one and to raise our caution so to prevent ourselves from falling to his deceit especially at the end of time. There is an arch enemy who sets himself to destroy the people of God. His intention in beckoning Eve in the Garden was not innocent or good in any sense of the meaning. He accomplished his purpose largely through deceit, that is, falsehood. This is why each of us need to be trained in the truth of God's Word.

The Serpent's Line of Questioning

The conversation between the serpent and Eve reveals a number of things about how the evil one still tempts and ensnares God's people today. Notice that more details of this conversation are given than the one between God and Adam. The purpose for this section is to train us in discernment. Genesis 3 records two statements from the devil (Gen 3:1, 4-5). We can learn a lot about him and his ways by carefully studying his statements.

Statement #1

"Has God indeed (really) said, 'You shall not eat of every tree of the garden'?" (Gen 3:1)

The serpent was obviously familiar with both God (notice his deliberate lack of using God's Name 'Lord–

Is God to blame?

Is God to blame for all that goes on in life—especially the bad? Why should he allow evil to happen?

Sometimes we talk as if God is the only player in our world and dismiss the true culprit for the havoc. When we view Him this way, it's easy to become angry with him, hate him, find ourselves tolerating him, or not want to have anything to do with Him until we really have to.

Is God to blame? Am I not a player too? And who else is? Why should God blame me or hold me responsible if he calls all the shots, has predestined everything, and knows what I am going to do anyway and has preprogrammed me to do that?

All of us (mankind) shall answer to God – no one is exempt irrespective of what we believe, feel or practice.

Yahweh') and His words. The serpent's words were carefully crafted around what God had said. He was not seeking information here but presenting doubt. He evidently knew what God had said. He used the question format to cast a negative glare about God and craftily made it sound that God was not being very nice, causing Eve to negatively focus on God's prohibition. Perhaps we could expand this in our own words,

Oh, you mean that the God who supposedly takes care of you and loves you told you not to eat from the trees in the garden? How just like him!

The serpent by his question covered up his motive and guided Eve to doubt her trust in God. We cannot say that he lied because it was a question, but the fact is, he introduced false

> **What was the serpent's motive or desire in these temptations?**
>
> - Take revenge against God.
> - Gain dominion over man and creation.
> - Steal what authority God had given man.
> - Control over God's creation and so look powerful like God.
> - Become Godlike by ruling over God's creation. Jn 10:10, Mat 4:9-10.

thoughts that he used to confuse her. The fact was that God had given all the trees to eat from except one, but his question caused her to think that God had withheld the best from her. Where he was subtle in the first statement, he was much more direct in the second statement.

Statement #2

> You will not surely die. For God knows that in the day that you eat of it your eyes will be opened, and you will be like God, knowing good and evil (Gen 3:4-5).

The Serpent goes much further here. In this second statement, he lapsed into outright denial and contradiction of what God had communicated. As yet they did not know death, and they had not lost the fellowship of

God. They trusted that God loved them and meant what He said. They believed God had their welfare in mind and would provide everything they needed including even this prohibition. All this soon changed, however.

The serpent spoke in outright contradiction to God's word. Eve knew and practiced God's Word, but an appealing promise caught her off guard. Note the nature of the promise. You do not have a way of independently testing it without disobeying or setting aside God's clear warning and its negative consequences. How is this like some modern marketing tricks? This is important concerning temptation.

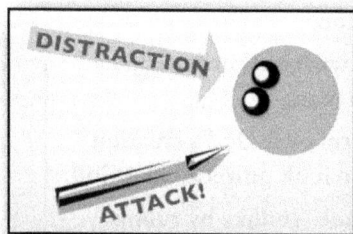

The serpent never clearly defined his purpose in all this. A stranger causes all this doubt to fly through her formerly pure mind in one short moment. Perhaps we underestimate the place thoughts can have in our minds even when we do not 'believe' them.

She knew God's Word. She evidently learned it from Adam. Genesis 2:16 clearly states that God commanded Adam rather than Eve. "And the LORD God commanded the man, saying, "From any tree of the garden you may eat freely" (Gen 2:16). Adam, as head, rightly communicated God's commands to her. Perhaps the evil one chose to speak to her rather than Adam because she heard the command indirectly through Adam rather than directly from God. He attacked the side rather than the head. Her immediate and proper response to the serpent in Genesis 3:2-3 demonstrates that she knew what God wanted.

> And the woman said to the serpent, "From the fruit of the trees of the garden we may eat; but from the fruit of the tree which is in the middle of the garden, God has said, 'You shall not eat from it or touch it, lest you die" (3:2-3).

Since the recommendation by the serpent was so clearly in conflict with God's word, the decision boiled down to whom Eve trusted. Either God, whom she had known well from the beginning and from whom she derived her being and all her position, or the serpent who she did not know at all.

She could have protected herself by considering who was most trustworthy, or by simply focusing on the Lord's command. Her willingness to decide to listen to the serpent in the end had great ramifications. Before discussing these, though, let's first look more closely at why Eve decided to forsake the one she trusted for one she hardly knew.

In order to discern error, we must ask, "How does what I hear or think differ from what God says?" In order to do this, though, we must know God's Word! In what ways are you making sure that God's Word is at the front of your thoughts?

Discussion question

- Have you ever thought one way even though your feelings did not fully reflect the facts? Should we trust such feelings? (Comment on Proverbs 28:26.)

Eve's Decision-making Considerations

The scriptures are quite clear on the process by which Eve chose to disobey God. We are not told whether Eve asked more questions. Perhaps it is unimportant. The longer she toyed with the idea of eating the attractive fruit, the more she allowed her mind to focus on the suggestion of disobedience, and the less she thought of God's clear command.

How did someone go from full trust in God to making such a blunder? Remember that the directive from the serpent openly challenged God's clear command. The subtlety of the devil's first statement was nowhere to be found in the blatant contradiction of the second. How could the evil one convince a sinless person made in the image of God to disobey God? If she could be so blinded, where does that leave us? Jesus wisely reminded us to seek extra protection from these temptations in the Lord's prayer, "And do not lead us into temptation, but deliver us from evil" (Matthew 6:13). Let's look closer at the reason she submitted to the evil one. There were three clear reasons stated in Genesis 3:6 as to why Eve was persuaded.

- good for food

- pleasant to the eye

- desirable to make one wise

Some have wisely seen these three inward attractions (i.e. lusts, desires) to be behind John's admonition in 1 John 2:16-17. The food is the lust of the flesh or the appetites. That which the eye sees becomes something that catches our attention. That which makes one wise closely aligns itself to how one thinks others might perceive oneself. In this case she thought she would be wise.

> For all that is in the world, the lust of the flesh and the lust of the eyes and the boastful pride of life, is not from the Father, but is from the world. And the world is passing away, and also its lusts; but the one who does the will of God abides forever (1 Jn 2:16-17).

Desires have their place in our lives. God has given us these desires to help us explore and discover different ways that He has wonderfully provided for us. But when we allow our desires to go counter to God's clear purposes in order to fulfill them, then the desires lead us away from God to find fulfillment on our own. This 'choice' characterizes our modern world.

We should not think that her decision was lopsided against her favor. God, actually, had heavily prepared the first couple with many wonderful words, acts, and reminders of His care for them. They had every reason to trust God. After all, He'd just given Adam that special woman! Here are a few items that should have fostered a right decision:

1. God personally revealed Himself to them (note: His name Yahweh) and talked with them.

2. The Lord provided clear and unambiguous words as to what was right and wrong.

3. He provided an abundant supply of food to meet their appetite.

4. Her beloved husband also told her what not to do.

5. The Lord warned them of death's consequence for disobedience.

6. The Lord created a lovely garden to enhance their trust in Him.

So why did Eve still sin? She allowed herself to focus on what was not true and was therefore unable to allow the truth to shape her decision. Adam was a different case. Eve was deceived, but Adam chose to go along with Eve. Perhaps he thought that he would lose Eve. His sin was the worse and ultimately brought the world into sin.

> For it was Adam who was first created, and then Eve. And it was not Adam who was deceived, but the woman being quite deceived, fell into transgression (1 Timothy 2:13-14).

Adam's Response

Adam, the leader of the home, the one who named woman, should have known to act better. But surprisingly, the Bible is silent on whether Adam put up resistance at all. Perhaps there was a delay of time when he thought what would happen to her. He might have also suffered a trio plague of desires: flesh, eyes, and pride as he thought about losing his companion. He took the serpent's cunning bait through his wife, 'hook, line, and sinker'.

Man deferred from his leadership role of carrying out God's commands. Man was clearly responsible to lead the wife. Not only was he first created and particularly addressed by God, but Eve was designed to help him carry out his roles. Notice in Gen 3:17, Adam is reprimanded for obeying his wife. It was wrong because what she suggested countered what God commanded, but the following of her initiating was wrong too. Adam should have initiated proper carrying out of God's teaching, but failed.

- Why didn't Adam implement any kind of filter to protect Eve from the serpent's words?

- Should our fascination with or love for our spouses set aside our responsibility of obedience toward God?

Marriage is not only between man and woman, but in truth it is between the couple and God. God, as the Creator, is the overseer of marriage. It is each person's responsibility to maintain a healthy relation with God, which will strengthen the bond between the two people.

The point here is to underscore the order of priority of man's loyalty in relationships:

- Unique personal relationship of God with man

- Relationship of man to His wife preceding all other 'inter-human' relationships

- Relationship of man to other creatures under God's sovereignty

Discussion questions

- Is anyone important enough to be able to set aside the Lord's clear word, will, or purpose aside?

- Is anything, any glory, prestige, reputation, or promise, great enough to disregard or contravene God's word?

- Does God ever ask us to set aside His precepts in order to obtain His promises?

Reflection on Temptation

We have gained a lot of insight into how the evil one tempts humans. He largely uses distraction and manipulation of thought. In this case, we saw the serpent shaping how Eve thought. He introduced subjects for her to think about. He caused her to look at things from a certain slant. The evil one knew how to manipulate Eve's thoughts by the clever introduction of newer thoughts. He used the first thought to distract her and the second to attack. Attack, in this context, meant to have her forget what was true and adopt what was not true so that she would act upon it. He first preyed on her defenses and then did his mental 'hacking.' Is this just true for Eve? I think not.

Satan first approached the woman. She might have been easier to attack because the Lord gave the instructions to Adam, and thus she heard them secondhand. Or maybe he targeted her because women are more subjective, while men objective. She lacked Adam's drive to objectivity. Both are valid observations. But this does not mean that men are not prone to temptation as well. The devil uses the same methods of distraction to cause him to forget God's truth, but the way he does this will be different. Each individual is different. If the devil is seeking us, he knows our weaknesses. He has been observing us. We conclude that, although Eve might have been more susceptible to temptation and deceit, the evil one widely uses the same methods to tempt everyone.

He is a manipulator of thoughts because he knows when to insert thoughts into our minds, in hopes that we adopt them for ourselves. The mind is largely influenced by thoughts, which in the end become words. Temptation then occurs through words that come into our minds. We might be allured by what we see, but there will be a suggestive thought (or series of thoughts) from the evil one to cause us to think according to his way. His thoughts seem like our own. Although the devil cannot make us do things, he can manipulate our thoughts, causing our minds and emotions to foster a judgment in his favor.

If God's people can understand temptation, they can learn how to break the stronghold of bad habits, depression, anxiety, anger, and fear. This is why Paul calls us to renew our minds.[56] With Christ in our minds, the evil one cannot easily deceive us. The firmer the habit, the more uncontrollable the impulses will seem. The evil one, in these cases, controls our thought patterns, which are based on lies and deceit. However they can be broken when identified and matched with the truth of God. Eve later noticed the deception, but in many cases people do not. They are bound.

Why is it that Adam sinned? The account relates it as if there was no tension in Adam's mind. "She gave also to her husband with her, and he ate" (Gen 3:6). It seems so simple and innocent as passing food around the dinner table. 1 Timothy 2:14 clearly tells us that Adam was not deceived like Eve. "It was not Adam who was deceived." This seems to mean that at the time when Adam ate the fruit, he was aware that he was going against God's command. Eve, at least for the moment, had forgotten. Adam was clearly aware of the choice. He chose to disobey. It is safe to conclude that Adam chose to disobey. He put his loyalty and affection elsewhere. He had up to that point obeyed God. He buttressed that loyalty by regularly obeying, but when he ate the fruit, he passed his loyalty elsewhere.

We do not know whether Adam was with Eve all the time when the serpent was speaking. Some suggest this. It is possible. Both scenarios are possible and therefore we must be careful not to base conclusions on

---

[56] *Reaching Beyond Mediocrity* clearly shows how to overcome these temptations, even ones that have continued to ruin our lives to now.
www.foundationsforfreedom.net/Help/Store/Intros/Reaching-Beyond.html

unsure facts. More importantly, we should note that Adam deliberately made a wrong choice. This is very much like man's weakness. They know something is wrong but still choose to do it. This sometimes involves looking at pornography, having an affair, stating a lie, etc. They are being tempted through their desires, and like the woman, give in to them. We could discuss this further by asking, "What made Adam change what he valued so much that he would go against the very God who treated him so kindly?"

Our guess is that he began to treasure the gift of God to him, his woman, more than the Giver of that gift. We cannot be sure of this, but it seems quite possible. We see his descendants all doing the same thing in this materialistic world. It appears that he just took and ate that fruit as if nothing unusual was happening, but underneath a great war of values was taking place. He chose to love things over God. Adam's sin brought us all under God's condemnation.

Conclusion

Genesis 3:1-6 records God's test for man. God did not tempt man. The Lord wanted man to succeed, and He provided that possibility by providing all the resources necessary for overcoming. Instead, we find that Eve was deceived and fell into sin while Adam, not being deceived, turned his heart away from God and unto his own desires.

From this terse passage we see how sin entered the human race and spoiled the earth. Any study of the environment must include the study of man's sin if it is going to be effective. Satan continues to use temptation to keep the human race at his bidding.

From more of a philosophical standpoint, many of man's major questions of life are answered in this momentous passage. Man had everything. There was no real reason for the fall except the evil one's devious ways. Fortunately, we not only learn how the evil one tempts us, but also how God has brought a cure for the very problem man caused, a cure achieved through the glorious Savior and prince, Messiah Jesus.

The Fall into Sin (Genesis 3:7-13, 22)

7 Then the eyes of both of them were opened, and they knew that they were naked; and they sewed fig leaves together and made themselves loin coverings. 8 And they heard the sound of the LORD God walking in the garden in the cool of the day, and the man and his wife hid themselves from the presence of the LORD God among the trees of the garden. 9 Then the LORD God called to the man, and said to him, "Where are you?" 10 And he said, "I heard the sound of Thee in the garden, and I was afraid because I was naked; so I hid myself." 11 And He said, "Who told you that you were naked? Have you eaten from the tree of which I commanded you not to eat?" 12 And the man said, "The woman whom Thou gavest to be with me, she gave me from the tree, and I ate." 13 Then the LORD God said to the woman, "What is this you have done?" And the woman said, "The serpent deceived me, and I ate" (Gen 3:7-13).

There were two contesting consequences that resulted from Adam and Eve's disobedience concerning the tree of the knowledge of good and evil.

- God's "You **shall surely die**" (Gen 2:17).

- The serpent's "You **shall not surely die.** For God knows that in the day that you eat of it your eyes will be opened, and you will be like God, knowing good and evil" (Gen 3:4).

Serious subversion is expressed through counter-questioning the nature of God and His supremacy. In a similar way, telemarketers appeal to potential victim's vulnerability but hide the real cost. Let's look at both the short term (immediate) and long term results of our forefather's sin.

Immediate Results of Their Sin

Eyes were opened (Gen 3:7).

They got to know good and evil, and in that sense became like God (3:22), so the serpent's promise came true.... but they got MORE than just knowledge. While God has knowledge of good and evil, evil never has a controlling part. This shows God's remarkable will and holiness! But for man, this knowledge of good and evil came by becoming subject to the control of evil, transferal of their rulership to Satan, and loss of the ideal life as God designed it.

In knowing good and evil, they lost the free access to the tree of life, which, had they had eaten from after their sin, would have allowed them to live forever.

The irony is that the excellence of their faculties was infinitely depressed. This is where mankind is today; he does not have a proper perspective of God, His creation, the future, goodness, and the other attributes God originally gave to man. His will, mind, and heart were all at once stained. Man might consider himself good, but when we take a minute to observe the general world or a particular person, the debate is quickly over. Man has fallen into a world of sin, which is a fact supported by ample proof.

Guilt, shame, lost innocence

A number of things happened as a result of the guilt they felt after disobeying.

- They knew they were naked (Compare Gen 3:7 with 2:25)

They were ashamed (unlike supporters of nudism that deny its shame), and as a result of that shame, they tried to cover up their nakedness with sewed fig leaves. God considered it inadequate and provided a better set of clothing (Gen 3:21).[57]

- They hid from God's presence (Gen 3:8 -10)

---

[57] In order to get the clothes needed there needed to be the death to the animal. This is a spiritual symbol of the inadequacy of our own coverings and would, in the end, need God's provision through the death of Jesus Christ to find real forgiveness and restoration of relationship.

They had to hide because of sin. Sin does not make us want to go to God because it causes us to fear His presence, which is distinctly different from the healthy fear and awe that pushes us into God's presence. "For everyone who does evil hates the light, and does not come to the light, lest his deeds should be exposed" (John 3:20).

- They passed the blame (Gen 3:12)

Adam and Eve also fell into blaming others ('buck-passing') and denial of their own responsibility in their disobedience. Shielding themselves from responsibility of their sin was just another way they hid from God. It is much easier to bring attention to another person's wrong than to admit that we are responsible for our own wrong doing.

- They deceived and made excuses (Gen 3:13)

The woman, while placing responsibility on Adam, also admits that she was deceived. Unfortunately, the fact of her deception is only noticed after the goal of deception had worked to its end, achieving its devilish purpose.

Deception, the essence of the enemy of God and of our souls!

Why would anyone deceive?

The use of deceit is an admission to inferiority and arrogance. The serpent is evil because he deceives to get what he otherwise could not have. The serpent could only bait mankind through deceit, and it was through deceit that he caused his own fall. Furthermore, he used deceit to sow rebellion among mankind. So what did the serpent get for his deception? Control. But, that control is permitted for only a short time, "He must be released for a short time" (Rev 20:3) before his catastrophic and humiliating end. His devastating end is already calculated out. The evil one can only continue his operations as he continues to pass on his dark understanding to others. When God's truth is revealed, his power wilts—much like how light destroys darkness.

- Did the serpent's promise that "you would not surely die" come true? No. Death closed in rapidly immediately destroying their relationship with God, and yet, physical death was delayed to bring the promise of salvation.

- Did they 'surely die'? Yes (Rev 20:14-15).

The death they experienced can in no way be compared to the reward of obedience. The contrast is so great that we can hardly comprehend why both Eve and Adam fell into disobedience. The unfolding drama of their sure death continues on in the following chapters. The physical death was delayed, but spiritual death took place instantly and pervades human history (Rom 5:14, 21). Only in Christ Jesus do we see God interrupting this cycle of death with the gift of renewed Life in Christ (Rom 5:20).

2. Long Term Results

Adam subjected his progeny to the dominion of sin. Later on we will see that it was God, in His wisdom, mercy, and grace, who immediately took steps to

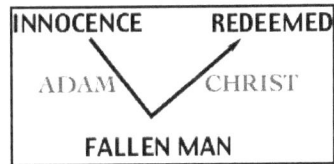

prevent this catastrophic fall from happening in a way that could not be reversed (Gen 3:23-24).

Disorder is intrinsically linked to disobedience. Where there is disorder, there is sin. The calamity that falls to man was not because of some error on God's part, but because the evil one inspired man to join him in rebelling against God. Tranquility, peace, and love was suddenly replaced with disturbance, struggle, and enmity.

Man is fallen. Even the best of us struggle with the dominion of sin in our souls. Paul says, "The body is dead because of sin" (Rom 8:10). We are holed in a world of sin which has even prided itself of complex and advanced human cultures and societies, but God's standard is infinitely higher than those achievements. Romans 5:17 summarizes the long-term results of sin. Fortunately, the Lord has reversed the curse to bring about positive long-term effects through Christ Jesus: eternal life. Jesus Christ becomes the tree of life for us.

> For if by the transgression of the one, death reigned through the one, much more those who receive the abundance of grace and of the gift of righteousness will reign in life through the One, Jesus Christ (Romans 5:17).

The Fall of Man

Volumes have been written about the fall of man. We will only introduce this debate to avoid forgetting the purpose of Genesis 3:1-13.

Man was made in the image of God. Varying viewpoints of this teaching differ because of the way it depends on what they think man lost in the first place. If, for example, we consider our ability to make decisions through reason as part of being created in the image of God, then we are asserting the belief that man did not completely lose the image of God after the fall. He can still make such decisions, even if they are made in the context of a corrupt will. The larger argument is debated in whether man completely or partially lost the image of God.

The consequence of the pain males face can be traced back to the act of eating from the forbidden tree. The mentioned sorrow, sweat, and pain would be different from woman's, but it would again make his calling to provide for food so much more difficult. Woman's main task was to bear and raise children while men would work the fields. They will be associated difficulties. Disobedience brings disorder, which in turn brings pain and suffering, and, but due to God's grace, from that suffering Jesus is born and redemption comes.

Colossians 3:10 lets us know that we now are being renewed in our creation as the image of God because Christ lives in our lives. "And have put on the new self who is being renewed to a true knowledge according to the image of the One who created him" (Col 3:10). John tells us, however, that this image will not be completed until we see Christ.

Beloved, now we are children of God, and it has not appeared as yet what we shall be. We know that, when He appears, we shall be like Him, because we shall see Him just as He is (1 John 3:2).

Man has fallen. We see the shame, the loss of the glory of God, rebellion and disconnection. But the Lord, in His wonderful and gracious way, has made a way through Christ where our stain is not only removed, but that can we gain through faith the righteousness of Christ (i.e. justified) that covers our moral nakedness and enables us to live uprightly (Col 3:12).

Conclusion

- In choosing to ignore God while exercising their free will, Adam and Eve suffered the consequences of God's warning. Though mankind has free will, he is still responsible to God for his actions. With freedom there is responsibility; with responsibility, accountability. As a people, we need to trust God enough to obey Him, otherwise we will be consumed by our desires to gain what is vain.

- If only Adam and Eve had taken God at His word! They would not have fallen. They only had to put the Lord and His will above their own, and all would have been fine.

- In making decisions, small or great, we need to persistently prioritize the defined will and principles of God. God will never ask us to set aside His will to obtain His promises (John 17:17).

- Natural man is no longer innocent; he is fallen. However, through faith in Christ, the second Adam, the people of God are alive and able to live in obedience.

Reflection

1. How would you answer someone who makes the following claim: "Why should God blame me or hold me responsible for my mistakes if he calls all the shots and knows what I am going to do anyway?"

2. If you were Eve or Adam, how would you have combated the serpent's temptation? How do you combat him now?

3. Compare this episode to Matthew 4:1-10. All the people involved in the situation knew the word of God, including Satan. Write down how each one handled or used God's Word. What accounted for the triumph of Jesus Christ?

GENESIS

Genesis 4:1-12
The Penetration of Evil

When studying the Bible, it is not only important to observe what is said, but also the reason for its inclusion. In this case, we need to find the connection between Genesis 3 and 4, but first let us summarize the foundational lessons we have learned from Genesis 1-3.

The Basic Worldview (Gen 1-3)

In the first two chapters of Genesis we discover that everything was made by God and for God, and can be described as good, wonderful, and awesome, including the creation, design of man and woman, and the institution of marriage.

Understanding God (Gen 1-2)

One would think that God did not need to include in the Bible the part of Genesis 4 that describes the murder of Abel, and Genesis 3 altogether. But if the full truth did not come out about the evil we find in everyday life, then the Bible couldn't continue without incriminating God. Genesis 3 through 5 acts as a bridge that allows us to gain a foundational understanding necessary to the establishment of some of life's most basic facts:

- God is a creative God.

- He is powerful, but good

- God wants the best for mankind

This enables us to ultimately trust and seek God rather than blame and avoid Him. This is the Gospel bridge of the Old Testament.

Understanding Evil (Gen 3)

The Lord could easily have elaborated on the creation of the world, but more importantly He desired to provide us with a proper worldview to help us guard our hearts and minds.

An attempted mass-killing near our church shocked and horrified us, but is it not true that we know, and maybe even expect, such things will happen? Like it or not, we are very acquainted with evil.

The Lord wanted to help us properly understand evil or we would never be able to trust our Creator God (this is same theme found in the Book of Job). How we view evil is one of the main tasks of religions and philosophies, and many of the concepts of evil have evolved over time.

There are many beliefs about evil in today's world. Here are five. The first two groups do not intellectually believe in evil; the remaining three do believe in the existence of evil.

- Cut-throat evolutionary: Anything is good if you want to do it and can get away with it.

- Constrained evolutionary: There is no such thing as evil, but we ought to get along the best we can and don't bother others.

No such **thing** as evil	Evil is **bad**
• Cut-throat secular	• Perplexity
	• Religious
• Constrained secular	• Biblical

- Perplexity: I don't know why there is so much evil and wish the world would be better.

- Religious: Evil is bad, but I will try to be good.

- Biblical: Evil is bad and has stained me. I need God to do a special work in my life so that His goodness will arise from my life.

The Biblical worldview has been with us from the beginning because God knew the important role it would have on our willingness to trust Him. This is why the truth about our restoration with the Lord is called "good news" (lit. the gospel).

Connecting Genesis 3 and 4

Genesis 4 largely exists to help us connect the presence of evil in the world with the evil found within ourselves. More than this, God wants us to realize that the reason evil exists is because we have excluded Him from our lives. Deep down, we believe that there is a better way than God's and so we resort to lies, and suffer under the decisions we make outside of God.

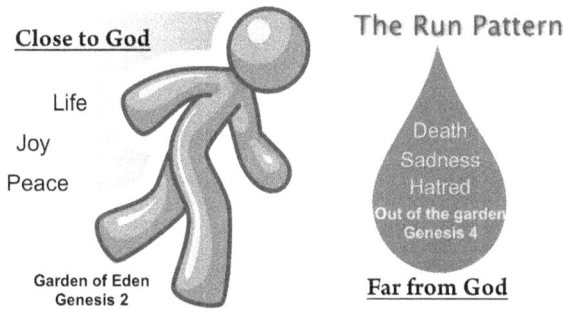

Out of the Garden, Out of God's Presence

The message could not be clearer: without God, man's life and joy is gone. The reason for this is highlighted in the last lines of Genesis 3. God had escorted Adam and Eve out of the Garden of Eden because they were no longer able to live in God's presence:

> Therefore the LORD God sent him out from the garden of Eden, to cultivate the ground from which he was taken. 24 So He drove the man out; and at the east of the garden of Eden He stationed the cherubim, and the flaming sword which turned every direction, to guard the way to the tree of life (Gen 3:23-24).

God would have at once destroyed them because of His wrath, but delayed it by covering them and putting them out of His immediate presence. They did spiritually 'die', but physical death was delayed. Genesis 4, therefore, describes man's life apart from God's presence and an absence of the trusting relationship they once had with God.

Our Present Situation

God does provide a little perspective here, though, starting at the end of Genesis 3 and continuing right into Genesis 4 and even Genesis 5. Genesis 3 shows the entrance of evil into the world, not through God, but through another. Genesis 4 paints a clear picture of how this act of disobedience in chapter 3 damaged the heart and home of man with the cold-blooded act of murder. Genesis 5 uses a long genealogy to show the full effect of this sin by the way it spreads out its evil to all men (see Romans 5:12-21).

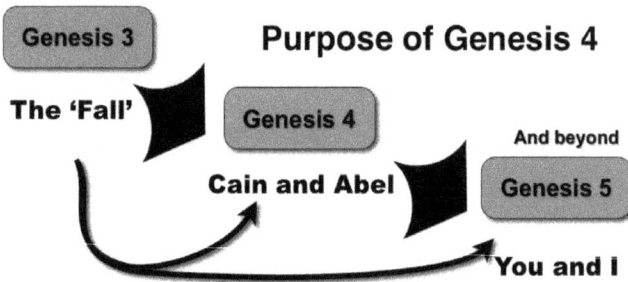

Purpose of Genesis 4

More grace

But we also see something else. God defines grace early on by the way He pursues man, even after his rebellion against God. This is an early picture of God's person: Just and yet merciful. He is the Opposer (kicks sinners out: Just) and supporter (reasons with sinners: gracious).

This scene is repeated throughout history. God's grace perseveres because, from within judgment, mercy is constantly being ushered in and the great love of God displayed.

In fact, what we see in Genesis 4 could be reported in today's news. A happy column reports the birth of a second son. Twenty years later, a another report states that the older son, Cain, recklessly killed his younger brother, Abel, because of a family quarrel. Though we might be shocked at this news item, we are not utterly surprised, are we? No, because this is life as we know it.

On a greater scale, we might watch a video of a nation bombing another nation killing thousands on the history channel. Horrible. But the same thing still happens today. The place, time, and people have changed, but the destruction of lives goes on and on, nation to nation just like one of my biblical instructor friends in India who was poisoned to death.

Race, religion, culture, and language separates us, but evil unites us. This is the main point of Genesis 5. There is only one human race; we are all interconnected through evil's inner poison.

But wait a minute …

Most people observe this evil but have not been able to comprehend what it means. They only see part of the picture, more specifically the evil acts themselves, and fail to comprehensibly understand the whole, and especially their part in it. They superficially conclude that some bad people caused the problem, rather than perceiving that the whole system is flawed and broken.

I once met a pastor who talked about his seedy past in gambling and various other things. I asked him, "What changed?" and he replied that his uncle one day brought him around to the back of a race track, away from the glamour of it all. A number of huts were assembled with pieces of metal and plastic. Nothing happened that moment to him, but it helped him see that is not where he wanted to end up.

If we are alert, we would notice this manifestation of evil in our own homes, including pastors' homes. Otherwise, why would we argue, fight, and live out petty jealousies with those we love? We focus so much on the problems of others that we can hardly perceive the larger problem of what we call evil in this world.

An Ugly Picture

People mean to bring harm to others because of their innate selfish desires. Where God is good to others, man is evil. God plans to bring about good while man insists on using his power and privilege to hurt the people around him.

There is a second side to this observation, however, that is important to note. Evil resides in us. "Therefore, just as through one man sin entered into the world, and death through sin, and so death spread to all men, because all sinned" (Romans 5:12). Our lives are compromised. It is not just bad judgment that causes bad things, but an evil motivation that lives in our hearts.

Religious people and others hide beneath a veneer of so-called good works. They focus on these good works and yet are not willing to acknowledge how evil shapes their lives. Paul aptly describes the world in one short sentence, "For all have sinned and fall short of the glory of God" (Rom 3:23).

The Question of Evil

This is why the question of evil still stands as one of the most perplexing problems man faces. How could such a thing happen? There is no way an older brother should plot and kill his younger brother. Or later, we see Lamech (Gen 4:23-24) killing someone who merely wounded him. Here are some questions on evil to assist us in thinking more deeply about evil:

- Why does man hurt others?
- What is God doing by allowing evil people to live?

- Why does God try to carefully advise and relate to evil people even after being arrogant for so long?

- Who is the serpent that dared to counter God's mighty Word? Why did God allow him to get away with his deceit?

- Why did man so easily believe the strange evil one and despise his good God who kindly prepared the Garden of Eden for him?

There are many such questions that are raised early in the Bible. Several of them are not answered until the very end in the Book of Revelation.

The Infiltration of Evil (Gen 4:1-5)

Although there exists so much evil about us, we still all hope and dream that things will go well with us. Chapter 4 of Genesis begins like many a good story, or much like we hope our lives will turn out: marriage, family, home, job, etc. The young are typically full of this ambition and hope. But evil enters the world, our hearts, and homes.

Life rarely stays hopeful, however. There might come an experience or a series of issues that finally make us realize that this world is not all it promises to be. There are hardships, sickness, accidents, etc. Oftentimes, people are oblivious as to how many others have not been able to gain the ideal happy life. Maybe someone was diagnosed with multiple sclerosis, another's parents got divorced, or a spouse faced a layoff. We figure that somehow we will miss those challenges, or if they come, we will worm our way out of them.

One pastor friend in Nigeria who had just been blessed with a new daughter went through a trying time when his older daughter was on the verge of dying from malaria. Something is desperately wrong with this world: its broken relationships, death, misery, famine, etc. We have to work so hard to get ahead. We might have a baby, but the pain of pregnancy and birth reminds us that we are sinners in a broken world. Rachel, Jacob's beloved wife, finally gave birth to her second child,

Benjamin, but died in childbirth (Gen 35:18). This is the result of what it means to live apart from God.

This degeneration of life's quality is what we see here in Genesis 4. It starts off so nicely but quickly regresses into a horrible, unbelievable nightmare. It takes a while to understand death's first victim to living beings. Youthful aspirations fight off the rugged picture of evil for as long as possible before swallowing it. Hopes quickly fade away being soured by realism. God is trying to point out here the connection between what happened in Genesis 3 and 4, and our own lives.

Marriage, Sex, and Work (Gen 4:1-2)

> Now the man had relations with his wife Eve, and she conceived and gave birth to Cain, and she said, "I have gotten a manchild with the help of the LORD. 2 And again, she gave birth to his brother Abel. And Abel was a keeper of flocks, but Cain was a tiller of the ground (Gen 4:1-2).

Marriage is a grand ordinance designed by God, and the fruit of that relationship is children, blend of the two parents, affirming the glory of oneness.

They were, no doubt, astonished by the child-bearing process, even as we marvel on how a new human can be born today. Just two chapters prior, we learned how God made Adam and Eve with His own hands. I'm sure God revealed these things to Adam (he *was* knocked out when Eve was made), but this way of 'making' other humans was new to them.

They didn't have a baby boy, like most of us would say. They had a 'manchild' or literally human being. They still saw God's help in this seen in the idea associated with Cain, his given name, "With the help of the Lord" (Gen 3:1).

Thoughts on family planning

Modern 'family planning' is an actual sham because it goes directly against the purpose and plan of God. God has literally made us to reproduce starting nine months after marriage and end before reaching our senior years. Who, for example, would start a business and not assure that it was well-maintained? Without proper care, the house, or business, would quickly decline. God granted us reproductive abilities to build up His world but the curse of selfish narrow thinking is literally destroying societies. When we place ease, comfort, and money before God's greater purposes, then His curse comes upon us which is exactly what we see happening in our world.

We admit that the Lord has given us many years to rightly care for our children. It is a very important job that requires much work and dedication. Parents invest in their children because their children will be the future world. This value can be seen in how people spend tens of thousand of dollars just to have a child, whether through adoption or fertilization techniques.

Family planning with its near accuracy is relatively new. God has shown His intention that we use this God-given power to properly bear and care for children within the context of a solid home. Putting off children is not proper unless, perhaps, some extenuating health circumstances. God gives us nine months to prepare. That is enough. We need to stop considering marriage to be a trove of pleasure rather than a place of responsibility before God to raise godly children.

The world looks at children as a burden and financial obligation rather than what they are: a gift from God. May God purge this pagan perspective from our lives! Love your children, and they in turn will bask and return in that love. Focus on the trouble they cause, and you will breed a hateful generation that knows little of God's love.

Trouble in the Offering (Gen 4:3-5)

So it came about in the course of time that Cain brought an offering to the LORD of the fruit of the ground. 4 And Abel, on his part also brought of the firstlings of his flock and of their fat

portions. And the LORD had regard for Abel and for his offering;
5 but for Cain and for his offering He had no regard (Gen 4:3-5).

Not everyone is as bad as they can be. Abel seemed to do a good job of integrating his life as an act of worship to the one true God. Life was more than living because, to him, it was living in a relationship with God.

This relationship affected the way he lived. This faith and understanding urged him to make offerings to God. There is no clear scriptural teaching that Abel was instructed to make a sacrifice or even an offering, but as with the rest of mankind, it is considered appropriate and right. This is the religious nature within man. Abel, however, went beyond that with an offering based on faith. He believed God would accept it.

By faith Abel offered to God a better sacrifice than Cain, through which he obtained the testimony that he was righteous, God testifying about his gifts, and through faith, though he is dead, he still speaks (Heb 11:4).

Society's Rules and Laws

One great difference exists between Cain's time and ours, though. Most of us wonder how Cain could kill his brother. We would never do this!

This has to do with the difference in society. Sure Cain heard God's voice, but there was not much of what we would call a society, with all its laws and education. Although our culture's influence has waned due to a weaker family and media distraction, each of us has a strong world culture constantly engaging us. The society becomes another voice warning us. We hear of prisons and fear the law. So though we might get angry, we would not, under most circumstances, kill someone.

Jesus has said, though, if the restraint of laws were not around us, perhaps we would be more open to expressing our rage and selfishness.

Isn't this what happened in the UK when people saw that they could raid a shop and not get caught?[58]

> You have heard that the ancients were told, 'YOU SHALL NOT COMMIT MURDER' and 'Whoever commits murder shall be liable to the court. But I say to you that everyone who is angry with his brother shall be guilty before the court; and whoever shall say to his brother, 'Raca,' shall be guilty before the supreme court; and whoever shall say, 'You fool,' shall be guilty enough to go into the fiery hell' (Mat 5:21-22).

Murder is wrong, but so is anger and rage against people. The law doesn't say, 'Thou shalt not get angry,' because the law was a judicial law which needed clear evidence. However, if we love our neighbor, we won't get angry or incite spite, hate, jealousy, or arrogance.

The real problem is not murder but those desires that are innate in all of us that lead to murder. We might not dare to kill anyone, but are we willing to curse, get into a rage, plot revenge, murmur against, etc.? Are we more innocent than the killer who does something that is in his heart? For others, one's pet sin might not be jealousy and hatred, but lying and deceit, or engaging an adulterous spirit.

Theology of Man

When man rebelled against God, he left the grace that made him able to love like God. This is the selfish streak in each one of us and only as we become aware of it will we really seek God's grace in our lives. In this sense, we must die to ourselves before we find life. We need to:

- Carefully observe this principle of death that operated in Cain so that we better understand how it similarly works in us.

- Cautiously listen to God's counsel to learn how to overcome these self-seeking desires.

---

[58] "They just went in and grabbed what they could. Why not?"
(http://www.mirror.co.uk/news/uk-news/london-riots-young-rioters-say-146880).

- Remember the great principle of life from God that regenerates us and brings hope in what otherwise would be a gruesome world (Gen 3:36).

The Lord conversed with Cain, and yet Cain was willing to hurt others by acting on those innate desires. Those strong desires still live within man now and can overrun his sense and sanity.

Most importantly, for us, is the confidence derived from God's Word, that through the truth of God we can overcome the evil that lives within us. This was God's point.

Cain's Anger (Gen 4:3-5)

3 So it came about in the course of time that Cain brought an offering to the LORD of the fruit of the ground. 4 And Abel, on his part also brought of the firstlings of his flock and of their fat portions. And the LORD had regard for Abel and for his offering; 5 but for Cain and for his offering He had no regard. So Cain became very angry and his countenance fell (Gen 4:3-5).

So why did Cain get angry? And why did God reject Cain's offering and accept Abel's? Part of the problem is that nowhere do we see a clear explanation of what would distinguish a good offering from an unacceptable one. We can guess that somehow God had revealed to Cain that his offering was not acceptable.

There are two things to consider in answering this question: the kind of offering and the faith behind the offering.

The Kind of Offering

Some suggest that only meat offerings were acceptable. This is certainly possible, and further support can be found in the fact that God found it necessary to use skins to cover Adam and Eve. The death of the animals were required to cover man in order to hold off God's wrath. Perhaps, their nakedness revealed a loss of glory that earlier covered them. This offering would be symbolic of Christ's future sacrifice of

Himself on the cross and the covering of righteousness that God's people would gain through faith in Christ.

Though there are no clear indications that offerings were expected, God had his own expectations of what was considered to be a good or poor one. Able offered a good offering and Cain did not. If the offering problem consisted of what was being offered, then Cain could simply have purchased some animals for this purpose. He did not seem to care. God had His expectations, but Cain did not go out of his way to make a proper sacrifice.

The Faith Behind the Offering

Others suggest that it was not the kind of offering but the presence or absence of faith. There are several reasons for this suggestion.

- Sacrificial animals can never wholly satisfy God. "In whole burnt offerings and sacrifices for sin Thou hast taken no pleasure" (Heb 10:6). (Counter: Though this is true, God still used animal sacrifices to temporarily appease His wrath in the Old Testament.)

- It is the faith, not the sacrifice, that pleases God. This is affirmed by the New Testament. "By faith Abel offered to God a better sacrifice than Cain, through which he obtained the testimony that he was righteous, God testifying about his gifts, and through faith, though he is dead, he still speaks" (Heb 11:4). Faith pleases God. (Counter: Others would suggest that it was faith along with the sacrifice, not one or the other.)

In the end, we should conclude that the kind of offering was important, but less relevant to our lives. Jesus has now become our sacrifice. More clear is the fact that Cain was unwilling to offer the proper offering even after God confronted him. He was content with a mediocre offering.

Though Cain heard from God, he was not a man of faith, but of sight. He lived by the world's ways (and later largely shaped the world at that time!). He did not give regard for the things of God. God clearly states the importance of faith. "And without faith it is impossible to please Him, for he who comes to God must believe that He is, and that He is a rewarder of those who seek Him" (Heb 11:6).

The Lord points out the curse of the religious spirit. It is not that Cain did not do anything. He did make an offering, which still required some effort and cost. But why did he do it at all?

Cain evidently made an offering before his brother did (4:3-4). Perhaps it was motivated by his parents expectations, or a request from God. We don't know. We do know, however, that it was not because he was trying to please God. He took the religious shortcut that dooms men to hell and hatred.

The Nature of Religion

- Religious activities are those outward spiritual activities done to pacify God or others without the inward spiritual love and faith toward God and others.

- Religion is a self-expression of spirituality that pleases man but stinks before God.

- Religion is an outlet where man's worst can be shown because man believes his hideous prideful thoughts and actions are okay because his religious activities balance it all out.

- Religion's greatest danger is the way it keeps people from God. In that sense, it would be better not to be religious. One at least might find God that way.

Snares & Freedom

Religion is a war man fights on earth.

In biblical Christianity, one's life connects with the eternal God.

- Religious works are spiritual activities one does without any conscious presence in the Lord.

Nice activities that you think make you acceptable before God.

- The giving, serving, praying, etc. you engage in with a reason to appease your conscience and increase your pride more than please God.

Most people are affected by religion and its comprehensive theologies that provide incorrect answers to life's perplexing problems. Religious people are unmoved by God Himself for they have no genuine faith. They are stirred by their conscience, perhaps, but justify their righteousness through their good works rather than perceiving the evil within.

Religion has a mediocrity about it that kills. People will do a little for 'God' but it really is for their conscience sake. The world is filled with this deadly religion, including a religious Christianity.

People like to make a big difference between the evil people out there and themselves (the religious ones), but they carefully ignore their offenses against God. They believe their offerings will make enough difference that God will not care about their past wrongs.

Are your spiritual thoughts and activities void of faith?

- Offerings (Will God reward you?)
- Prayers (Does God hear you?)
- Bible reading plans (Is God teaching you?)
- Helping others (Do you serve in God's strength?)
- Attending church (Are you there to please Him?)

There is the test of love of God against the love for the world. We know we love the world when we try to get by with less in our relationship with God. Perhaps, a sign of our religiosity without a genuine faith in

God is that we are not very devoted. We do only what satisfies our consciences rather than what pleases the living God.

B) The Confrontation of Evil (Gen 4:5-12)

Genesis 4:5-12 provides a brilliant model of biblical counseling. We actually get to see God counseling someone who is in the middle of deciding to commit a serious wrong.

It appears that besides being a great model of how we need to confront evil, we also get a great insight into how God intervenes in evil rather than blankly judging it. This, of course, is a great sign of His grace.

In the following verses, we can spot different aspects of good biblical counseling. It's a shame that the Christian community as a whole often refuses to imitate God's way and instead chooses to be influenced by the world's voices.

God's Confrontation (Gen 4:5-7)

> But for Cain and his offering He had no regard. So Cain became very angry and his countenance fell. 6 Then the LORD said to Cain, "Why are you angry? And why has your countenance fallen? 7 If you do well, will not your countenance be lifted up? And if you do not do well, sin is crouching at the door; and its desire is for you, but you must master it" (Gen 4:5-7).

God pointed out the inadequacy of Cain's offering. It would have been in Cain's best interest to learn from this and change, but the hardened heart adamantly resists the words of truth. Below is a chart that more clearly identifies the key aspects of biblical counseling.

"Why are you angry?"	Points out the problem is rooted with his heart rather than another. Promotes honest evaluation.
"And why has your countenance fallen?"	Carefully observes. Identifies his poor attitude by reminding him of his angry countenance.
"If you do well, will not your countenance be lifted up?"	Shows how one's sinful behavior and guilt is associated with sadness.
"And if you do not do well, sin is crouching at the door."	Brings a warning of the ensuing dangers if an alternate path is not chosen.
"And its desire is for you, but you must master it."	Provides hope that something can be done and hints on how to conquer this inner evil.

BIBLICAL COUNSELING (GENESIS 4)

Cain, Evil, and Us

Evil has existed in this world for a long time, but not forever. Remember Genesis 3? More importantly, we know evil entered into our personal lives with the dawn of our physical life. This spiritual disease has infiltrated even the best of us. While Adam welcomed evil, it was passed on right into his children and his children's children–including us his descendants.

Because of Adam's sin, we were born with a sinful nature and all its cravings. Galatians 5 gives us a great insight into all of that. 5:19 says, "Now the deeds of the flesh are evident, which are immorality, impurity, sensuality, etc."

There is a verse that gives us an understanding of how the devil is connected to our sinfulness. We cannot blame the devil as though we had not our own choice. "The one who practices sin is of the devil; for the devil has sinned from the beginning" (3:8).

Do you see that key phrase, "of the devil?" John repeats it in 3:10, "By this the children of God and the children of the devil are obvious: anyone who does not practice righteousness is not of God, nor the one who does not love his brother" (1 John 3:10). The devil's mind and ways have invaded our lives.

"But you must master it."

The Devil's Plans (Gen 4:8-12)

> And Cain told Abel his brother. And it came about when they were in the field, that Cain rose up against Abel his brother and killed him. "Then the LORD said to Cain, "Where is Abel your brother?" And he said, "I do not know. Am I my brother's keeper?" 10 And He said, "What have you done? The voice of your brother's blood is crying to Me from the ground. 11 "And now you are cursed from the ground, which has opened its mouth to receive your brother's blood from your hand. 12 "When you cultivate the ground, it shall no longer yield its strength to you; you shall be a vagrant and a wanderer on the earth" (Gen 4:8-12).

Adam got sucked into the devil's plans, so now every man is born under Satan's power. Our physical bodies are not inherently evil, but because of our desires, our thoughts are swayed, and the body carries out sinful action. From the beginning of time, Satan has been strategizing how to sabotage God's plan. He is the ultimate terrorist, turning good to evil, and light to darkness. He is behind the antichrists around us.

Although this passage does not speak of the end in very clear language, we know from other verses that both spiritual death and physical death are a result of sin. 'For as through the one man's disobedience the many were made sinners' (Rom 5:19). And in 5:21, "Sin reigned in death."

We see this practically worked out in the case of Cain and Abel. Abel sought the ways of God, but Cain didn't like them. Without a society around to restrain evil, he did what he wanted. He desired to eliminate the presence of goodness seen in Abel's life, and the resulting hatred and bitterness ended up with bloodshed. Without restraints around us, our hatred would indeed have room to flare like Cain's.

Facts of Murder (Gen 4:10)

Murder takes away a life that God has made. God does not permit this. Although children are born from two parents, we, as a human race, must acknowledge that our children do not inherently belong to us as parents, but to God, as their Creator.

We might be jealous of someone, like Cain was of Abel, but murder is still murder. God takes it as a personal affront to His good plans. It is something He deals with severely, "The voice of your brother's blood is crying to Me from the ground."

Sometimes people kill from hatred, but more and more often people kill out of convenience. In terms of abortion it doesn't so much have to do with denying her choice more than it has to do with preserving God-given life. God granted Cain a choice, and the choice he made resulted in evil. In a similar way, the choice of abortion is evil and incurs God's wrath.

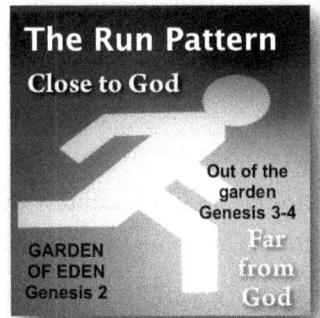

The Run Pattern

Close to God

Out of the garden Genesis 3-4

GARDEN OF EDEN Genesis 2

Far from God

Several times a year, a scene comes to my mind of all the millions of babies in a pool of blood crying out to God. We have prioritized our preferences and convenience over God's and have taken action contrary to what He has told us in Exodus 20:14, "You shall not murder."

God's commands help us walk uprightly–especially when we have not thought through the implications of our behavior. God has told us what is best and what to refrain from. Man is made in the image of God, so taking the life of another person is leagues apart from taking the life of a bug, horse, or chicken.

The Murder and its Results (Gen 4:8-12)

The seeds of sin were sown by Adam and Eve by trusting the devil and acting against the clear command of God. This led to death—a state in which sin has dominion in their lives and is passed on to subsequent generations. Cain went on and married and had his children. Cities developed. Innovation came about, but sin's stain penetrated the best works of man. The cities became a grand display of man's evil, glossed over with a veneer of religiosity.

As we examine the lineage of Adam via Cain to the 6th generation, we see the characteristics of the acquired sinful nature unfold even more. Two horrible murders further ruin the descendants of Cain: Cain is unable to offer a sacrifice acceptable to God but his brother Abel is. Out of jealousy and anger, Cain kills his brother for outperforming him before God! Lamech, out of vengeance, kills a young man for hurting him.

Evil has not only generally penetrated our world, but our own hearts and homes. May we confess our sin and seek God's grace while there is still time. God is warning us. Make the better choice. Cease evil.

Application
- Do you have the signs of religion but not faith?
- Are you afraid of getting too involved or devoted to God?
- Do you tolerate mediocrity rather than excel?
- Live for sight (for man), not by faith (in God)
- Are you afraid to confront? Chastise?
- Are you paying attention to what God is speaking to you?

GENESIS

Genesis 5 Patriarchal Chart: Since The Beginning of Time

The Patriarchal Chart (Gen 5)

The *Genesis 5 Patriarchal Chart* below shows the comparative ages of the patriarchs ranging from Adam to the period of the Flood. Specifically, you can find the chronological relationship between different men like Adam, Seth, Enosh, Enoch, Methuselah, Lamech, and Noah.[59]

Enoch's Secret Word: Methuselah (5:21-25)

Methuselah in Genesis 5:21-25 speaks about Enoch's son and how he named him Methuselah because of a special prophetic vision given to Enoch.

> And Enoch lived sixty-five years, and became the father of Methuselah. Then Enoch walked with God three hundred years after he became the father of Methuselah, and he had other sons and daughters. So all the days of Enoch were three hundred and sixty-five years. And Enoch walked with God; and he was not, for God took him. And Methuselah lived one hundred and eighty-seven years, and became the father of Lamech (Gen 5:21-25).

---

[59] www.foundationsforfreedom.net/dl/biot/OT_Law/Genesis/Genesis05_Geneaology_Chart.pdf

From the
Beginning of Time
Genesis 5

Eternity
Flood
1656

Eternity
God

From Methuse-lah's name we understand that the flood was sent after his death. However, because of God's great mercy, we also find Methuselah lived the longest life.

Measurements are nearly exact +/- 1cm
1 cm = 100 years

1rt Adam 130 — 930
2nd Seth 105 — 912
3rd Enosh 90 — 905
4th Kenan 70 — 910
5th Mahalalel 65 — 895
6th Jared 162 — 962
7th Enoch 65 — 365
8th Methuselah *"death and sent"* 187 — 969
9th Lamech 182 — 777

10th

When did this prophecy come about? We sense it was given to Enoch before Methu-selah's birth. Enoch then built this prophecy into his son's name, Methuselah (death and sent). Enoch lived a very short life comparatively. Because of his righteous-ness, he was taken alive to be with God.

Shem 500 — 600 Flood 2/17/600 2/27/601 — 950
Ham 600
Japheth

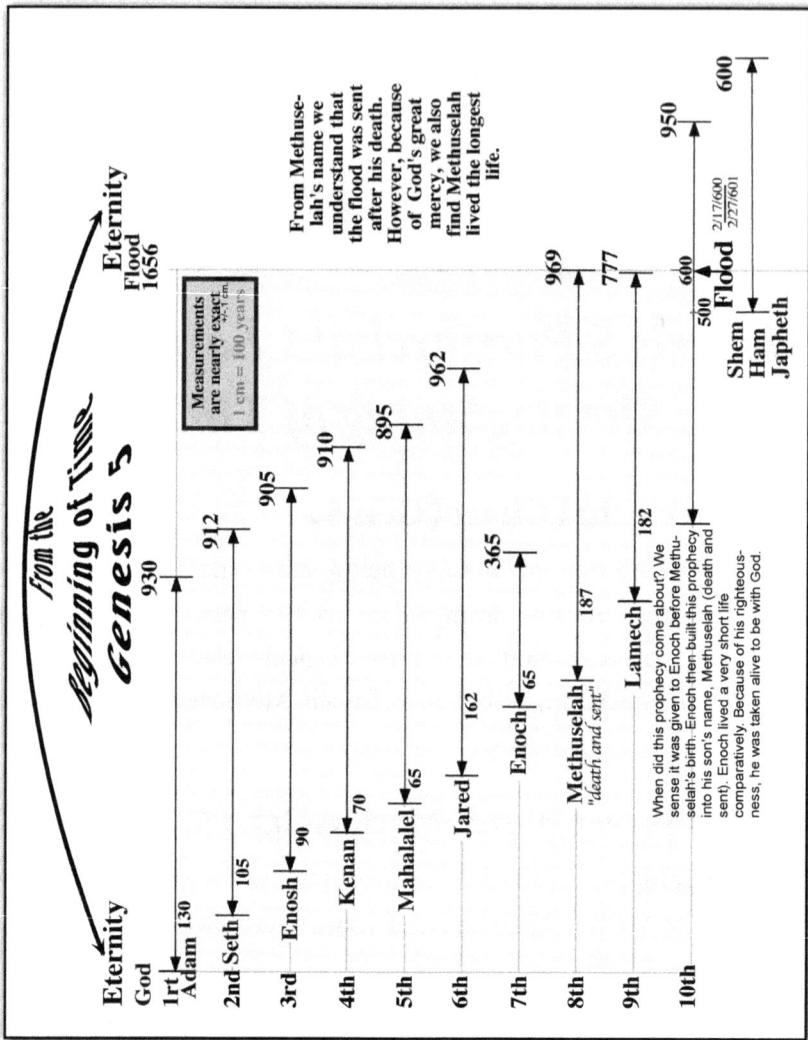

DIAGRAM OF GENESIS 5 GENEALOGY

Names have significant meanings in the Bible and in many eastern countries. They are in a sense prophetic of a person. Jacob means "crooked." Abraham means "father of many nations." Enoch means "dedicated."

Methuselah means "death and sent." The objection to this interpretation is that the word for death has a letter out of place. But no godly man like

Enoch could put "death" into his son's name ('Death' became a famous god's name at some point in history.) Instead, the letter was switched to make 'death' hidden and yet present. We need to ask, "Why?"

Two significant events that confirm this prophetic aspect.

1. A Cosmic Happening

First, something great and tremendous was sent almost immediately upon Methuselah's death in 1656 (from Adam's birth counting). What was sent? Right after Methuselah's death, a great judgment would be sent upon the world. This judgment was none other than the world-wide flood that swept the then-known world into oblivion. Only eight people survived the sea of death (see Genesis 5 chart).

2. The Great Prophecy

Secondly, in further confirmation to Methuselah's significant name was the great prophecy given to his father, Enoch. We would not know of this prophecy except from Jude 1:14-15.

> And about these also Enoch, [in] the seventh [generation] from Adam, prophesied, saying, "Behold, the Lord

came with many thousands of His holy ones, to execute judgment upon all, and to convict all the ungodly of all their ungodly deeds which they have done in an ungodly way, and of all the harsh things which ungodly sinners have spoken against Him (Jude 1:14-15).

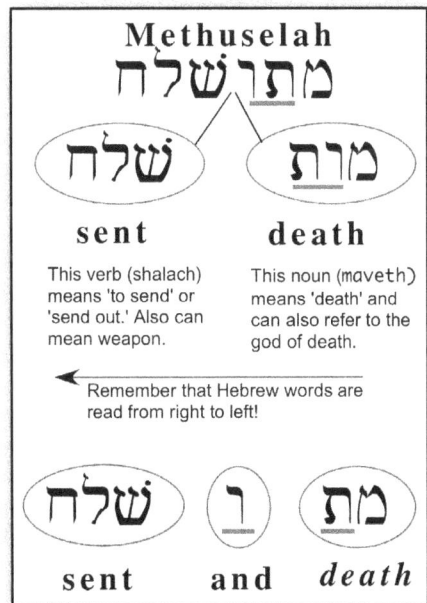

Methuselah

מְתֻשֶׁלַח

שֶׁלַח	מֻת
sent	**death**
This verb (shalach) means 'to send' or 'send out.' Also can mean weapon.	This noun (maveth) means 'death' and can also refer to the god of death.

◀ Remember that Hebrew words are read from right to left!

שֶׁלַח	וּ	מֻת
sent	**and**	*death*

When did this prophecy come about? We believe this prophecy was given to Enoch before Methuselah's birth. Enoch then encoded this prophecy into his son's name, Methuselah (death and sent). Enoch's prophecy of great judgment would come right after his son died. His son's name Methuselah was Enoch's secret word. We understand there might be suspicion to this name because some books interpret Methuselah's name to be "man of the dart." This is possible, but that interpretation has a problem. There is the oddly placed conjunction "and" in the middle of the two words "man" and "weapon." We favor "death and sent."

Conclusion

In summary, "death and sent" is a very meaningful name given the context of Methuselah's life and death along with his father's important vision. God revealed his judgment of the wicked at Methuselah's death, and Enoch incorporated this prophecy into his son's name.

Perhaps the most confirming aspect of all of this is God's stamp of grace. Everyone knows (don't you?) that Methuselah lived the longest of all men recorded in the Bible–969 years. The longer he lived, the longer the judgment was put off. This gave man a longer time to seek God and avert judgment. God clearly shows His great patience with man by sending judgment at the very last moment. We see the words of Ezekiel here, "For I have no pleasure in the death of anyone who dies," declares the Lord GOD. "Therefore, repent and live" (Ez 18:32).

One might question whether Methuselah died before the flood or by the flood. The evidence strongly leads in favor of before the flood.

1. Methuselah was of the godly line (Luke 3:27). He was in the line of ten godly descendants that preserved the godly promise. There no doubt

are others that are not mentioned. It is likely that he did not die as the rest of the world did. He was not in its judgment because he chose to live God's way.

2. Methuselah also was the oldest of all known mankind. At 969, he drew closest to the seeming ideal of 1000 years old. Long life is associated with the blessing of God. This is the way the scripture presents long life.

3) And lastly, Methuselah itself means 'sent death.' I suppose one could also argue that he died by the sending of the flood. His name would have no special significance if he would die by the flood for that would be true for all the ungodly at that time. God instead seems to have taken the oldest man living and then send the flood.

A Future Judgment

We know that judgment is soon coming upon the present earth too. This next time it will not be a flood, but fire that closes this phase of the earth. Jesus told us to be alert. Be ready. The oldest man in the Bible lived 969 years. Methuselah died right before the flood. This depicts the greatness of God's patience and mercy.

Don't fall away like others. Look to His return. Now is the day to repent– before judgment comes. He has already put off the judgment we deserve because of our great and many sins, but soon His judgment will come in God's heaped up wrath. If the Lord came with thousands of his holy ones to execute judgment upon the fraction of the people living in the time of the flood, we should understand that our judgment will be much greater; not with water, but with fire.

GENESIS

Genesis 6:1-13
The Pre-Flood Compromise

The Cause of Judgment (Gen 6:1-4)

> Now it came about, when men began to multiply on the face of the land, and daughters were born to them, 2 that the sons of God saw that the daughters of men were beautiful; and they took wives for themselves, whomever they chose. 3 Then the LORD said, "My Spirit shall not strive with man forever, because he also is flesh; nevertheless his days shall be one hundred and twenty years." 4 The Nephilim were on the earth in those days, and also afterward, when the sons of God came in to the daughters of men, and they bore children to them. Those were the mighty men who were of old, men of renown (Gen 6:1-4).

God told man to multiply and it was happening, "men began to multiply on the face of the land." The problem that urged the coming of the flood was not the number of mankind but their violence and corruption (6:12-13). Without correction, man's evil worsens as numbers increase.

Although we cannot be sure of the identity of the Nephilim and "sons of God," we can be sure that what they did came to God's notice, "My Spirit shall not strive with man...." (6:3). This is where God would shorten man's life span by bringing on the flood and modifying the atmosphere (i.e. mist to rain) and limit the gene pool to Noah's three sons. Whatever interpretation is chosen, the interpretation must further affirm God's wrath.

Identifying the Nephilim

There is much debate as to who the Nephilim were. The term is only used twice in the scriptures and literally means giant. There is great divide on this answer probably because of its limited usage; fewer words provide more room for imagination. Fortunately, it does not matter.

The Nephilim were referred to before and after the flood, but they didn't necessarily refer to the same group. The Book of Numbers refers to them as physical giants. Genesis 6:4 interestingly comments the Nephilim existed before and afterwards. This does not mean we should quickly conclude those in Moses' time (Num 13:33) south of Canaan (around 1500 BC) and those before the flood (around 2300 BC) were the same. After all, all the Nephilim perished in the flood. More likely, the second reference of the Nephilim, "also afterwards," identifies the period when the Sons of God came to intermarry, "...also afterward, when the sons of God came into...." (Gen 6:4).

It is unclear whether the daughters of men refers to the daughters of the Nephilim. Either the Nephilim are mentioned due to their daughters being involved in intermarrying or because the identification of the pressures of that period when the sons of God compromised their faith.

Identification of the "sons of God"

There are three major interpretations as to who the "sons of God" refer to in Gen 6:2 and 4. Again, it does not matter because in each case we are warned on how compromise of our faith often begins by intermarrying, which legitimizes Paul's caution against marrying out of one's faith (1 Cor 7:39).

(1) Fallen Angels

Some suggest that devils (i.e. fallen angels) somehow took on human nature to intermarry and interbreed with the human race. This suggestion does give sufficient reason as to why they could have brought on the judgment of God through the flood. The human race got increasingly depraved with the advances of these evil beings, but there is no basis for an interpretation with intermarrying angels.

A comment Jesus made in Matthew eliminates this possibility, "For in the resurrection they neither marry, nor are given in marriage, but are like angels in heaven" (Matt 22:30). What is true with the good angels is true with the wicked ones, that is, they do not marry nor do they bear children (6:4). Furthermore, there is no suggestion that they are angels. In order to consider it as a fair interpretation, there must be more clues than just a few scriptural passages from one book referring to the "sons of God."

The phrase "sons of God" is used in only two contexts in the Old Testament, one here in Genesis 6 (6:2,4) and the other in Job (Job 1:6, 2:1, 38:7). In the New Testament, however, 'sons of God' clearly refers to God's children and never to angels (Matt 5:9, Luke 20:36, Rom 8:14,19; Gal 3:26). Jesus in the New Testament is not afraid of calling God's people "sons of God." A son bears the likeness of his Father. Evil angels had no likeness of God, while the faithful angels did– if these were angels, they were not virtuous ones.

(2) Great and Powerful Rulers

Another possibility is that the "sons of God" referred to men of renown such as kings or rulers. This interpretation, however, does not add anything new for it is a common practice of powerful men to take women they like. How would that drastically worsen the pre-flood world situation so to incur God's wrath?[60]

(3) Seth's Godly Line

We favor the interpretation that associates the "sons of God" with the Seth line, the godly line that kept communion with God. This line of

---

60 Kline's suggestion that they were tyrannical 'divine kings' is similar, though from a different perspective (The Westminster Theological Journal, 1962: 199).

thinking is strongly supported by the strong emphasis of the godly line pictured in chapter five. The compromise of the godly line, furthermore, could feasibly provoke judgement. With the godly line sullied, what hope was there of a growing godly influence? "Salt is good; but if the salt becomes unsalty, with what will you make it salty again?" (Mark 9:50)

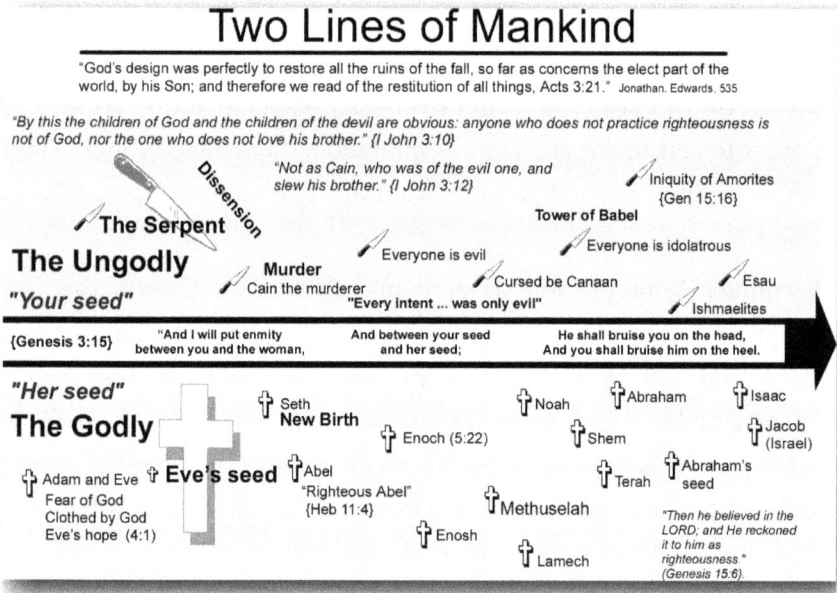

Two Lines of Mankind

"God's design was perfectly to restore all the ruins of the fall, so far as concerns the elect part of the world, by his Son; and therefore we read of the restitution of all things, Acts 3:21." Jonathan. Edwards. 535

"By this the children of God and the children of the devil are obvious: anyone who does not practice righteousness is not of God, nor the one who does not love his brother." {I John 3:10}

Selecting a Mate

The sons of God were markedly different from the sons of man. Up to this point there was a distinction between the men who sought after God and the ones who had forgotten God. They were known by their commitment to their father's God. This tension to preserve godliness is the same tension we face in our secular world today.

These godly men should have paid more attention to their heritage and preserved their distinctiveness. Without a vision of godliness, senses take over. These sons of God "saw that the daughters of men were beautiful."

Their reasons for choosing their wives became faulty because they did not carefully govern what they saw. When we compare, we notice different parts and fix our eyes on what pleases us. Once we notice their beauty, we deliberate on it, and our minds influence our body. This is the reason we dare not look at pornography or any programs that entice us to pay attention to a woman's attractive physical features. Once beauty becomes the focal point, our senses steer our life decisions, utterly corrupting our world making us worthy to be judged.

"They took wives for themselves"

Once beauty became their reason for choosing a woman to marry, these decisions shape their wider life decisions. They lost the ability to reason and reflect. The flesh seized control, and they never got it back. By the way, we are not saying that a beautiful wife is bad! Sarah was beautiful. "Delight in the wife of your youth."

The issue is that beauty controlled their desires. The way a woman talked, looked, and walked gained the attention of these men. God's guidance took a second place to the 'counsel' of a woman's beauty. They became indiscriminate in their choices.

"Whomever they chose"

This statement asserts that the men of God took wives that did not share their perspectives. Genesis goes on to describe the headlong fall of society after this point. One doesn't need much dirt to ruin purity. This is true with holiness too. It stands as the highest priority to train our sons and daughters to spiritually judge things rather than physically or emotionally 'feel' things.

The LORD responded to this right away. He did not have to wait for a generation to prove His conclusion.[61] Once the godly seed is lost among the ungodly, it is lost. God had no choice but to shorten life expectancy in order to preserve man, otherwise the ungodliness would soon destroy the world.

A godly person must marry a godly person. Balaam's big payoff came about because of insight into this very principle (Num 31:16). Godliness must be protected. A church must carry on discipline. A family must have rules. A government must have laws to preserve itself. If what distinguishes God's people is lost, even for just one generation, then it is lost forever.

Judgment Decided (Gen 6:5-8)

> 5 Then the LORD saw that the wickedness of man was great on the earth, and that every intent of the thoughts of his heart was only evil continually. 6 And the LORD was sorry that He had made man on the earth, and He was grieved in His heart. 7 And the LORD said, "I will blot out man whom I have created from the face of the land, from man to animals to creeping things and to birds of the sky; for I am sorry that I have made them." 8 But Noah found favor in the eyes of the LORD (Gen 6:5-8).

The "then" at the beginning of verse 5 shows the continuity of this passage. Because of the former wickedness, then wickedness increased. This wickedness caused God to bring severe judgment.

God's reasoning for His grief was communicated in verse 6, "And the Lord was sorry that He had made man on the earth, and He was grieved in His heart." God's decision is expressed in verse 7, but God's reluctance to take such steps is important for us to understand. God is slow to anger (9 out of 14 times the phrase is used, it is describing God) (Ex 34:6, Ne 9:17); man is to be like God (James 1:19).

---

[61] But even still judgment took at least as long as it took Noah to build the ark.

God's judgment was thorough to wipe life from the face of the earth. The only hope for the future can be found in Noah because he found "favor in the eyes of the Lord." And God chose to work through Him to reestablish the godly line.

Noah is Chosen (Gen 6:9-13)

> 9 These are the records of the generations of Noah. Noah was a righteous man, blameless in his time; Noah walked with God. 10 And Noah became the father of three sons: Shem, Ham, and Japheth. 11 Now the earth was corrupt in the sight of God, and the earth was filled with violence. 12 And God looked on the earth, and behold, it was corrupt; for all flesh had corrupted their way upon the earth. 13 Then God said to Noah, "The end of all flesh has come before Me; for the earth is filled with violence because of them; and behold, I am about to destroy them with the earth" (Gen 6:9-13).

Genesis 6:9 begins the fourth record comprising the Book of Genesis (6:9-9:29), "These are the records of the generations of Noah." His genealogical connection with the godly line was established in chapter five and his righteousness affirmed here in chapter 6. Notice the three affirmations of Noah's righteous in verse 9: righteous, blameless in his time, and "Noah walked with God." That last affirmation reminds us of Adam and Eve in the Garden and encourages us to strive in our relationships with the Lord. Though we are a sinful world, God highly values those who esteem Him and His values (Ez 14:14, 20).

Verses 11-12 summarizes God's judgment of mankind at that point in history, "It was corrupt; for all flesh had corrupted their way upon the earth." Again, the emphasis is on the compromise of the godly line. In verse 13 and onward, God speaks to Noah about this judgment, "I am about to destroy them with the earth." With this solemn judgment, Noah faithfully works with God as described in chapters 6-9 of Genesis.

Preservation of God's People

Danger	*Solution*	*Means*
• Intermingling by marriage	• Destroy the wicked	• Noah and the Ark
• Strong power of the world	• Weakened by isolation	• Create multilingual world
• Swallowed up in pagan culture	• Separate a nation from others	• Call Abraham out from Ur
• Dependent on world power	• Keep separate from Egypt	• Place Joseph to keep them.

GENESIS

Genesis 6:14-9:29
A Nasty Spring Cleaning

After clearly demonstrating the wickedness of mankind and their deserved judgment, a pattern that is replicated in the Book of Revelation, God first reveals His plan to carry out the destruction of His earth as a warning. Although the great wrath of God unleashed upon the earth is attention getting–and we should not miss warning as it becomes an example for later days. God spends many more verses (i.e. chapters 6-9) revealing His patient plan to preserve mankind and work with them. It would have been much easier to simply eliminate the whole human race, but God instead laid out elaborate plans that took over a hundred years to accomplish!

The Instructions for the Ark (Gen 6:14-22)

14 "Make for yourself an ark of gopher wood; you shall make the ark with rooms, and shall cover it inside and out with pitch. 15 "And this is how you shall make it: the length of the ark three hundred cubits, its breadth fifty cubits, and its height thirty cubits. 16 "You shall make a window for the ark, and finish it to a cubit from the top; and set the door of the ark in the side of it; you shall make it with lower, second, and third decks. 17 "And behold, I, even I am bringing the flood of water upon the earth, to destroy all flesh in which is the breath of life, from under heaven; everything that is on the earth shall perish (Gen 6:14-17).

This carefully laid out design of salvation, popularly called Noah's Ark, is only replicated in the special plans given to Moses regarding the temple in Exodus and to Ezekiel/John in Revelation regarding the heavenly temple/city (Ez 40-48; Rev 21-22). Regarding the ark, there is no mention that the measurements represent anything, though the tabernacle was designed after a heavenly temple. We must assume the measurements only had to do with building a seaworthy ship that would safely deliver Noah, his family, and the animals to the shores of the newly washed earth. Verses 14-16 provide the scale of the ark while verse 17 the reason for such a craft, namely to withstand the tremendous judgment that would through a worldwide flood wipe out every living thing.

Local or Global Flood

There is much unneeded debate on whether the flood was global or local. First, God's plan to save the animals would have been ridiculous if the flood was only local because animals in other parts of the earth would still exist. Second, the Lord clearly tells us His purpose: "to destroy all flesh in which is the breath of life, from under heaven; everything that is on the earth shall perish" (17). If God was destroying every living thing that has the breath of life (i.e. that breathes air), then that was what He was doing. The suggestion of a local flood makes God look foolish (Why have a boat for animals, etc.?), but a global one provides a persistent warning to mankind that God holds people everywhere accountable for their actions and will one day judge everyone across the face of the earth.

Another support for a global flood in chapter 7 is how the Lord clearly identifies the flood going 15 cubits (45 feet) higher than the mountain tops. The Lord was keeping records and passed them on to us to make this local flood argument totally unneeded.

> 19 And the water prevailed more and more upon the earth, so that all the high mountains everywhere under the heavens were

covered. 20 The water prevailed fifteen cubits higher, and the mountains were covered (Gen 7:19-20).

In summary, there was no doubt that God justly judged the world and simultaneously wisely used the flood to create fossil fuels from all the submerged forests during the flood.

Promise and Hope

18 "But I will establish My covenant with you; and you shall enter the ark--you and your sons and your wife, and your sons' wives with you. 19 "And of every living thing of all flesh, you shall bring two of every kind into the ark, to keep them alive with you; they shall be male and female. 20 "Of the birds after their kind, and of the animals after their kind, of every creeping thing of the ground after its kind, two of every kind shall come to you to keep them alive. 21 "And as for you, take for yourself some of all food which is edible, and gather it to yourself; and it shall be for food for you and for them." 22 Thus Noah did; according to all that God had commanded him, so he did (Gen 6:18-22).

Verses 18-21 give special expectations and directions to Noah. Most important to note is God's willingness to make a new covenant with Noah. God is revealing a new future plan with Noah and his family. Although God is very upset with the evil of many, He delighted in righteous Noah, who, along with all the animals that Noah brings aboard, would be saved from the devastation. The Lord did not hint at how long this might take, but they were instructed to take the necessary food for them and all the animals. Whether Noah had a special way to preserve the food or that God miraculously blessed it, we do not know, except that it worked.

People speculate on whether these animals could actually fit on the ark which was as long as a football field or that they could have brought so many animals on board that are living today. The Lord brought representatives of "kinds" of animals from which all the other variants came. For example, only one male and female cat with a rich gene pool needed to be brought aboard to give us the variety we enjoy today.[62]

Noah and his animals survived because he obeyed the Lord (22). God was the gracious one passing His plans on to Noah so he could prepare for the event. Disobedience would have brought destruction to all.

Entering the Ark (Gen 7-8)

7:1 Then the LORD said to Noah, "Enter the ark, you and all your household; for you alone I have seen to be righteous before Me in this time. 2 "You shall take with you of every clean animal by sevens, a male and his female; and of the animals that are not clean two, a male and his female; 3 also of the birds of the sky, by sevens, male and female, to keep offspring alive on the face of all the earth.4 "For after seven more days, I will send rain on the earth forty days and forty nights; and I will blot out from the face of the land every living thing that I have made." 5 And Noah did according to all that the LORD had commanded him. 6 Now Noah was six hundred years old when the flood of water came upon the earth.

The time came for Noah to board. The Lord was carefully watching the whole building process and now, with His wrath ready to be released on the wicked men of the earth and with the ark fully built, God directed Noah to board. God repeated what was going on in His mind in verse 4, "I will blot out from the face of the land every living thing I have made." But nothing is said of what was going on in Noah's mind. We can imagine them looking at this strange earth, speculating how this thing will spare them from raging waters. God includes again the most important point, "Noah did according to all that the Lord commanded" (7:5). This is, after all, what marked Noah off from everyone else. He obeyed when they disobeyed.

---

[62] *Answers in Genesis* specializes in such research: https://answersingenesis.org

Noah was to take two of every kind of animal on board, of course one male and one female for the purpose of reproducing more, along with seven of the birds and "clean" animals, which could be used for eating and sacrifice. Of course, up to this point, they did not eat animals but were vegetarians. Others might have eaten flesh, but Noah closely followed God's commands that were passed on down from Adam (Gen 1:30). It is only after the flood that the Lord will give permission to eat animals (9:3).

A few interesting points. First, Noah is said to bring the animals on board but in one verse God alludes to His part in bringing all the animals on board, "two of every kind shall come to you to keep them alive" (6:20). Although Noah was commanded to bring them on board (7:9,16), it appears God brought them to the ark itself, which would have saved Noah from an impossible job, assuming he could ever find them on his own.

Second, God closed the door. After Noah, his family, and the animals boarded, "the LORD closed it behind him" (7:16). It appears that Noah could not have closed it on his own, and so the ark becomes an illustration of salvation. God had a saving (i.e. evacuation) plan before judgment day would come, and the Lord passed His plan onto a righteous man who would save the world. God saved those trusting in Him, and Noah, being faithful, fully executed his part and thus the world was saved for God's covenant purposes.

The New Testament and Jesus refer to this flood without any hesitation, "For as in those days which were before the flood they were eating and drinking, they were marrying and giving in marriage, until the day that Noah entered the ark, and they did not understand until the flood came and took them all away; so shall the coming of the Son of Man be" (Mat 24:38-39; Luke 17:27). The early part of Genesis 6 similarly speaks of the world before the flood living in rebellion from God. This all is an illustration of how God's wrath will increase until Jesus Christ comes back to save His people. It is only those who are in Christ (i.e. in the ark) that will be saved from God's wrath. "And did not spare the ancient world, but preserved Noah, a preacher of righteousness, with seven others, when He brought a flood upon the world of the ungodly" (2 Pe 2:5).

Timing

There are several aspects about timing that we should pay attention to, including when it happened, how old Noah was, how long it took to build the ark, the time for the flood, and the time waiting for the earth to be readied after the waters receded. There is no date for when God first notified Noah about the ark, so the time of building it is unknown, though an educated guess indicates it to be less than forty years.[63]

With verse 7:4, the Lord gives us the first time specification: forty days will be the length of the flood, the "forty days and forty nights" speaks of the ongoing persistence of the flood throughout that time. This forty days would start after seven days. Noah, his family, and the animals were to board a week in advance. It was a process and would take time to prepare, but the signal was clear–the boat was ready. No more work on it. Verse 13 says that Noah, along with his sons and his wives and all the animals, actually boarded in the same day.

Noah was 600 years old when the flood came upon the earth (7:6). Before this time, his three sons were born and had found wives. In verse 11, the Lord expounded on the actual date with reference to Noah's life more exactly, "In the six hundredth year of Noah's life, in the second month, on the seventeenth day of the month, on the same day all the fountains of the great deep burst open, and the floodgates of the sky

---

[63] Shem was not the oldest, though first mentioned. He was 98 when entering the ark. So giving years to grow up and marry, we can see that it took about forty years to build the ark. "These are the records of the generations of Shem. Shem was one hundred years old, and became the father of Arpachshad two years after the flood" (Gen 11:10).

were opened" (7:11). They probably used the lunar calendar and in the second month, 17th day the flood occurred.

We should note that all the water did not simply fall from the sky but also came up from the great deeps. It appears that there was one supercontinent at the time and that great caverns of water were pushed up from underneath maybe separating the continents. Some suggest that a canopy surrounding the earth also freely gave of its tremendous amount of water. The point is not whether we fully understand where the water came from, though that is very interesting, but that God used the water to destroy all living creatures except those on the ark.

In 7:24 the Lord tells us that the earth remained flooded for 150 days, probably excluding the forty of the flooding. The flooded land began to be relieved only after four months, and then the waters started to recede. Actually, later in 8:4, the Lord points out the specific day the ark landed, "And in the seventh month, on the seventeenth day of the month, the ark rested upon the mountains of Ararat" (8:4). After the water started to recede, the ark finally rested on some of the tall mountains. Here are some time markers that were very significant to Noah and his family:

- Flood started when Noah was 600, 2nd month, 17th day (7:11).
- Flood stopped after 40 days (7:17)
- Waters started receding after 150 days (8:3)
- The ark touched bottom (on Mount Ararat): 7th month, 17th day (8:4)
- The top of the mountains became visible: 10th month, 1st day (8:5)
- Noah opened the window and released a raven (11th month -40 days) (8:6-8). Afterwards twice released a dove.
- Water was dried up from the earth: 601 year, 1st month (8:13).
- The waters receded sufficiently to exit: 601 year, 2nd month, 27th day (8:14)

The whole flood story is fascinating, especially with how the Lord used it to judge the world and at the same time save a people for Himself.

After the Flood (Gen 9)

9:1 And God blessed Noah and his sons and said to them, "Be fruitful and multiply, and fill the earth. 2 "And the fear of you and the terror of you shall be on every beast of the earth and on every bird of the sky; with everything that creeps on the ground, and all the fish of the sea, into your hand they are given. 3 "Every moving thing that is alive shall be food for you; I give all to you, as I gave the green plant. 4 "Only you shall not eat flesh with its life, that is, its blood (Gen 9:1-4).

Many huge changes took place for Noah and his family, including the great destruction of mankind and the new beginning. The ark served as an indication that God had a good plan in mind for Noah, and His assertion of this blessing upon Noah brought great relief (9:1). So, after the flood, what would remain the same and what would be different? We need to compare Genesis 1-3 and Genesis 9 to see the differences.

Noah still had to live in the hope of God's promises, and he still had to multiply. This commandment in itself spoke volumes of God's attitude toward mankind. If God detested man, why would He command them to increase their number? God wants mankind to the fill the earth with people and was willing to risk another mass rebellion against His ways in order to accomplish His greater plans (Rev 5:9-10).

We also see that the relationship between man and animals would be broken. "And the fear of you and the terror of you shall be on every beast of the earth and on every bird of the sky; with everything that creeps on the ground, and all the fish of the sea, into your hand they are given" (Gen 9:2). Terror will be instilled in the animals so they will not approach man.

Along with this, we notice that every moving thing was able to be served as food. Before the flood, man could only eat the plants, but now he has been given a wider menu. "Every moving thing that is alive shall be food for you; I give all to you, as I gave the green plant. Only you shall not eat flesh with its life, that is, its blood" (9:3-4). Some say, mostly affected by

Hinduism in the New Age or Buddhism, that one can better himself if he doesn't eat meat. There is not any solid proof for this. Vegetarians still die around seventy, and some of those who eat meat still live to be a hundred.

There is only one ongoing requirement for eating food. Man could not eat an animal with its blood. Some think of this new policy of eating flesh as too cruel. The Lord did instruct us on making sure the blood drained out after killing the beast. Though eating flesh became permissible, it's good to note that it was not a command.

Also spoken clearly here is the command against murder, "Whoever sheds man's blood, By man his blood shall be shed, For in the image of God He made man" (9:6). We already know that the value of man rests in the fact that he is made in the image of God (cf. Gen 1), even after he fell into sin. Therefore, no one, including beasts, should dare to put harm to God's special creation. Murder is out. God will take personal vengeance upon anyone or thing that kills another. Abortion is not an exception.

Along with the protection of life, is the command to increase it. If we are not convinced by verse 1, we should be by verse 7, "And as for you, be fruitful and multiply; Populate the earth abundantly and multiply in it" (9:7). God was not at all concerned with overpopulation. We are not only to populate the earth, but to populate it abundantly and multiply in it. We don't see simply additional increases but multiples of increases. One might think this command was just for Noah and his sons, but this command is perpetual because its end is so far ahead of our reach. They say our earth is full now, but it's not full enough. We are actually killing off millions through abortion so not to fulfill this command!

God reassures Noah, his family, and the animals as if they could understand. God made a covenant with them, that He would never again judge the earth by a flood. The rainbow stands as a heavenly reminder that God will not again judge mankind with a massive watery destruction (9:16-17).

A Population Explosion

So both man and animal reproduced and filled the earth. "These three were the sons of Noah; and from these the whole earth was populated" (9:19). Noah evidently did not have anymore children, and with all other human beings being gone, everyone now alive descended from one of Noah's three sons: "Shem and Ham and Japheth" (6:13; 9:19).

A Dark Event

> 20 Then Noah began farming and planted a vineyard. 21 And he drank of the wine and became drunk, and uncovered himself inside his tent. 22 And Ham, the father of Canaan, saw the nakedness of his father, and told his two brothers outside. 23 But Shem and Japheth took a garment and laid it upon both their shoulders and walked backward and covered the nakedness of their father; and their faces were turned away, so that they did not see their father's nakedness. 24 When Noah awoke from his wine, he knew what his youngest son had done to him. 25 So he said, "Cursed be Canaan; A servant of servants He shall be to his brothers." 26 He also said, "Blessed be the LORD, The God of Shem; And let Canaan be his servant. 27 "May God enlarge Japheth, And let him dwell in the tents of Shem; And let Canaan be his servant." 28 And Noah lived three hundred and fifty years after the flood. 29 So all the days of Noah were nine hundred and fifty years, and he died (Gen 9:20-29).

Everything would seem great with the new start except we discover that evil has crept back into the world, even as it did shortly after the first creation in Genesis 3. The scriptures reveal Noah the righteous got drunk, and Ham committed a shameful act (9:22), which could have been making fun of his naked father or making play with him, but in any case, the other brothers were more noble and covered up their father.

The repercussions that came to the three sons and their descendants would somewhat reflect this scene. He blessed both Shem and Japheth, but designated Canaan, a son of Ham, to be cursed. This will be seen a bit more clearly in the following chapters when we look at the expansion of mankind, which has brought our world where it is today. Canaan is the same land that God would later appoint Israel to judge (cf. Joshua).

Noah lived another 350 years after the flood to stabilize the new world community, who would learn from him how to seek after God. But then after a full 950 years Noah died, and he became embedded in a legend with the ark. Over 200 ancient cultures hold an ancient flood story in their histories, which originated from the real story but over time certain facts were changed. The Chinese have such an ancient character named Nu-wah. The Chinese character for boat is interestingly composed of three parts: the

船

boat
number 8
people (lit. mouths)

boat on the left, the number 8 on top, and people on the bottom right. So even to this day the whole story of God's judgment and salvation is seen encrypted in this one common character for boat.

GENESIS

Genesis 10-11
Unity & Diversity: Noah's Sons and Babel

Genesis 10 and 11 help us understand the development of the nations. They not only enable us to trace Abraham's line back to Noah but also discover the keys to understanding our modern society's linguistic and societal groups.

Objectives:

- Show the connection between the ancient and modern worlds through genealogical records.
- Establish the development of languages.
- Deepen our faith and commitment to the God of the scriptures.
- Expose the subtle threats and dangers of today's world culture.

When we distance ourselves from the world revealed in the scriptures, we tend to distance ourselves from God and His great plan. We might think, "God lived in the ancient world, which is not relevant to our own age with modern economies, web connections, educational systems, easy international communication, and pollution problems."

What Genesis 10-11 does is bridge the gap between the ancient and the modern worlds, and they do this through detailed genealogies and careful explanations of 'modern' phenomena like the diversity that derives from the multiethnic societies and multitude of languages.

It is absolutely fantastic to discover links between our modern world and the ancient world in God's Word, which was written thousands of years ago. Ancient cultures never could look beyond their own culture. They would always brag of their accomplishments and speak excessively of them. Only in God's Word do we find this detailed and honest revelation of the history of the world. God wants to link our modern generation to the ancient world because it is only then that we will gain a full understanding of the Lord of history and His purposes among mankind.

Why is this so important? Secularism is dependent on a disconnect from the ancient past. If people realized that we share roots with those who are mentioned in the scriptures, they would have to face the God who designed and made them. Secularists believe that religion developed with ignorant men in response to fear. History shows a completely different story which links modern man with the creation.

Genealogy: Unity & Diversity (Gen 10)

Genesis 10 and 11 are closely tied in their message. Genesis 10 provides the backdrop not only for Genesis 11 but also for modern history. Genesis 10 is a collection of genealogical records of the three sons of Noah: Ham, Japheth, and Shem. Genesis 11 includes both a record of the Tower of Babel as well as charts a thousand years of Shem's line. An extended chart of Noah's descendants and his three sons is given later.

Sin had followed Noah into the new world and stained it early on. The Genesis 11:1-9 record of the Tower of Babel shows us how the world, from Noah's time onward, again declined into an intolerable state requiring God to use some special ingenious device to slow the decay.

Genealogy – Noah's Three Sons **Genesis 10:1-32**	**Shows how the different races developed under Noah's grandsons.**
Narrative – Tower of Babel **Genesis 11:1-9**	**Reveals the reason for the many thousands of languages forming barriers between cultures.**
Genealogy – Shem's line **Genesis 11:10-32**	**Keeps us focused on the line of men through which God revealed His truth and would send a Savior.**

AN OVERVIEW OF GENESIS 10-11

The genealogies of Genesis 5 and 11 work together to unite ancient history with modern history through Abraham. They have several similarities.

- They both mark ten generations.

- They end by noting the three sons of the last person, Noah and Terah, Noah's father.

- The genealogies are accurately self-referenced. This is done by giving both the age of the father when he died and when his son was born. Although providing great internal accuracy, it does not give reference to the world's chronological timeline.

Evil increased over time, and the pattern of evil becomes more evident as the history of man rolls along. The wickedness of man expanded more quickly and widely as time went on, which was perhaps a result of the lessened influence of the great patriarchs. The first long decline tumbled on for 1656 years before God stepped in with the flood. In comparison, the escalation of evil that manifested itself at the Tower of Babel only took a couple hundred years. God stepped in and used a whole new drastic method of restraint to slow down this growth of wickedness that would impede the speed by which man's depravity would grow. This, in hindsight, became a form of salvation for man because this act held off God's righteous wrath being poured out upon mankind.

The genealogy of chapter 10 shows how all the people of the world derived from these three sons of Noah: Japheth, Ham, and Shem. Shem's generations are recorded in chapter 11. Notice the introductions characteristic of the Book of Genesis (toledot sections). Genesis 10 and 11 both begin with this type of introduction:

- Genesis 10:1: "Now these are the records of the generations of Shem, Ham, and Japheth, the sons of Noah...."

- Genesis 11:10: "These are the records of the generations of Shem...."

Genealogy of Genesis 5 and 11: Two Millenniums from Adam to Terah

The genealogy takes a different course with this second millennium. Chapter 10 does not record dates, and we find no information on how old Shem, Ham, and Japheth are. We only know about Shem's line from Genesis 11, which is how God shows us that He is only concerned about tracing the line from which the Messiah would be born. God shows how He is fulfilling the promise He first made in Genesis 3:15. This genealogical strategy was also utilized during the formation of Israel. Only the Levite's line was shown to continue (Exodus 6).

Millennium #1 Genesis 5 Adam to Noah   **Ten Generations**

God saved the world from wickedness through the ark.

Adam	Seth	Enosh	Kenan	Mahalalel	Jared	Enoch	Methuselah	Lamech	1000 Creation	Noah
0	130	235	325	396	460	622	687	874		1056

930   987
Adam   Enoch
died   taken

Millennium #2 Genesis 11 Noah to Terah   **Ten Generations**

God saved the world from wickedness through confusion.

1000 Creation	Noah		Shem		Arpachshad	Eber	Reu	Nahor		Abraham	2000
	1056		1558		1658	1723	1787	1849		2008	

Shelah Peleg Serug Terah
1693   1757   1819   1878

1656   1871?   Noah
Flood   Babel   died

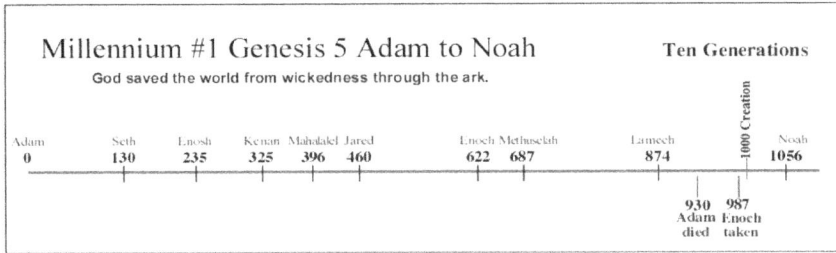

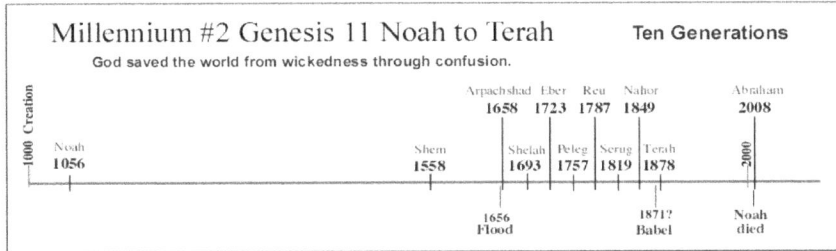

GENEALOGICAL CHARTS FROM GENESIS 5 AND 11

A United People under Noah (Gen 10)

In Genesis 10 we find the descendants of Noah; sixteen grandsons can be traced into the different parts of the world where they went. Genesis 10 shows that the world is linked to what God is doing in history. Secularists want to categorize all religions as myth, but Noah's ark and the genealogical record of Genesis 10 presents such a startling perspective of how we are all linked together. Secularism is scared to face the facts. They want to believe in an old earth rather than consider the possibility that the earth has only entered its 7th millennium.

A United History (Gen 10:6-11)

There are many examples of how the ancient world is connected. One example is found in Genesis 10:10-11. The larger context says,

And the sons of Ham were Cush and Mizraim and Put and Canaan. And the sons of Cush were Seba and Havilah and Sabtah and Raamah and Sabteca; and the sons of Raamah were Sheba and Dedan. Now Cush became the father of Nimrod; he became a mighty one on the earth. He was a mighty hunter before the

LORD; therefore it is said, "Like Nimrod a mighty hunter before the LORD." And the beginning of his kingdom was Babel and Erech and Accad and Calneh, in the land of Shinar. From that land he went forth into Assyria, and built Nineveh and Rehoboth-Ir and Calah (Gen 10:6-11).

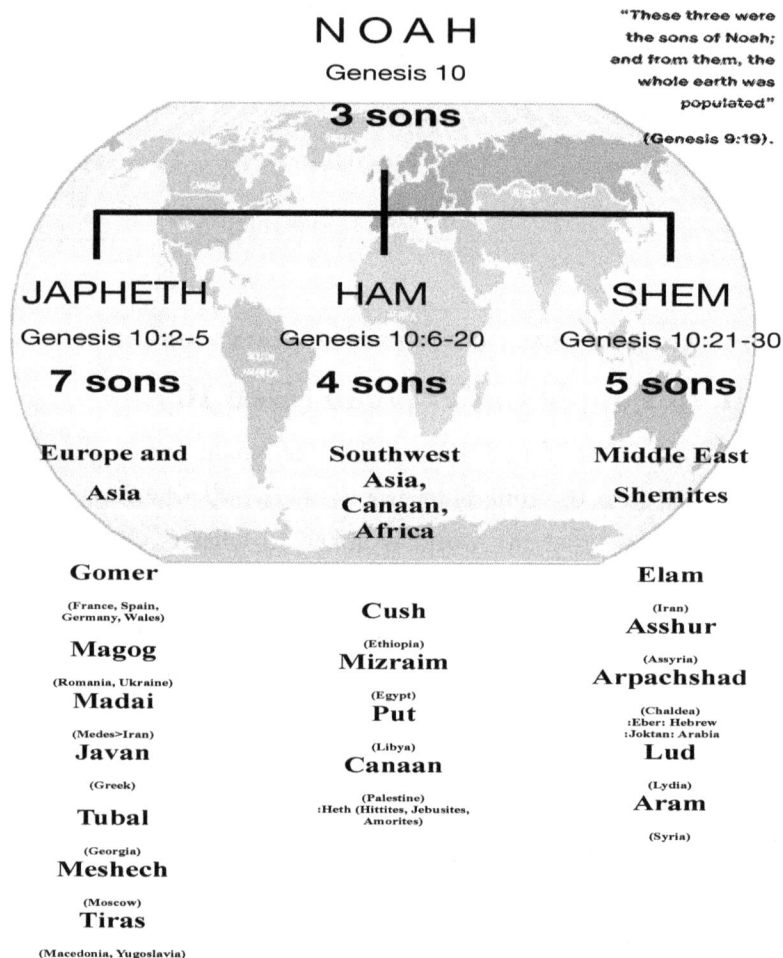

NOAH
Genesis 10
3 sons

"These three were the sons of Noah; and from them, the whole earth was populated" (Genesis 9:19).

JAPHETH	HAM	SHEM
Genesis 10:2-5	Genesis 10:6-20	Genesis 10:21-30
7 sons	**4 sons**	**5 sons**
Europe and Asia	Southwest Asia, Canaan, Africa	Middle East Shemites

Gomer		Elam
(France, Spain, Germany, Wales)	**Cush**	(Iran)
Magog	(Ethiopia)	**Asshur**
(Romania, Ukraine)	**Mizraim**	(Assyria)
Madai	(Egypt)	**Arpachshad**
(Medes>Iran)	**Put**	(Chaldea) :Eber: Hebrew :Joktan: Arabia
Javan	(Libya)	**Lud**
(Greek)	**Canaan**	(Lydia)
Tubal	(Palestine) :Heth (Hittites, Jebusites, Amorites)	**Aram**
(Georgia)		(Syria)
Meshech		
(Moscow)		
Tiras		
(Macedonia, Yugoslavia)		

GRAPHIC DISTRIBUTION OF NOAH'S GRANDSONS – GENESIS 10

At first, this might look like a very boring list of names. As we take a thorough look, however, we will find a summary of ancient history. Ham was the son of Noah. Cush was one of Ham's sons. Cush had his own son and named him Nimrod (great grandson of Noah).

This summarized history has references to the same places ancient historical books do. Archaeological studies are regularly uncovering and thus confirming with greater clarity many of the once questioned biblical references. What the Bible records is most significant, namely, Nimrod's building of a number of large cities, many of which we know from ancient history.

Nimrod started his city-building campaign with Mesopotamia, which was in what we now know as southern Iraq in the plains of Shinar, the land between the two rivers.[64] Babel (Gen 10:10) is Babylon (near modern day Bagdad). Accad (Akkad) is known for the ancient language Akkadian. Erech is suggested to be Uruk of Gilagamesh's epic. Many scholars assert Gilgamesh is indeed Nimrod himself.[65] Cush's city, Kish, was named after him.[66]

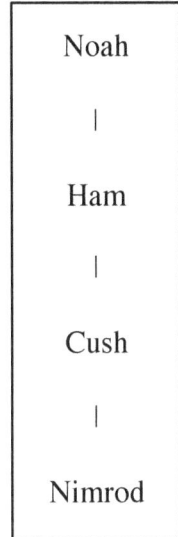

Noah
Ham
Cush
Nimrod

Genesis 10:11 says that Nimrod went to the north and started a number of cities there. "From that land he went forth into Assyria, and built Nineveh...." Nineveh is the most well-known city along the Tigris both in and outside Biblical context. The historical mounds of this huge city that had a wall eight miles long with fifteen huge gates. Many historical artifacts exist from this time. One of the mounds where Nineveh is (outside Mosul) actually is named 'The prophet Jonah" obviously related to the Prophet Jonah that visited that

---

64 In Hebrew the sound 'sh' and 's' are similar except for a dot. Some have difficulty with certain sounds and so word sounds adapt accordingly. It is hard to understand this because we are focused on how it is written when they imitate the sound. Note 'Uruk' and 'Erech.' We are less sure of Shinar's origin (Sin is moon goddess).

65 See http://www.ancientdays.net/nimrod.htm for more discussion.

66 Ethiopia also comes from Cush, but Cush's descendants might first have settled in Kish before going to the Ethiopian region. We are not sure.

city.[67] Calah is another city in modern day Iraq, twenty miles southeast of Mosul, that was also mentioned in Genesis 10:11. The awareness of the city has again come alive because of the Iraq war, it being the center of the Babylonian kingdom, the place of the first great cities and civilizations.

Genesis 10 provides a clear background of the Tower of Babel. Genesis 10 and 11 cannot be separated. Neither should modern history be disconnected from ancient history as it is described in the scriptures.

Genesis unashamedly confronts secularism. Secularism asserts that man has no roots back to God and His original creation. They live for the moment. Genesis states the world around us and man's origins are founded by and for God. This makes us dependent upon Him. Man is made for God and can find personal fulfillment only by having God's purpose accomplished in his or her life.

The Tower of Babel (Gen 11:1-9)

Now the whole earth used the same language and the same words. 2 And it came about as they journeyed east, that they found a plain in the land of Shinar and settled there. 3 And they said to one another, "Come, let us make bricks and burn them thoroughly." And they used brick for stone, and they used tar for mortar. 4 And they said, "Come, let us build for ourselves a city, and a tower

---

[67] Jonah's tomb was only recently destroyed.
http://www.cnn.com/2014/07/24/world/iraq-violence/index.html

whose top will reach into heaven, and let us make for ourselves a name; lest we be scattered abroad over the face of the whole earth." 5 And the LORD came down to see the city and the tower which the sons of men had built (Gen 11:1-5).

Man's Assessment (11:1-4)

Man was hesitant to spread out across the earth (11:4) because the cities offered so much more. They were right in one sense (11:6), but God forced their hand and dispersed them according to their various languages. This force to conquer and explore grew at different times and places, perhaps summarized by the phrase, "Go where no man has gone!"

So man communicated their plan to be a powerful people by:

Step #1: Readying the materials

Step #2: Building a city and tower

Their purpose was to become famous, an attraction point. They actually built the city and the Tower of Babel that reached far into the sky (11:5).

The Tower of Babel

Genesis 11 starts with a record of what happened in Babylon at the Tower. This event drastically reshaped the world's cultures. Genesis 10 paints a broad picture of what was happening throughout the world regarding who was filling the world, and to some degree where, but this event in chapter 11 further shows God's hand in history in the way the multiplicity of languages has affected the world.

The world is trying to overcome the barriers of language and culture, and it is getting closer to accomplishing that goal. The quest for power and money drives the machine of world culture, but God has His own purpose in humankind overcoming the barrier of language and culture: He wants to see people of every language giving praise to Him.

The sin of Noah and his sons was included in scripture (Gen 9:20-27) to remind us of the inherent flaws of the new societies that would form after the flood. God was not disillusioned; people are always hopeful of the discovery of some utopia, a perfect society, but God's Word assures us that this ideal world will not be found after the flood in Noah's new world. Sin follows mankind because it has infected the nature of man.

Ziggurat in Babylon

(Etemenanki - temple of the foundation of heaven and earth).

The Tower of Babel is one of many ziggurats that were built in the early Mesopotamian plain. They each seem to have a temple on the top of them, which is what the Biblical account suggests. It was not only a military lookout station but also served as a place for the people to commune with the gods. Most interesting is a quote from King Nebuchadnezzar referring to the reason those building the Tower of Babel (Babylon) abandoned it, because "Since a remote time, people had abandoned it, without order expressing their words."[68] This no doubt refers to the language confusion. Words were "without order".

The temple mound of Babel is still there today, and can be seen in a Google Earth satellite picture. The tower deteriorated, but the rubble was covered up with dust and dirt and formed a mound that is higher than the ground around it.[69]

The Date of the Tower of Babel

The Tower of Babel event recorded in the Bible shows how the wickedness of mankind again got out of hand, which caused God to judge the earth. God provided grace by separating mankind into a number of different groups. Each language group no doubt was based on a family. We find 70 people groups in Genesis 10.

---

[68] https://en.wikipedia.org/wiki/Etemenanki

[69] The picture above is current and from Google Earth.

The date of the Tower of Babel event is not certain, but it does fit into the ancient history of the Sumerians. We do not know, however, where it fits in the above genealogical chart. The flood is quite clear because it was person specific, that is, Noah's sons were already grown up (Shem was 100 hundred years old) and dates were supplied.

The Tower of Babel account in Genesis 11:1-9 does not have these dates, so it is difficult to pinpoint. Some have suggested that Genesis 10:25 refers to the Tower of Babel. "And two sons were born to Eber; the name of the one was Peleg, for in his days the earth was divided; and his brother's name was Joktan" (Gen 10:25). Those that hold to this interpretive point consider the division referred to in the verse is the actual division of mankind that occurred due to the varying languages. "So the LORD scattered them abroad from there over the face of the whole earth; and they stopped building the city" (Gen 11:8). Others suggest that this division in Peleg's day refers to the splitting of the continents. The division of mankind seems more likely. Genesis 11 did not follow after the genealogy of chapter 10. The genealogy was complete.

We simply do not know when the Tower of the Babel happened, but we do know that it had a great impact on the history of mankind. When I travel to the villages and cities in India, China, or Africa, I constantly need to find translators. Language has formed a barrier of information and thus created a 'natural' separation. The unknown always creates a tendency to protect and suspect.

The Lord mixed up language to preserve mankind from pooling his filthy ideas and working for the mass detriment of humankind. The church's first miraculous event found in Acts 2 found people speaking all sorts of languages without knowing them beforehand. The crowd heard the Gospel in their native tongues. Although this was a special occasion, it helps us realize that from that point on, the Gospel was to go out to the whole world and break the language barriers, starting the great missionary movement.

God's Assessment and Judgment (Gen 11:5-9)

Yahweh (LORD) came down to look at the city and tower that they had built. We should realize that the tower was only part of a big complex, the featured building of the city.

Unified purpose with one language gave them the potential to do anything that they wished. "And now nothing which they purpose to do will be impossible for them." God's observation is astonishing especially in light of His knowledge of man's capabilities.

God did two things. He first confused their language. The confusion came about because they no longer mutually understood one other as they had before. The scene was quite remarkable no doubt. We are not sure how large the groups that still did understand each other were. Was it a family or a great grandfather and his descendants that still understood each other? We are not sure. But whatever the case, each of these groups were forced to spread.

Related to the first, the Lord also scattered them about on the earth. We are not sure whether this 'scattering' involved anything beyond the confusion of languages. It is quite possible that something like bad weather or suspicion and a sense of protectionism came over them to the point that they desired their individual places. As a result of no longer understanding each other, they went across the earth looking for a place to establish their own societies, becoming the groundwork for our modern international world.

Diversity of Mankind (Gen 11:1-9)

Josephus, the Jewish historian around Jesus' time described the diversity of mankind in this way:

> When all men were of one language, some of them built a high tower, as if they would thereby ascend up to heaven; but the gods

sent storms of wind and overthrew the tower, and gave everyone his peculiar language; and for this reason it was that the city was called Babylon.... After this they were dispersed abroad, on account of their languages, and went out by colonies everywhere; and each colony took possession of that land which they lighted upon, and unto which God led them; so that the whole continent was filled with them, both the inland and maritime countries. There were some also who passed over the sea in ships, and inhabited the islands; and some of these nations do still retain the denominations (i.e. names) which were given to them by their first founders; but some also have lost them ...[70]

> **MAN VERSUS GOD**
> **(Gen 11:1-9)**
>
> Genesis 11:1-9 are composed of only a few sentences but gives us an astonishing social, linguistic and theological perspective of the world.

Development of Language (Gen 11:1-9)

A mono-lingual world is difficult for a world traveler to comprehend because different currencies, dress, customs, and languages are to be expected. It seems incredible for there to be only one language and culture across the earth. Same language, same words.

Since the scriptures only state that the one language was confused, it is possible that there is one original father language.

Much work is being done on the history of languages. They compare the words from the major language families (See the attached graphic).[71]

---

[70] Josephus, *The Works of Josephus: New Updated Version* (USA, Hendrickson Publishers, 1987) p35.

[71]

http://freepages.folklore.rootsweb.ancestry.com/~sturnbo/files/oldest/Table%20of%20Nations%20and%20Genealogy%20of%20Mankind.htm

Reflections on Cultures and Language

Man was confused before he was scattered. The language barrier not only made them drop their building plans but caused them to become isolated groups according to language. The confusion was selective though. People in the same groups could understand each other. People who speak the same live together – Chinatown! Isolated groups of people formed their own cultures. This explains why cultures have slight but distorted memories

Language Groupings

* Indo-European (Northern India/Europe)
* Afro-Asiatic (Northern Africa/Middle East/Southwestern Asia)
* Kartvelian (Caucasus Mountains/Southern Russia)
* Uralic (Northern Europe/Central Siberia/Eurasia)
* Altaic (Eastern Europe/Central Asia)
* Dravidian (Central & Southern India)
* Sino-Tibetan (Northern & Eastern Asia)
* Malayo-Polynesian (Southeastern Asia/Pacific Islands)
* Austro-Asiatic (Eastern India/Southwestern Asia)
* Niger-Congo (Western & Central Africa)
* Nilo-Saharan (Northeastern Africa)
* Khoisan (Southern Africa)
* Eskimo-Aleut (Northeastern Siberia/Alaska/Aleutians)
* Algonkian, Athapascan, Iroquoian, & Mosan (North America)
* Uto-Aztecan, Oto-Manguean, Mayan, & Macro-Chibchan (Central A)
* Carib, Andean-Equatorial (South America)
* Torricelli, West Papuan & Sepik-Ramu (New Guinea)
* Bunaban, Ngaran & Yiwaidjan (Northern Australia)
* Pama-Nyungan (Central & Southern Australia)

(see footnote for reference).

of main biblical events such as the flood–they all experienced it in the early development of their history before they were divided by language.

Some speculate that Hebrew was the original language (Edenic language). Isaac Mozeson, author of "The Word: The Dictionary that reveals the Hebrew roots of the English Language" is convinced of this. Below he writes,

> Percentage-wise and vocabulary-wise, English is more obviously a dialect of Hebrew than of Latin, Greek or French.

> More impressive than the Hebrew motto of Yale College is the title of Harvard College's first dissertation: Hebrew Is the Mother

Tongue. When Noah Webster's original dictionary traced many English words beyond German, French, Latin and Greek to their "Shemitic" origin, no one raised an eyebrow. Every learned person knew that Hebrew was the Mother Tongue.

The Oxford English Dictionary is so troubled by a biblical source for BABBLE (Babel), that it warns readers that "no direct connection with Babel can be traced" and declares the term to be of "unknown origin.""[72]

The Destruction of Cultures

Cultures are protected from fast decay because of an unspoken agreement on standards and stories that serve to uphold those values. Cultures begin to break down when outside 'stories' are introduced and different ways of life seem possible.

The isolation of different groups has restrained the growth of wickedness by establishing many different cultures across the globe. Each holds and protects its own values. The isolation of these cultures originated at the Tower of Babel. What has happened in the last generation is a fast degeneration of these many diverse cultures.

The desire of many different cultures to create a world culture, united by the web, will further accelerate the spread of wickedness. People from different cultures are able to communicate with people from different areas. Education has increased the usage of world languages like English. Automatic translation services on the web and elsewhere are rapidly enabling others to transfer information to others. The 'impurities' seeping into each culture bring them closer and closer to losing their individuality to the world. We need to be careful as we step into the 7th millennium!

---

[72] Isaac Mozeson, "Edenics (Biblical Hebrew)." Interchangeable Letters. N.p., n.d. Web. 07 Jan. 2013.

Danger of the Modern Culture

When we look back at Genesis 11:1-9, the seed of isolationism was planted. Wickedness now is increasing with the breakdown of the cultures, but we can find hope in how the Gospel is also spreading because of the spread of world culture. 4,000 new churches were planted in the Ukraine in the past ten years, and India, with its vast number of isolated villages with their own languages, is fast becoming evangelized. Over the last twenty years, an amazing 400,000 churches have been started across the world. Increasing urban populations that are international, multilingual, tolerant to modern standards, and shaped through the modern educational system spread their ideas over the world wide web. It is incredible to see the places people can now access this web, even in the poorest countries in the world. God's wrath might not be held off much longer.

The development of these tall towers in the ancient world is significant. Each tower resulted from the ambition of man to show himself as greater than his neighbor. The destruction of the Twin Towers is at least a warning from God to man, reminding him not to glory in himself. This does not restrain man, however; man goes bigger and taller, with Dubai being the biggest bidder now.

Observations

- Diverse cultures are reminders of God's preservation of mankind so that His plan of redemption can be worked out in earth's history through our Savior Christ Jesus.

- We should not be fooled into thinking one culture is better than any given other. Each has positive and negative traits. Instead we should remember that the problem of each of these cultures is connected to the sin that plagues our native cultures. It entered the human race through Adam and was passed on through Noah's sons, through Noah himself.

- Time is now short. War and disease can devastate large numbers of people on earth, and unless technology is taken away from us, we have the capability of combining our arrogance in a secular world culture. Temptation and sin will increase. How can we escape the world culture encroaching on our lives?

Reflection

- The battle with temptation will increase as this modern 'one world' society grows. What spiritual disciplines help protect you from these worldly intrusions upon your love for God and His ways? Be specific.

GENESIS

Genesis 12:1-9
Our Journey of Faith

Your Journey of Faith

Now the LORD said to Abram, "Go forth from your country, And from your relatives And from your father's house, To the land which I will show you; 2 And I will make you a great nation, And I will bless you, And make your name great; And so you shall be a blessing; 3 And I will bless those who bless you, And the one who curses you I will curse. And in you all the families of the earth shall be blessed." 4 So Abram went forth as the LORD had spoken to him; and Lot went with him. Now Abram was seventy-five years old when he departed from Haran (Gen 12:1-4).

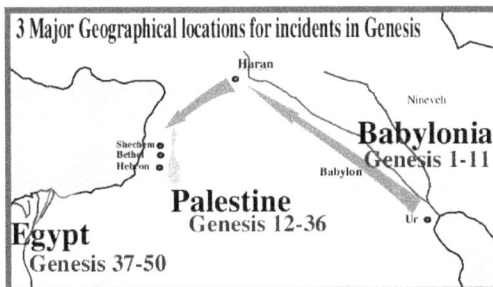

3 Major Geographical locations for incidents in Genesis

Haran

Nineveh

Babylonia
Genesis 1-11

Shechem
Bethel
Hebron

Babylon

Palestine
Genesis 12-36

Ur

Egypt
Genesis 37-50

God wants to extend His blessings through us to others. God is not stingy with His goodness. The issue that arises in the carrying out of this blessing is the problem of finding faithful servants to give His blessing to so that they can pass it on to others. Here are some questions that you should keep in mind to make the most of this study.

- Does God really want to give me His blessings?

- How does God bless me?

- What does it take in me to receive His blessings?

- Why does God bless me?

- How can I pass these blessings on to others?

- Why am I so slow in believing God's good intentions, and so quick to doubt Him?

The good part about studying the life of Abraham is that he seems so typical of most of us both in background as well as in his journey of faith. Galatians 3:6-9 says,

> Even so Abraham BELIEVED GOD, AND IT WAS RECKONED TO HIM AS RIGHTEOUSNESS. Therefore, be sure that it is those who are of faith who are sons of Abraham. And the Scripture, foreseeing that God would justify the Gentiles by faith, preached the gospel beforehand to Abraham, saying, "ALL THE NATIONS SHALL BE BLESSED IN YOU." So then those who are of faith are blessed with Abraham, the believer.

Notice that if we indeed are genuine believers in Jesus Christ, then Abraham is not just the father of Isaac, but is also our spiritual father. Through his faith we are participants in God's great blessings in this world. "Now not for his sake only was it written, that it was reckoned to him, but for our sake also, to whom it will be reckoned, as those who believe in Him who raised Jesus our Lord from the dead" (Romans 4:23-24). But the vision gets even greater than this. God is passing on these great blessings right now, not only in our lives but through our lives.

If you feel bored with your faith, it is because you do not realize God's cosmic plan that incorporates all of eternity. If you look at evangelism as a negative and fearful command, then you have not grasped both the goodness of God and how God's love can help each and every person.

As Christians, we are all on a journey of faith like Abraham. There is the beginning of this faith, the development of this faith, and the outcome of this faith. Today, we are going to focus on how a person actually gains this faith. We will see that the faith that saves us is the same faith that drives us. Faith is not a confidence in our knowledge of God but a willingness to obey God in the way He has revealed Himself to us.

Let us go back to Abraham's life now and see how his meeting with God changed him in five radical ways. Each change played an important process in how God would bring His blessing to mankind around the world.

He Left What Would Perish

The first life-changing fact about Abram is that he left what would perish. Instead of living for this world, he came to live in this world in such a way that prepared him for his life in the next world. But what is it that makes such a change in a person? What would cause him, or anyone else for that matter, to leave home?

The famous theologian, Augustine, one of the church fathers, wrote a book titled *The City of God*. He well knew the world and, like Abraham, left it for something better. In Genesis chapters 1-11 the "city of God" begins to take form with the call of Abraham and his response in faith. God took that little faith and graciously worked with Abraham over a long time.

The world, the society that still lives and animates most human beings, is decisively shaped by satisfying itself with what can be seen. God's new society, city, or family, however, is shaped by the invisible. From Genesis 12 onward, even into the rest of the scriptures, this new society is featured as a people who are shaped more by the invisible God and what He has said than what is seen.

God's close watch over His people can be seen from many different perspectives. Just mentioning Abraham's promised line (Isaac, Jacob [Israel], etc.) reckons back to the biblical records of God's interaction with many individuals for His greater purposes.

There is no doubt that as Abram prepared to take this big step in life, he would have been mocked by those around him. His people liked what they had and were uneasy thinking about things that would unsettle their plans and hopes for the future. They were confused as to why he would be willing to leave the best behind.

When I went to the mission field, my relatives and non-Christian friends covered up their dismay at my being a missionary by talking about the excitement of travel. I never could identify with this kind of conversation because I don't like traveling and would rather stay home in a more predictable environment with those who already love me. Abraham no doubt faced the desire to remain with what was familiar.

Abram must have faced disgust, discouragement and despair from those he was leaving. The fact of his departure from what is sure for what is promising implies that he had found something better. We can see this through the men of faith referred to in Hebrews 11:15, "And indeed if they had been thinking of that country from which they went out, they would have had opportunity to return."

Ur was not a bad place. Ur was one of the major cities of the most advanced civilization in the world then:

> As one of the important Sumerian cities it possessed an elaborate system of writing, advanced means of mathematical calculations, religious records, refined specimens of art, a school system, and much else that modern man equates with civilization and refinement.

After the rule from Akkad, rule over the Babylonian area from Ur came about. A general, named Ur-Nammu, was able to become independent and succeeded in bringing the whole of Babylonia under his control within a very short space of time. He probably received his post in Ur from the local ruler, Utuhengal of Uruk. This new era was called the Third Dynasty of Ur, a reaction of Sumerians against Akkadians. A total of five rulers from this dynasty ruled for a total of 109 years (Ur-Nammu's =18). Shulgi, Urnammu's son and successor, ruled 48 years. (pp. 185-190) The period around 2000 B.C., roughly in the period of the Third Dynasty of Ur.... [*The Early History of the Ancient Near East*][73]

They were advanced in mathematics, literature and, many other subjects. In contrast to other places at that time, Ur was like a star at night or sun by day. Man had every reason to get there and very few to stay away. Anyone can tell you that large cities hold more potential for greater success. Think of places like New York City, or Tokyo.

Where was he going, if indeed he was living in the place all men wanted to be? What made him think that there was something better out there? It is interesting that in the first three verses it only says, "To the land which I will show you." God was intentional to reveal this to him later. It seemed rather clear, though, from Genesis 11:31 and 12:5 that it was Canaan.

Earlier on around 2400 B.C., Palestine did have a number of city states, but they were destroyed by a nation in the North. By Abram's time, the area was not as well rebuilt and was under the control of Egypt. It certainly was not a 'couldn't turn down' offer.

When American settlers heard they could get a piece of land in a new colony for nothing, they set their hearts on it. Many families packed up everything they had, left the country and society they knew, and went on to seek the promise of something better. Abraham packed up and

---

[73] "Third Dynasty of Ur." Wikipedia. Wikimedia Foundation, 01 May 2013. Web. 07 Jan. 2013. http://en.wikipedia.org/wiki/Third_Dynasty_of_Ur

moved on, but he never settled. He wandered back and forth across the land, living in tents and shepherding the flocks. The last statement on the issue in Hebrews 11 is fairly clear. Abram never received what he was promised.

> By faith Abraham, when he was called, obeyed by going out to a place which he was to receive for an inheritance; and he went out, not knowing where he was going. By faith he lived as an alien in the land of promise, as in a foreign [land], dwelling in tents with Isaac and Jacob, fellow heirs of the same promise (Heb 11:8-9).

> All these died in faith, without receiving the promises, but having seen them and having welcomed them from a distance, and having confessed that they were strangers and exiles on the earth. For those who say such things make it clear that they are seeking a country of their own (Heb 11:13-14).

God & Society Genesis 1-11	God's New Family Genesis 12-50	
• God's creation of the world. • The world rebels from her Creator. • The world sinks into despair and evil; the world is the society. • The world then is very similar to our world today.	• God starts a new family/society. • This new society is based on trust in Him, which implies a relationship. • This family is focused on in rest of Genesis.	Abraham Isaac Jacob Joseph

GRAPHIC OUTLINE OF GENESIS

There is no doubt that our past contributes to what makes each of us special. Our motherland, our language, our rearing, our education, etc. Abram, a man from the East, also had his life pre-call. But something happened to him that radically changed the way he thought of his life.

Something beyond the world's culture brought a strong and powerful influence upon his life. He met God. Who would have thought that he would leave his family? Who would have thought that he would leave his culture and his home? Who would have thought that he would have left the old gods?

After gaining our education, it is hard for us to go back home because our minds and perspectives have changed. Think about how it would be to not only got to a foreign place with a different language, but to a place that was more backward in how they approached life. There was something in Abraham's experience with God that so challenged and moved him that he was willing to leave it all for the promise of God. Everything that he pinned his hopes and security on all of a sudden meant nothing compared to what God had promised him.

What is it that makes a person willing to leave his home, land, family, and religion for something different? We don't know if God had appeared to Abram once or many times. We don't know what actually happened in his experience with the divine. But it was enough that Abram made a decision to actually obey God. When a person meets God, he is required to use faith.

How would Abram or ourselves ever be able to convince our parents, friends or children that running after houses and professional degrees is not life itself? It only has the appearance of life and success? Like everyone else, you will end up saying good-bye to loved ones, and later on, you will be in the same position as those who have died before you. All the things you once pursued and gained mean nothing at that point. They mean less than nothing; they will mock you. Only by encountering God did he change course.

The way to a better life is to see a better course. One cannot change people by criticizing what they have done. You can say all sorts of things about what people are doing, but all those words will do no good until you can communicate that there is something better. What they do, whether it is gambling, drinking, smoking, or seeking success at all costs, is irrelevant. Everyone ends up similarly in the end. Yes, there are different stories to tell on how they got there, but it is still the same ending.

Christians don't love money, don't get drunk, don't gamble, don't lie, etc. not because there is a set of rules out there telling them not to. If this was the case, they would probably fall right back into what they prided themselves in saying they did not do. Most bad habits are not broken because behind the habit there is a love for what is being done. A Christian is one who has seen the brokenness of his life and at the same time has seen a hope for a better life.

What did Jesus say to that most successful, educated, and wealthy Jewish leader named Nicodemus? "You must be born again." (John 3:7). It would seem ridiculous that anyone would think that someone doing so well would need to start over from scratch–i.e., to be born again.

Karl Barth commented once on a Billy Graham sermon, saying that it was good, but "I wish you didn't stress 'you must be born again.'" There must be a disdain for what we have on earth before we can begin to gaze upon eternity. If we love what we have on earth, we will never love what is in heaven.

Abram had it made where he was. He was not laid off; his wife didn't divorce him. He was at the top of the world in Ur of the Chaldees. It wasn't a pursuit of what the world offered Abram that took him on his journey thousands of miles away to an unvisited land. If he was looking for such things, he would have stayed home. Hebrews 11:9 says, "By faith he lived as an alien in the land of promise, as in a foreign land, dwelling in tents with Isaac and Jacob, fellow heirs of the same promise."

How many of us would move from comfortable homes to tents? How many of us would give up our engineer jobs to care for sheep or tend the fields? God met Abram and radically changed his perspective and hopes for life, which in turn changed his goals in life. All the things he had meant nothing to him.

Application

Have you reached the point in your life where you finally see that what you were chasing really means nothing in the long term? Has God ever met you in such a way that he has shown you His blessing, and afterward nothing you wanted before meant anything anymore?

Someone has rightly said repentance and faith are two sides of the same coin. Once we see God, our past lives fade to vanity and emptiness. We realize that we have pursued the wrong thing, and that we have neglected to obey the One who made us.

He Obeyed the Invisible God

The second radical change in Abram was his willingness to obey an invisible God. Some people challenge God by thinking, "Who is this God who demands our attention but hides in the background?" Why is God so subtle? Why doesn't He make His power more obvious and visible?

No more can we say He can't be found. No more need we demand a set of miraculous proofs establishing God's existence. Actually, Romans chapter 1 clearly says He has made Himself clearly known but we have rejected Him. When Abram stepped out to obey this invisible God, we all became openly accountable. What is it about God that so challenged Abram? Who is He? Why would He call Abram? What makes a meeting with the LORD cause such an abrupt change in his life? How can I meet Him in such a way?

First, let's recognize that all that Abram had to look forward to depended upon whether God would be true to His Word. If someone came up to you and said he had a special gift that he would like to give you, would you believe him? If he was a stranger, you would probably believe him to be a hustler.

We don't know what God said or did to convince Abram. Maybe he heard the story of Noah and the flood that was passed down to him from his grandfather. Maybe he dreamed of meeting the Maker of the heavens and the earth. We often confuse a knowledge of God's existence with an understanding of what Christ did in knowing God. When God met Abraham, he did what the invisible Maker told him to do.

We say we have met Him, but we deny it when we keep doing what we want to do. But indeed, as children of Abraham, we must share that experience of meeting the God of all gods, the King of all kings, a meeting that we never want to forget and always ready to repeat.

As much as people like religion, they do not really want to know God. I am not saying that when we meet God that we completely know or understand Him. Not at all! We see that Abraham's faith had to grow. He met God at different stages and places in his life. It is significant though, that the next time it records God appearing to Abram is in the Promised Land after many years. Only when He obeyed, did God further reveal Himself to Abram.

Application

Have you ever got to the point in life where you wanted to see things a bit clearer? You wanted God to do something special, to give you clarity? If you find yourself in such a situation, remember that first you must obey what He has instructed you to do. If at any point you need further revelation or direction along the way of obedience, He will provide that. We just must go along in obedience. This is the life of faith.

When God first called me into the ministry, I was into my first year of university   studying engineering. I could have stayed at university, studying something I loved. But God, however, wanted me to move on. On one hand, if I stayed, I would be completely financially secure, but on the other hand, if I went into ministry, I would have no money. I changed schools to further equip me for the ministry that God had called me to, and He provided–just barely. I worked a semester before I started my studies, and continued to work for most of the remaining semesters.

Our experiences of God come in many different forms and at many different times, but at the most basic level, it starts with an awe of His person and a conviction of sin. God's intention was never to leave us in such a hopeless state. This is why He sent His only Son Jesus Christ into the world. He provided for those who would ask for forgiveness. He would forgive and restore. He doesn't keep us down, but in His grace provides help to those who see their impoverished life.

This invisible One revealed Himself as LORD–as Jehovah. God told Abram His name. At this point we must believe that it was something like when Moses heard God speak His name to him, "I am that I am." He is the ever existing one.

Second, we see that God was stepping into Abram's life; he was not making room for God. God is too big to just make room for in our lives. It is completely idolatrous for us to elevate man to a level where he thinks he can accommodate God in his life. It is not about how He came for me but that He has come to call me to serve Him. This is what Abram and every true believer does. We come to God to listen to Him. There is no doubt that God intends for every believer to remember that to come to Him as a Christian one must die to his own life and live for God.

Application

Abram left everything in obedience to God. His whole life would now orbit around God. He left what he could take confidence in for the One who would take care of him. A couple of problems with our faith as believers is that having met God, we have forgotten how special He is.

We have forgotten about His awesome holiness and love. We have gone back to the world to be enchanted with computer games and stock markets. We live in this world as if it is what gives meaning to our lives. True meaning in life comes by keeping the Lord as the head of it.

He Hoped in Future Promises (Gen 12:2-4)

If we live for the present, we will be a disappointed people. After his obedience, everything that made Abram's life have meaning was in the distant future. He trusted God to bring it all about. Some might call him a fool, but when we look at our lives, perhaps we are the fools. Abram became Abraham. The childless became the father of many nations. Where is there a land that the people do not have a faith like their father of faith Abraham?

He gave up the world to gain the eternal. He rejected his earthly inheritance to gain his eternal inheritance. The blessings that God promised him were all in the future. He trusted God to make him great rather than try to become great by his own power. He waited for God to make him a blessing in His way rather than pretend to be a blessing.

He could not make himself into a great nation. Only God could (and did) make a nation from his son. Here is this man from a pagan culture, who stood out in God's eyes by his faith. He met God and he obeyed Him. We should not give up faith because of our age or because of our past sins. God's grace is greater than all of these things. There is a lie that says that we must make ourselves great. This lie leads to death. Greatness is not something that corrupt and pass away. God wants to make us, His people, a great people.

He wants to impart His blessing into our lives just as He did with Abraham. We need to move forward in our faith. We must not think that we can make ourselves great, nor must we think that the way to making ourselves great is through the world's means. God does expect action from our lives, but that action should always be in obedience to His will.

Now the LORD said to Abram, "Go forth from your country, And from your relatives And from your father's house, To the land which I will show you; And I will make you a great nation, And I will bless you, And make your name great; And so you shall be a blessing; And I will bless those who bless you, And the one who curses you I will curse. And in you all the families of the earth shall be blessed. So Abram went forth as the LORD had spoken to him; and Lot went with him. Now Abram was seventy-five years old when he departed from Haran (Gen 12:1-4).

By faith Abraham, when he was called, obeyed by going out to a place which he was to receive for an inheritance; and he went out, not knowing where he was going. By faith he lived as an alien in the land of promise, as in a foreign land, dwelling in tents with Isaac and Jacob, fellow heirs of the same promise; 10 for he was looking for the city which has foundations, whose architect and builder is God. 11 By faith even Sarah herself received ability to conceive, even beyond the proper time of life, since she considered Him faithful who had promised; 12 therefore, also, there was born of one man, and him as good as dead at that, as many descendants AS THE STARS OF HEAVEN IN NUMBER, AND INNUMERABLE AS THE SAND WHICH IS BY THE SEASHORE.

The personal challenge

Do I love the world or God more? The test forces us to decide between the two.

The personal hope

Is God's will so wondrous that I would leave all and run for it?

---

13 All these died in faith, without receiving the promises, but having seen them and having welcomed them from a distance, and having confessed that they were strangers and exiles on the earth. 14 For those who say such things make it clear that they are seeking a country of their own. 15 And indeed if they had been thinking of that country from which they went out, they would have had opportunity to return. 16 But as it is, they desire a better country, that is a heavenly one. Therefore God is not ashamed to be called their God; for He has prepared a city for them.

17 By faith Abraham, when he was tested, offered up Isaac; and he who had received the promises was offering up his only begotten son; 18 it was he to whom it was said, "IN ISAAC YOUR

DESCENDANTS SHALL BE CALLED." 19 He considered that God is able to raise men even from the dead; from which he also received him back as a type. 20 By faith Isaac blessed Jacob and Esau, even regarding things to come (Hebrews 11:8-20).

The Promises

As we take a closer look at Genesis 12:1-3, we will discover many different promises that the Lord made to Abraham. Before looking into these promises though, let's first think of what God is doing by giving these promises. In Genesis 12:1 we find the condition of the promises. God is asking that Abraham give up what is sure, familiar, and easy, and do what is unknown and daring.

"Now the LORD said to Abram, "Go forth from your country, And from your relatives And from your father's house, To the land which I will show you;

2 And I will make you a great nation, And I will bless you, And make your name great; And so you shall be a blessing; 3 And I will bless those who bless you, And the one who curses you I will curse. And in you all the families of the earth shall be blessed." (Genesis 12:1-3).

The Condition

Is God's way more important to me?

The Promise

Is God's promises great enough for me to make the necessary sacrifices?

This is the personal challenge that God often (and probably always) brings into the lives of His people. The condition forces us to make a decision. Do we love God more than all the things that we see and have? According to the world, the believer is stupid to believe what he believes. Why risk everything for nothing? These life decisions require significant choices.

I remember making many of these significant choices in the past all requiring moving, sacrificing, and facing the challenge of the unknown. I am not an adventurer, but God has regularly called me into these risky situations. One challenge required that I leave my secure job, even though I had seven children at the time and no savings. Hudson Taylor said, "Unless there is an element of risk in your exploits for God there is no need for faith."

The world sees no substance in God's promises; the rewards are not apparent. Abraham didn't even know where he was going. All was speculation. But Abraham believed differently. He jumped into his trust in God's promises. He believed that the promises would cause a better life than staying where he was. In other words, his trust in God's promises became everything to him.

God wasn't looking for a perfect man (Abraham certainly was not that), but a man who simply trusted in Him. The promises would guide Abraham in his future journey. God does a similar thing in the lives of all of His people. It is for this reason our spiritual lives are considered journeys. The promises become life-shapers, and so, his anticipation of them guides his future decisions.

I personally have decided that it is better to obtain God's promises that one can keep forever than to gain the world and loose it all.

Dream big

Dream big. God is changing us by what He wants to do in our lives. Self-esteem shapes us when we stare into our pride or poverty. Faith, however, encourages us to envision what God can and will do in and through our insignificant lives.

1) I will make you a great __nation__ (12:2a)

2) I will __bless__ you (12:2b)

3) *I will* make your __name__ great (Gen 12:2c)

4) You shall be a __blessing__ (Gen 12:2d)

5) __I__ will bless those who bless you (12:3a)

6) The one who __curses__ you I will __curse__ (12:3b)

7) In you all the __families__ of the earth shall be blessed (12:3c)

7 PROMISES OF GENESIS 12:1-3

These promises in Genesis 12:2-3 are for Abraham as the condition was. We are not attempting to hijack them for our lives. Each promise was fulfilled in Abraham's life.

We need to learn from God's Word. We first can learn how God often instigates faith into the lives of His people. He is no doubt doing this all the time by general revelation. We do not know what drove God to speak so to Abraham, but this is not our concern here (check out Romans 9-11).

More important is the fact that God does do this and, throughout the rest of scripture, has done similarly in our lives. Of course, the condition and promises will differ. They are less important since they all issue from God, who wonderfully involves us in His good and great plan. Each of our lives are special situations where the Almighty steps in to work.

The risks that He asks us to take will be dependent on our own circumstances. So will the promises. There will be similarities, however, because of who God is and how He is drawing us to live in His presence and work out His good purposes.

Three Teachings on Blessings (Gen 12:1-3)

As we study these seven promises from God to Abraham, we will discover three significant aspects of God's promises to His people.

First, blessings are from God. Five times in these verses the Lord says 'I'. He takes charge of bringing the blessings to Abraham's life. This made Abraham totally dependent upon God and His blessings, and they didn't happen by chance because their occurrence were dependent on God's goodness and faithfulness to help him receive them. In the end, Abram ends up richly blessed. The Genesis account clearly points this out. Abram began to see this happen so regularly that he didn't even want to take spoils from a war to mar God's image of blessing.

And Abram said to the king of Sodom, "I have sworn to the LORD God Most High, possessor of heaven and earth, that I will not take a thread or a sandal thong or anything that is yours, lest you should say, 'I have made Abram rich' (Gen 14:22-23).

Second, we are reminded that blessings are to be shared. Blessings are carefully distributed among God's people so that we will share them with others. This is so counter to the world's perspective of building up savings and storing up a living.

"So you shall be a blessing." What

A) Blessings are from God (Gen 12:2a)	Dependent on Him	His blessings
B) Blessings are to be shared (Gen 12:2b)	Accountable to Him	His purpose
C) Blessings are to be multiplied (Gen 12:3)	Expectant upon Him	His abundance

does this mean but that others will be blessed through Abraham?

> In you all the families of the earth will be blessed." This is an amazing promise that is so true today. Jesus Christ was the seed of Abraham and so when others from the many nations believe in Christ, they are blessed through Abraham's promise. "Therefore, be sure that it is those who are of faith who are sons of Abraham (Gal 3:7).

Our lives as believers, then, should live accountably before God who has richly blessed us to magnify His Name by blessing others. "… But giving a blessing instead; for you were called for the very purpose that you might inherit a blessing" (1 Peter 3:9).

Third, we should understand that these blessings are to be multiplied. Abraham received many blessings, and as they went out from his life, they were greatly multiplied. Like Abraham, we should be people looking around for how God wants to pour out His wonderful blessings.

We should look at our lives and be expectant, and so we are when we see the sick, weary, and hungry. Pray and intercede for them and see how God might work. "I will bless those who bless you." "I will bless you." We see that God has made Abram and all his children to be those who are to continually look to the Lord to be blessed. This is indeed God's abounding grace.

Personal Reflections

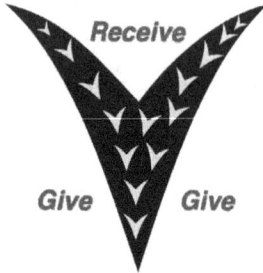

Are we poised to receive and distribute God's blessings? It might be a smile as we assist someone who needs a hand. The Lord might want us to share from our riches and resources. The point is that we are to not only be expectant on what God will give but how He wants us to distribute this blessing.

Application

- How has God's promises shaped your life?

- What decisions have you made because of what God has promised you?

- What did you have to leave behind?

- What challenges have you faced in the world?

- Perhaps, you have followed the world. You are still in 'Ur.' You never left. Is God's voice still lingering in your mind?

- In what way has God blessed you? What blessings does He have for your life?

Summary

So much happens when God meets us. Let our hearts be like Abraham's! We may not be innate adventurers, but let's be those who live and die in the promises of God. Abraham left behind what would perish, obeyed the invisible God and hoped in future promises. It is Abraham who ended up with everything. We should seek that the God of all blessing should come across our lives too.

He Faced Life Challenges (Gen 12:5-6)

> And Abram took Sarai his wife and Lot his nephew, and all their possessions which they had accumulated, and the persons which they had acquired in Haran, and they set out for the land of Canaan; thus they came to the land of Canaan. 6 And Abram passed through the land as far as the site of Shechem, to the oak of Moreh. Now the Canaanite was then in the land (Gen 12:5-6).

God never said it would be easy to follow his promises. The way to get these blessings might not be easy, but it is straightforward: always through obedience. Obey and wait.

There is no doubt that we will face significant life struggles as we learn to live by faith. Abraham did and so will we. Let's look at three particular life challenges that we will need to deal with, with examples from Genesis 12:5-6.

The Challenge to Move

The first challenge we must face is the challenge of adjusting our lives to the circumstances that God wants us to operate in. In many cases, we will need to move. I remember carefully packing all that we were permitted to take in seven trunks and boxes. It would be shipped to Taiwan where we would serve as church planters. Everything else needed to be tossed, given away, or stored.

Genesis 12:5 focused on Abraham's material possessions. Was this to emphasize that God's blessing was already being accrued? Probably. But in any case, these things also made it more difficult to make a move. Notice the phrases, "all their possessions," "had accumulated," and "they had acquired in Haran." Imagine how much easier it would've been to stay put. Yet when God indicates that we should go, then move we must.

Abram had to face this tension. He no doubt had to leave a lot behind. There were no big moving trucks and shipping containers to assist in the move. They had to walk it to where they were going. It's hard for people to believe all that they can accumulate in just a few years of living here or there. Abraham was the same: the temptation to stay must have been great. He already was blessed! He didn't need to make a move in order to become blessed. His move to the land of Canaan was significant because he was living for the promise more than for the comfort. It would have been so easy to stay there in Haran, especially seeing how God had prospered him. Do we believe that living in full obedience will bring the greatest reward?

The Challenge of Leaving Relationships

The second challenge is our relationships. Often the biggest problem is our relatives, but leaving our friends behind is a close second.

Abraham took Sarai his wife and Lot his nephew. It appears that Abraham was not completely faithful here in bringing his nephew. "Go forth from your country, And from your relatives And from your father's house" (Gen 12:1).

This fact of this act of disobedience is further supported by all the problems that originated with Lot. The story of Lot is continued in the next chapters of Genesis; peace was not obtained until Abraham and Lot separated. The problem of complete obedience is ever before us. To conduct God's ministry, God has His requirements, sometimes leaving our relatives.

Why is it so hard to leave our relatives? Our relatives are our family, and that's where we form our most meaningful relationships. Take them away and we feel vulnerable and lonely. With the great increase of travel and immigration, this issue might seem to be less of a struggle, but when you look behind the scenes, you will find souls struggling over the potential separation of their relatives.

Full obedience is key. Please note that when we disobey, things will not go well. Like Abraham, we will find much conflict until we reach the situation that God had originally appointed.

The Challenge of Obstacles

The third challenge came in the form of obstacles. Abraham clearly did not have the same faith he would have at the end of his life. Genesis 12:6 states, "Now the Canaanite were then in the land."

God promised Abraham the land and yet the land was occupied by others. He had just a few people with him, so he probably would've felt more secure had Lot and his family stayed with him. Just think what Abram would say to his potential enemies when they asked him what his purpose in the land was. "Oh, God wants to give me all this land." That wouldn't be easy to respond to.

God's promises are not always what they seem. God promised land and yet the land was occupied.

- How was the promised land Abraham's?
- Did he have to wait?
- What was he to do in the meantime?
- Did God want him to do something to get the land?

These questions are so relevant to the way God works in His people today! Promises, at first, are often seen as empty words. This again becomes a challenge of trust in His Words.

Will we endure in our feeble faith in His Word or take an alternate way? Surely our lives suffer today because many a saint took the path into the world. Praise God that Abraham stayed on the course of faith. He persisted. He would continue to struggle throughout his life, but he took the first step, which would lead to another step of faith.

Application

Is there a step God is now waiting for you to take? What is it? What holds you back? When will you step in obedience so that you and others might abound in His good blessings?

He Prioritized Spiritual Relationships (12:7-9)

7 And the LORD appeared to Abram and said, "To your descendants I will give this land." So he built an altar there to the LORD who had appeared to him. 8 Then he proceeded from there to the mountain on the east of Bethel, and pitched his tent, with Bethel on the west and Ai on the east; and there he built an altar to the LORD and called upon the name of the LORD. 9 And Abram journeyed on, continuing toward the Negev (Gen 12:7-9).

Obedience is Key

After Abram finally reached Canaan, the Lord appeared to him. "And the LORD appeared to Abram and said, "To your descendants I will give this land." God was waiting for Abram's final move to the Promised Land before He spoke further about the promise He had made.

How long had it been since God spoke to Abraham? It seems like it was in Ur (i.e. Mesopotamia) when he first heard God speak. God was waiting many years for Abram to move from Haran to the Promised Land.

And he said, "Hear me, brethren and fathers! The God of glory appeared to our father Abraham when he was in Mesopotamia, before he lived in Haran, and said to him, 'DEPART FROM YOUR COUNTRY AND YOUR RELATIVES, AND COME INTO THE LAND THAT I WILL SHOW YOU.' "Then he departed from the land of the Chaldeans, and settled in Haran. And from there, after his father died, God removed him into this country in which you are now living" (Acts 7:2-4).

The point is, years can pass before we hear God speak and clarify that all is well. This is the life of faith. We are not running on experiences with God but on our trust in the 'silent' God. But things can often be sped up. How? Obedience. Why? For several reasons.

First, obedience proves that we have learned to walk in faith. If we need another 'God' experience, does it not show that we have not responded to how God has already spoken? We should prioritize obedience for what God has already shown us.

Second, obedience leads us into new situations where further directions will need to be given. The first step has been accomplished. But now what? God will often supplement guidance as we need it.

Third, obedience leads us into desperate situations where our need for God becomes very evident. It might not seem that God wants to speak, but the opposite is true. God desires to speak often to us, but our obedience has not matured. Only after Abram finally left Haran and arrived in Canaan did God speak.

God Fosters a Relationship

So God is interested in building our relationship with Him, at least, that is how it appears from the way God came to meet with Abram once he arrived. Verse 7 states, "To your descendants I will give this land." God would affirm Abram's understanding of the totally perplexing situation. When we need comfort, guidance, and help, God is always there to provide it.

This verse not only mentions the fact that God further revealed Himself to Abram, but that Abram responded by deepening His commitment to God. "So he built an altar there to the LORD who had appeared to him."

Abram did not hold resentment in his heart, "It is about time that you spoke, Lord." Nor was Abram so threatened that he shied away from God. He sensed that building an altar was an important step in affirming these key moments of his life. He was now 75, not very young. Most of his years had passed. Though we do not know how young Abram was when he was called, nor how many years he spent waffling about in Haran, we do know how old he was when he finally did get to where God instructed him.

Now, Abram is able to move beyond his relationship with his father, Terah, and leave him. He began to establish the relationship beyond all human relationships, the most-important spiritual relationship with God. God doesn't just want us to believe in His existence but to enter a relationship with Him. This close relationship satisfies us even when others don't understand, or even when they spurn us.

Two Altars

Although we do not know how much time took place between verse 7 and 8, something deeper was certainly taking shape in Abram's life. When he went to Bethel, he pitched a tent in between the two cities of Bethel and Ai. Abram notably built a second altar.

The first altar was one of prompting. God had spoken. Abraham had finally completed the first run. This second altar, however, was one through which Abram took the initiative. He did not need God to speak in order to cause him to worship. No. Worship and devotion to this LORD Yahweh was now to regularly direct his life.

It appears that Abram began to reflect on the dead-end situation that he had fallen into. Here he is, a small group of foreigner nomads, surrounded by a pagan, perhaps hostile, culture. Abram no doubt felt very vulnerable and "called upon the name of the LORD" (12:8). He saw that there was no way that this would become his land unless the Majestic and Mighty God worked.

He staked his life and future upon the Lord. Similarly, God is looking for this second altar in our lives, the one where we see our hopelessness and cast our dependence upon Him. It was not until this moment occurred that Abram, and by extension ourselves, fully recognized that the blessings and help he gained are from God. This is the way these spiritual relationships work.

Our faith has to be specifically trained. It is moments like these that help us see this. I vividly remember a time that I cried out to the Lord for help when I was led into a corner. He heard. He answered. All that I have gained from that November day in 2000 can be attributed to His glory and power.

Life would go on for Abram as it does for us. He seemed to move onto the more deserted places of Canaan to the Negev, but some firm foundational blocks had been set for his life that would lead to the rest of God's work in his life.

Summary

Abraham was called out of a thriving pagan city to some unknown place by an unknown God, the same God of his ancestors, but little did he know of Him. Abram's obedience was only half-hearted at first because instead of leaving everything, he accompanied his father to Haran (Gen 11:31). But at least he was on the way.

God is patient. When his father died, Abraham, at 75 years of age, was finally willing to make the move to the unfamiliar and perhaps dreaded place that God had called him to. God recognized this step of faith, delayed though it may be, and met him upon his arrival. Abram felt so vulnerable for his life and family, which he moved to the desert, but he did not return to Haran. He stayed in the wilderness, in faith of God's promises.

Each of us are on a journey of faith where the Lord through many life circumstances, not very unlike Abraham's experiences, cultivates a deep and rich personal relationship with Himself, the Living God.

Application

- What does God want for your life? Is He content with a merely religious faith?
- Where are you on your journey of faith?
- Have you ever lived in semi-disobedience as Abram did in Haran? Explain.
- What is the significance of the two altars? Have you ever made any? Explain.
- What challenges do you face now? Are you 'hiding' in the desert?

GENESIS

Genesis 12-22
Abraham's Journey of Faith

Let's look at Abraham's life and note four ways that we can build our own faith. Abraham's growth in faith can be traced to God's revelations to him (calling, promises, visions) as well as his own obedience in responding to God. See Appendix 3 for a graphic summary: Geographical Summary of Old Testament.

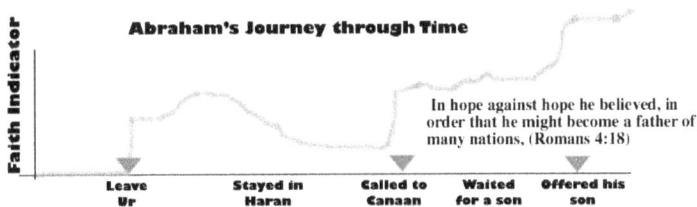

Abraham's Journey through Time

In hope against hope he believed, in order that he might become a father of many nations. (Romans 4:18)

| Leave Ur | Stayed in Haran | Called to Canaan | Waited for a son | Offered his son |

ABRAHAM'S JOURNEY THROUGH TIME

The Call of Abraham (Gen 12:1)

Now the LORD said **to** Abram,

"Go forth **from** your country,

And **from** your relatives

And **from** your father's house,

To the land which I will show you."

Looking Forward

> When God speaks, listen carefully. Ask questions. You might not hear from Him for a while!

When God's grace begins to pour into our lives, movement takes place. Note the three 'froms' and the two 'tos.' Motion and direction of God's believers cause disruption in the flow of the world and enable God's plans to be implemented.

Looking Back

Born in Ur (2008 years since creation)
Age 75: Leaves Haran for Canaan. (2083 creation)
    LORD appears to him in Shechem.
Age 86: Ishmael born in Hebron.
Age 99: Promise of Isaac (Gen 17)
Age 100: Birth of Isaac (Gen 20-21)
Age 120?: Offering of Isaac on Moriah (Gen 22)
Age 175: Abraham dies in Hebron (Gen 25)

A pattern from Genesis 1 and 2 is again being repeated. God's goodness is being expressed. Where God's goodness goes, transformation and blessing follows. This, of course, is no different from the power of the Gospel–God's grace. It is all the same.

God wants us to pay attention to His ways. As Abraham's children of faith, God has destined His great and glorious goodness to be poured through our lives. As Christians, we need not strive for blessing as much as we should strive to open our lives to His blessings and work. We see the pattern called 'The Flow' ebb into our lives nonstop, pouring out into the lives of others around us.

THE FLOW

We will see that this goodness of God was never meant to end with our lives but should flow out to the people and contexts around us. We need to make sure that as individuals, families, and churches we are open to God's purpose of spreading His goodness through the world.

If 'The Flow' is stopped, then it begins decaying. Backsliding describes either closing our lives to God's goodness (maybe because of bitterness) or an unwillingness to share what blessings God has given to us (maybe because of worldliness or selfishness). Solutions are easy.

The Method (Gen 15)

The means by which God's grace flows into our lives.

> By faith Abraham, when he was called, obeyed by going out to a place which he was to receive for an inheritance; and he went out, not knowing where he was going. By faith he lived as an alien in the land of promise, as in a foreign *land,* dwelling in tents with Isaac and Jacob, fellow heirs of the same promise; for he was looking for the city which has foundations, whose architect and builder is God (Heb 11:8-10).

God creates situations in our lives where we are given the opportunity to gain more faith and incorporate more of His grace into our lives so that His goodness might reach more people. Consistent faith is crucial to this process, not just the initial faith, but the pursuing faith.

God could easily have given Abraham a son earlier, or many of them. He only gave Abram a promise of many descendants, and when He gave that promise, Abram had no children. Surely anyone who heard of God's promise to aging Abram would laugh and mock him. This was the challenge of his faith that was embedded in his name, 'Abram,' meaning 'exalted father.'

> And He took him outside and said, "Now look toward the heavens, and count the stars, if you are able to count them." And He said to him, "So shall your descendants be." Then he believed in the LORD; and He reckoned it to him as righteousness (Gen 15:5-6).

Hagar   **Abraham**   Sarah

**Abraham's
Descendants**

Ishmael   **Isaac**

Arabs - Moslems
(Ge 37:25, 27, 28)

Esau   **Jacob
(Israel)**

Edomites (Dt 23:7; Nu 34:3
Nu 24:18; Jos15:1; II Sa 8:14)

(Leah)   (Bilhah) (Zilpah) (Rachel)
Rachel's maid   Leah's maid

Reuben, Simeon, Levi, **Judah**   Dan Naphtali   Gad Asher   Joseph Benjamin

Issachar, Zebulun Dinah   Manasseh Ephraim

David

x Reuben (Ge 49:3-4, 35:22)
x Simeon (Ge 49:5-7, 34:1-31)
x Levi   (Ge 49:5-7, 34:1-31)
✓ Judah   (Ge 49:8-12)

Jesus   *The Lord will not leave Judah, the staff will not depart from
his feet until Shiloh comes (Genesis 49:10).*

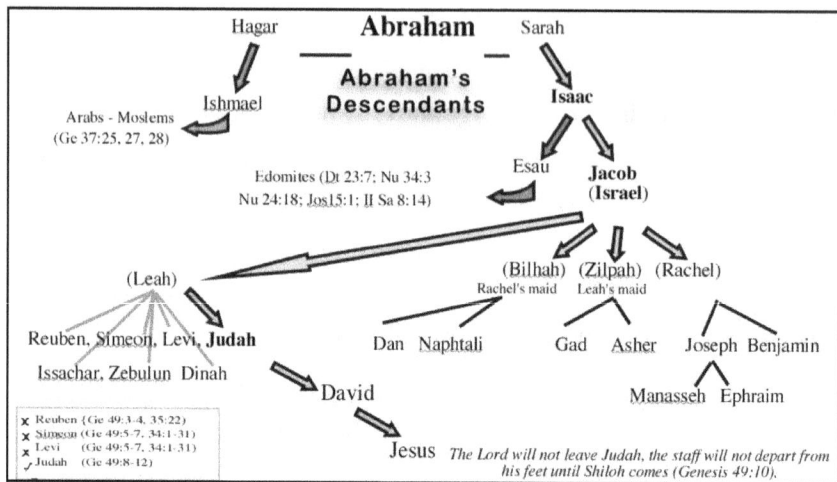

A CHART OF ABRAHAM'S DESCENDANTS

The Testing (Gen 22)

The means through which God's grace abounds in our lives.

Waiting for God's timing is a hard thing to do. Waiting for something to happen tests both the importance of what God has said as well as our belief that God will fulfill His Word. Genesis 22 leaps beyond this, though, with another kind of test, the test of sacrifice.

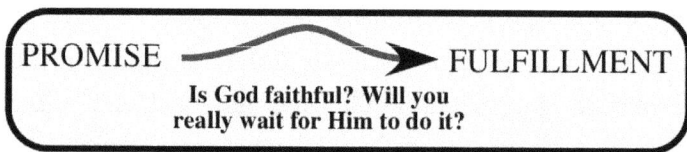

PROMISE ⟶ FULFILLMENT
**Is God faithful? Will you
really wait for Him to do it?**

The timing test tried Abraham on endurance and suffering. Many years he had to go without. The test to sacrifice his only son Isaac, however, tested his belief in the impossible as well as God's determination to accomplish what He intended. Abraham was asked to give up every glimmer of hope to fulfill the things that he waited for throughout his whole life.

No matter how much Abraham had prospered, the test was about who he would pass it down to. By offering Isaac to God, Abraham was willing to sacrifice all that he had or had dreamed of. He cared less for his dreams than obedience to what God wanted.

Morality of Sacrifices

Some ask about the morality of asking a father to kill his child. The issue is not easy to resolve unless you understand God's perspective. Let's first ask if it was immoral to offer up Jesus Christ (cf. Acts 2:23) on the cross? If it was immoral, then God is not holy. He has done something that violates His person. Since He is holy, we must accept the fact that God can ask others to give up their life by the hand of others, especially when there is a greater purpose involved. This is what we do in war, but the sacrifice of a child is much closer to home. In the case of Christ as the Son of God, it is the scene of redemption and salvation. The One who set the laws of the world established what is moral by who He is and what He wills.

Isaac was a strong teenager that was willing to give up his life. We do not read of any sort of physical struggle taking place to get Isaac on the altar. By carrying the wood (figure of Christ, carrying the cross), we know Isaac was at least a young man. It is possible that Abraham knocked him out, but the context doesn't lead us to this line of thinking. Instead we see an obedient son laying on the altar after being bound by his father. This is the perfect picture of Jesus who willingly gave up His life on the cross at His Heavenly Father's request. Isaac, it seems then, willingly gave up his life at his father's request just as Jesus did.

Faith grows the most in life's struggles through circumstances that God puts before us.

Application

1. Do the following graph assignment.

- Note what year you believed on the left and this year on your right.

- Mark key times of spiritual growth and obedience in your life with a triangle.

- Mark with an X any significant struggles and doubts that kept you down.

- Draw a line graph to connect the points.

Faith Indicator

_____ **Journey through Time**
(Your name)

Conversion date   **Today's date**

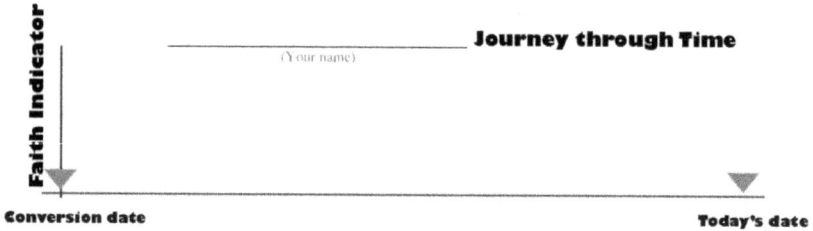

2. Describe one struggle of faith that you went through and grew from:

3. To allow 'THE FLOW' to fully operate in your life, you need to be ready to sacrifice all of your own desires, dreams, comforts, and loved ones. Meditate on Romans 12:1-2 along with Genesis 22. Picture yourself on the altar as a living sacrifice. Tell the Lord that you are willing to give up these things so that His grace and goodness might more effectively spread to the world.

Genesis 12-49
Abraham's Descendants - A Chart

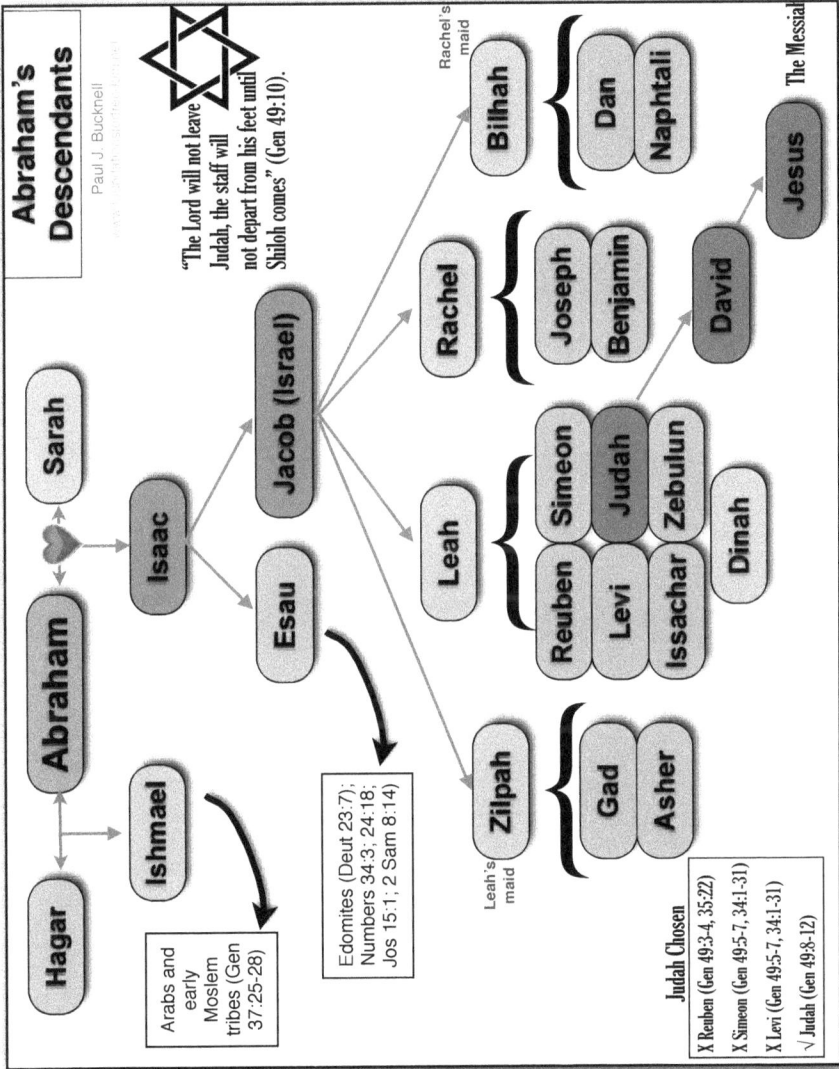

Abraham's Descendants

Paul J. Bucknell

"The Lord will not leave Judah, the staff will not depart from his feet until Shiloh comes" (Gen 49:10).

Hagar — Abraham — Sarah

Abraham — Ishmael

Isaac

Jacob (Israel)

Esau

Ishmael: Arabs and early Moslem tribes (Gen 37:25-28)

Esau: Edomites (Deut 23:7; Numbers 34:18; 24:18; Jos 15:1; 2 Sam 8:14)

Leah's maid — Zilpah:
{ Gad, Asher }

Leah:
{ Reuben, Simeon, Levi, Judah, Issachar, Zebulun, Dinah }

Rachel:
{ Joseph, Benjamin }

Rachel's maid — Bilhah:
{ Dan, Naphtali }

David → Jesus — The Messiah

Judah Chosen
X Reuben (Gen 49:3-4, 35:22)
X Simeon (Gen 49:5-7, 34:1-31)
X Levi (Gen 49:5-7, 34:1-31)
√ Judah (Gen 49:8-12)

CHART OF ABRAHAM'S DESCENDANTS

235

GENESIS

Genesis 12-16, 20
Abraham's Costly Detours

Objectives:

- Understand more of Abraham's weaknesses so that we can better learn from his life.

- Show how insecurities develop and avoid such paths.

- Become more aware of relativism and instead pledge to live by God's Word no matter what it costs.

- Stop making life decisions with our senses and prioritize faith.

We've all made some bad decisions in life

One would think that God would not be so hard on Abraham for his bad decisions. God recorded Abraham's mistakes adjacent to the LORD's great promises. The reading seems so awkward.

Disobedience always costs. God does not count how long you have been a Christian or what you have done for His kingdom. If anything, we find that those who get closer to God are held to a more scrutinizing standard than others.

We will have a difficult time understanding the consequences God brought into Abraham's life if we do not rightly understand God and His ways. God treats as holy those who are close to Him. We see this illustrated by the fire that came from Yahweh's presence to consume

Aaron's sons, Nadab and Abihu. Moses tried to calm Aaron down by explaining God's strong action in Leviticus 10:3

> It is what the LORD spoke, saying,
> By those who come near Me I will be treated holy,
> And before all the people I will be honored. (Lev10:3)

It was only after this that Aaron was willing to calm down. We find this same demand of holiness to be in Abraham, and we find the same standard to be held among all of God's people. Disobedience reveals an arrogance in our hearts that communicates that we find our opinions or judgments to be more worthy than what God has said.

With this theme in mind, we can learn from the mistakes of Abraham. We can also learn from the study of history, but in the end, history is the study of the decisions and consequences of decisions that certain individual have made.

> **When God speaks, listen carefully. Pay attention to details. They might not make immediate sense, but they are important!**

We will explore three detours that Abram took, which brought him off God's path and onto the path of sin. Let's take a good look at them. The reason they were recorded is to serve as a warning, to keep us from making the same mistakes in our spiritual journey.

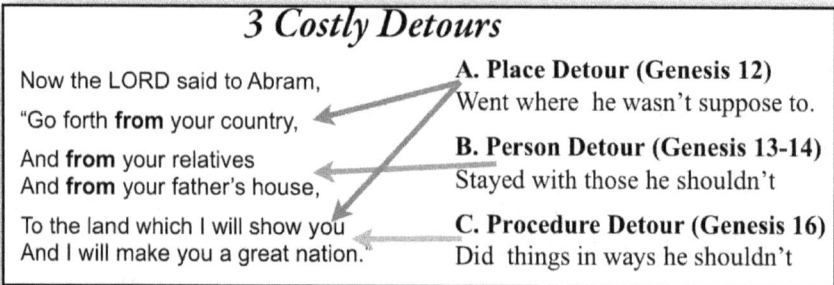

3 Costly Detours

Now the LORD said to Abram,

"Go forth **from** your country,

And **from** your relatives
And **from** your father's house,

To the land which I will show you
And I will make you a great nation."

A. Place Detour (Genesis 12)
Went where he wasn't suppose to.

B. Person Detour (Genesis 13-14)
Stayed with those he shouldn't

C. Procedure Detour (Genesis 16)
Did things in ways he shouldn't

A. Place Detour (Gen 12:10-20, 20)

"Is it God's will for me to go to this place or that place?" This is asked quite often. In order to answer it, we need to look at two basic questions that will help us grow in our discernment.

Abram's first detour took him where he shouldn't have been. In chapter 12 we find Abram in the middle of a famine in the land that God had directed him to go to. Things must have been desperate. Abraham was never called to go to Egypt. In Genesis 12:11, Abraham even foresaw that the famine might affect Egypt adversely, but he didn't let that stop him.

Insecurity always grows when you leave the place God has called you to. If insecurities are allowed to grow, they will lead to bad decisions because these decisions are not built on faith but on sight and fear. Here Abraham was willing to forsake his husbandly duty of protecting his wife, and even conspired with his wife that she should agree to pretend to be his sister. In this way they will not kill him and snatch her when they saw how beautiful she was. We do not have time to discuss how God helped Abraham out of this mess, but we will emphasize it was only by God's grace that he escaped the misery that he deserved.

By looking at Abram's weaknesses we find it remarkable that God would ever call him to such an important role. There was an obvious problem in their marriage where he allowed circumstances to dictate how he would act toward his wife, even to the point of allowing harm to come to her. This was an obvious example where he did not love his wife as he loved himself.

1. Where did the Lord originally send you and why?

The LORD told Abram to go to the land of Canaan, or Palestine. God revealed the "where" in two stages; Genesis 12:1 kept the place a mystery, but later in 12:7, we see the LORD clearly affirming His purpose:

> And the LORD appeared to Abram and said,
> "To your descendants I will give this land."

We are right to applaud Abram on getting this far. This was sheer faith that he acted in. This is the scene where God's promises would later be fulfilled in his son's life and ours through Jesus! God spoke clearly to His purposes. This was to be a long term place for Abraham to live.

Application

God doesn't often (if ever) reveal to us His whole plan for our lives all at once, at least not clearly. As we take one step in obedience, in His time He shows us more. He is never late in revealing what we need to know.

2. Has He asked you to go somewhere else?

The reason we ask 'Why?' on the first question is to see if God would put a time limit or have a special purpose in sending you to a certain place. Often, when this "short-term mission" is complete, you return to where you were before. God often sends a person to a place just for a short time; many of these instances involve studying or helping someone.

Two times Abraham left without clear direction from the Lord, and both times we see different motivations shaping him.

a) Abram went down to Egypt (Gen 12:10)

Abram went to Egypt because of famine. Of course, Egypt promised better things to him. It's easy to imagine that Abram fell into thinking that Egypt held more potential for his prosperity than God's promise to him did. From this we learn that contentment is important in following God.

He should have trusted in the Lord. Because he left the place in which God wanted him to reside, he exposed himself to temptation. Considering what happened to him in this instance, it is remarkable that this happens again in Genesis 20.

b) Abraham settled between Kadesh and Shur (Gen 20:1)

Abraham settled between Kadesh and Shur; then he lived in Gerar (Gen 20:1). Notice the step by step procedure. Perhaps the incident with Lot and Sodom created resentment in Abraham. Whatever the case, Abraham committed the same sin of deceiving others about his wife out of fear for his own life. He allowed his wife to become a part of another man's collection of women just so he could be safe!

Summary

Abram doubted God's directive. He chose to leave the place God told him to go, and because of that, he faced extra temptation. Through temptation, God revealed a weakness in Abraham's marriage and his faith in God. Despite Abraham's moral failures, God intervened and kept Sarah pure for the sake of the promised child. So despite Abram's failure, God kept her pure and still blessed Abram.

Unfortunately, Abraham's willingness to mistreat his wife caused severe marital problems, and because of his position as father, his attitudes would influence his sons attitudes toward and treatment of their wives.

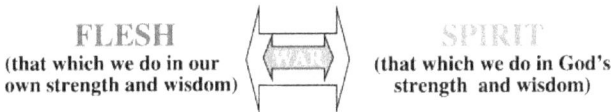

FLESH   SPIRIT
(that which we do in our   (that which we do in God's
own strength and wisdom)   strength and wisdom)

THE FLESH VERSUS SPIRIT DIAGRAM

Application

- As husbands, do we love ourselves more than our wives or vice-a-versa? We need to put away our great ambitions, or our lazy passion for entertainment, and start working on those projects around the home.

- Did you ever go anywhere God didn't want you to go? A job? A vacation? A visit? We need God's special grace to be where God wants us, less we face extra temptations. Don't make significant decisions unless called.

- What are some of the reasons you might go astray? Is it because of your awry values and desires? Read Galatians 5:17 and reflect on your tendency to value the things the Lord does not. "For the flesh sets its desire against the Spirit, and the Spirit against the flesh; for these are in opposition to one another, so that you may not do the things that you please" (Gal 5:17)

- Note the pattern below. Peace comes from obedience. Insecurity comes from disobedience. Do you face insecurities? What are they? See if they are related to any prior disobedience.

> If it was in modern times, Abram and Sarah might have joined the list of many others in seeing whether they could help the fertilization process along. They would check out the best hospitals but discover meager results. Or perhaps they would not have. They knew something that many of us do not know.
>
> In Genesis 16:2, Sarai, his wife, said, "Now behold, the LORD has prevented me from bearing children."
>
> The Lord was in charge of her fertilization. But if she really believed this, would she then have given Hagar her maid to Abram to lie with? We can sense the doubts and frustrations in this chapter.

Disobedience => Insecurity => Fears => Immoral decisions
Obedience => Trust => Peace => Good decisions

Person Detour (Gen 13-14)

• Being with those you shouldn't

The second detour that Abraham takes is uncovered in two different incidents, but it all revolved around being with someone God told him not to be with. Have you ever been with those you shouldn't have been with? This is a person problem. Many of Abram's problems developed because he brought Lot along.

Genesis 12:1 told Abraham "Go... from your relatives."

But what do we find in Genesis 13:1, "So Abram went up from Egypt to the Negev, he and his wife and all that belonged to him; and Lot with him." God gave Abram specific instructions in order to keep him from trouble; His positive instruction was a warning so to be spared from future problems. Disobedience always has its consequences. Chapters 13 and 14 record two big hassles Abraham could have avoided had he obeyed the LORD.

1. Abram and Lot's Workmen (Gen 13)

The first problem was over Abram and Lot's workmen. In verse 13:7 Abraham mentions that they were brothers and the real enemies were the Canaanite and the Perizzites. If they argued, they would become vulnerable to the enemy. In the end, they just couldn't get along with each other. In the end, Abram and Lot separated, and Lot and his men, attracted to the glamorous cities of Sodom and Gomorrah (13:10) left, and his family suffered forever because of it. Abraham settled in Canaan.

2. Abram's Rescue of Lot (Gen 14)

The second problem of having Lot nearby led to getting caught in a risky fight. When Lot was nearby, Abram was responsible for his safety and well-being. The evil one often uses this method to distract God's people from their main work. Abram would not have had any of these concerns had he just left Lot back in Haran. Abram risked everything to help rescue Lot. No doubt, Abraham showed his courage and concern for family, which is important, and God helped them to defeat the coalition army they went up against. But remember, it was not Abram's cleverness, but God's grace that got him out of trouble.

A LOT OF PROBLEMS

Application

Evaluate what difficulties you are going through at this point in time. See if it is at connected to disobedience. Examine relationships, marital problems, etc.

Procedure Detour (Gen 16-17)

Doing things in ways you shouldn't

The Difficulty

This third detour is the one I want to focus on: doing things in ways we shouldn't. Abraham's procedure detour is found beginning in chapter 16 and ending in chapter 21. The problem and the temptation are found in Genesis 16:1, "Now Sarai, Abram's wife had borne him no children, and she had an Egyptian maid whose name was Hagar."

There is no doubt that those who did not bear children were despised and looked down on in those days. But the problem was much greater than just Sarah's barrenness. In Genesis 12:7 we read, "And the LORD appeared to Abram and said, "To your descendants I will give this land."

The promise that brought Abram to the land was the promise of a great nation coming from his descendants. But what good is it to have a land with no descendants? Barren women were often despised by others in the ancient world. Sarai faced this 'reputation' problem, but even still, the lack of a child became much more a test of Abram's faith. It is like saying to a boy with only one arm that he will become a great baseball player. The promise, in a sense, teased Abram and provoked him to understand more of God. We can understand Abraham's perplexed state a bit more from Genesis 15:1-6.

> After these things the word of the LORD came to Abram in a vision, saying, "Do not fear, Abram, I am a shield to you; Your reward shall be very great." 2 And Abram said, "O Lord GOD, what wilt Thou give me, since I am childless, and the heir of my house is Eliezer of Damascus?" 3 And Abram said, "Since Thou

hast given no offspring to me, one born in my house is my heir." 4
Then behold, the word of the LORD came to him, saying, "This
man will not be your heir; but one who shall come forth from your
own body, he shall be your heir." 5 And He took him outside and
said, "Now look toward the heavens, and count the stars, if you are
able to count them." And He said to him, "So shall your
descendants be." 6 Then he believed in the LORD; and He
reckoned it to him as righteousness.

Every crisis that we face in life offers its own temptation. In Abraham's
case, he simply didn't have any children after many years of being
married. Along with the personal frustration came the social stigma. As
we can still see in several societies today, we can expect they faced
rejection from others because of their childlessness. Notice Yahweh's
repeated promises to Abram.

And the LORD appeared to Abram and said, "To your
descendants I will give this land." (12:7)

And I will make your descendants as the dust of the earth... (13:6)

Abraham's perplexed state can be seen from Genesis 15:1-6,

2 And Abram said, "O Lord GOD, what wilt Thou give me, since I
am childless, and the heir of my house is Eliezer of Damascus?" 3
And Abram said, "Since Thou hast given no offspring to me, one
born in my house is my heir" (Gen 15:2-3).

It would have been easier if God had never spoken to Abram, but He
did. In fact, to make matters worse, Abram's name means father. His
destiny was wrapped up in what he did not have. Abram did believe God
as verse 15:6 says, but God was developing and greatly testing this faith.
The real quality of endurance is not waiting until the fulfillment of a
promise was almost accomplished, but until it is actually fulfilled.

There was a common practice in those parts recorded in ancient records
found by Haran. If a couple were infertility, it was legal and acceptable
for the husband to impregnate his wife's slave girl. When the time of
birth came around, the wife would be there at the birth and receive the

baby, and they would treat it as her own. This is what is spoken of happening in Genesis 16:3-4.

> And after Abram had lived ten years in the land of Canaan, Abram's wife Sarai took Hagar the Egyptian, her maid, and gave her to her husband Abram as his wife. And he went in to Hagar, and she conceived; and when she saw that she had conceived, her mistress was despised in her sight.

We should remember it was not that they were impulsive. It seems that Sarah had mentioned this option ten years prior to him following up on it as 16:3 says. But as often happens, time tests our faith. We ask, "Did God really mean that? Maybe I misunderstood Him." But consider the problems that arose when they doubted and questioned God's timing for the promised child. In the same way, until we confront our sin, problems get worse and worse.

In Genesis 16:2-3, Sarah recommends the worldly way of getting God's work done. Abraham, at first, thought God would do it through his own, biological son. But time and the influence of other's doubt wore him down, which allowed him room to follow the world's way of resolving the issue. While the world might have thought this was appropriate, Abraham's action was disobedience to God.

In Genesis 16:4, the Egyptian servant girl came to think she was better than Sarai because she could have intimacies and children with her mistress' husband. Sarai said, "I was despised in her sight." Because of this new dynamic that had been accomplished in disobedience, Sarah's attitude was not right and this put all sorts of tension in the family that they hadn't had before.

In Genesis 16:5, Sarah made things worse by threatening her husband. The very spirit of rebellion that her slave girl was exhibiting, she was also expressing toward her husband. She put the ultimatum before Abraham, "May the LORD judge between you and me." She was demanding that either Abraham do something about her being belittled by her maid or she would. It seems evident that Abraham was reluctant to deal with the situation. After all, he thought Ismael, the son born to the Egyptian slave girl, to be the promised child. This leads us to Abraham's next desperate step in his procedure detour.

In Genesis 16:6a, Abraham tries to wash his hands from the mess he created. But he still didn't act responsibly and so told Sarai that she could do with the slave girl whatever she wanted. Now keep in mind that this would've been hard for Abraham. It's easy to see how he favored Hagar in his reluctance to deal with the issues that arose after Ishmael's conception. Sarai was very upset with him, maybe even to the point of leaving him, but what good is a great nation without his wife? So he had to forgo his hope that this child would be the promised son. Hopelessness and despair reigned over Abraham.

In Genesis 16:6b, Sarai not only told Hagar to pack up her things and leave but "treated her harshly." Just think about this: they require this woman to provide an heir, she does, and now she is abused! As a result of the abuse and command to leave, she fled from Sarah's presence. Why did Sarah, a woman praised for great qualities of gentleness and a submissive spirit in I Peter 4, abuse her slave girl? She was probably kicking herself for suggesting that Abraham do this whole thing, maybe because she didn't think he'd actually do it. But Abraham did it! She was thinking for him at that moment but not in a comprehensive manner. Great jealousy came upon her.

The Consequences

Our tendency toward self-reliance in getting things done will eventually be shown to be poor attempts at accomplishing what God has already promised to provide. When we try to accomplish things on our own, things will get worse and worse until, by God's grace, He steps in. When we do not do things according to God's timing and procedure, all sorts of bad things happen:

- Ishmael's descendants became, and still are, a major threat to Israel (of Isaac the Promised son).

- More problems developed in Abraham and Sarah's marriage.

- Unable to prove God's faithfulness in his own life.

- Poor testimony to the world.

God redeemed the situation that Abraham and Sarah made a mess of, and He even made a special appearance to Hagar to tell her two things:

1. She should humble her heart. She had been wrongly prideful. She should not exasperate the situation to her advantage. Hagar responded in humility and returned to Abraham and Sarah.

2. The Lord promised that her child would become a great man and that she should name him Ishmael. From this we see that Ishmael became the forefather of the Arabs and Moslems. They are a fighting people. They grow by war as we saw in North Africa when they conquered the Christians. I also believe that we will be given the opportunity to take the gospel to them, to greatly bless them and call many of them to know Jesus. Up to now, the mission field to the Arabs has been very difficult, which, I would say is in part due to the way we responded to their violence with violence, as in the Crusades. One important principle highlighted in Galatians is that the flesh is opposed to the spirit. Truly, Abraham's "work of the flesh" has produced a long-lasting consequence that we can see even today, 4,000 years after the fact. The Middle East conflict arises every time Israel is revived. After the captivity, Nehemiah faced great hostility (Nehemiah 2:19 "Geshem the Arab"). And, ever since the United Nations chartered Israel back into existence in 1948, the Middle East has been filled with hostility.

Summary

God had given a wonderful promise to Abraham, but he almost lost his family because he was doubtful enough to use the world's ways to accomplish God's will. God's promises and the world's ways are not compatible. Sometimes we will convince ourselves that God's ways are the same as the world's ways, but there is no compatibility. It caused great friction in his family, and as a result, we experience the result of that contention today in the Middle East. If God judged Abraham, who had received great promises of God, do you think that we will get off any easier? Obedience always will work out for our best.

Detecting Detours

God wants us to endure the test of our faith and endure through the enemy's temptation. Below I will summarize some of the suggestions of the world and compare them to what the Lord says in order to highlight the difference in approach and perspective. The incident with Hagar and Ishmael highlights these differences:

- 16:2: The world confidently tells us this or that way is best. God says the world's ways are always hard and never best. Eventually Hagar and her son Ishmael were thrown out. They could not live together. Work done in the flesh will one day be revealed.

- 16:3: The world places urgency on accomplishment, but God is not in a rush. It is not surprising to find ourselves pressured by the world to do things the way it suggests. We seem to think that we are doing God a favor by speeding up plans for His kingdom, but in fact we slow things down. God purposed that Abram wait many years before Isaac was born. After 10 years he tried to hurry things. The following 14 years was proof that hurrying God's plans takes even more time! Age 86: Ishmael (Gen 16:16) <> Age 100: Isaac (Gen 21:5)

- 16:4: The world only considers the things that it can tangibly do. God, however, often calls us to things beyond what we can do. The world focuses on what it can accomplish in its own wisdom and through its own resources, but with God's way, miracles are common place because man cannot accomplish what is needed on his own. In Abraham's case, Isaac was a miracle child.

The world prides itself on what it accomplishes on its own while God's people always exalts the Creator for what He has done. Man feels good by emphasizing that he's done everything he can with his talents, money, and reputation. Abram honorably used his resources and risking them (when saving Lot). Man's way exalts man; God's way always exalts God.

The world suggests that we live counter to the principles of God outlined in His Word. God doesn't want us to live counter to His Word because He knows whats best for us. The world, which includes much of the professing church today, believes in relativism. In Abram's case, the principles of marriage were broken. Deep down they knew it, but they chose to violate them anyway. God's ways are always in accord with His Word.

The world lives by what it sees, feels, and senses. God's ways are often oriented around faith. Man focuses on and is limited by what is happening around him; man is pragmatic, and is fixed on copying others. God, however, works in creative and various means all within the bounds of His Word.

COSTLY DETOURS

The World	The Godly	Evidence
World's ways are never best	God's ways are always best	Bad consequences
Seems compelling	Not really urgent	Waited 14 more years
Self-reliant	God-dependent	The miracle of Isaac
Prideful	Exalts the Lord	God supplies
Relativistic	Set on God's principles	Abraham's marriage
Lives by senses	Lives by faith	Abraham's faith

COSTLY DETOUR DIAGRAM

The big question is, will you avoid the unnecessary detours? Can you detect them? The above detours are used as examples to highlight the differences between the six differences between the world's way and God's way.

Conclusion

We will always have the opportunity to take a detour. God is waiting for His people to come back to Him, seek His face, and follow His ways; we don't need the latest organizational methods! May God unite our hearts in accomplishing the purpose of His heart so that the world may know of the glory of God.

GENESIS

Genesis 14
Abraham Saves Lot and Learns Much

God's training ground for Abraham

The first section of Genesis, chapters 1-11, revealed how God shaped the world at large while Genesis 12 and onward takes a more personal focus on how God shapes individuals. The assumption is that people need training, not just in knowledge and skills, but in making priorities and decisions, setting values, and especially in relating to God their Maker.

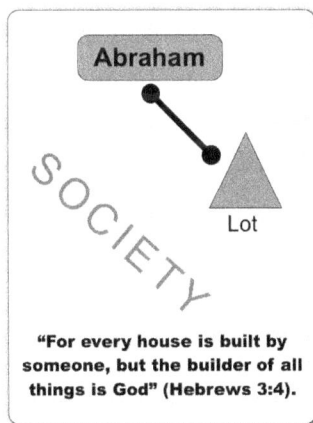

"For every house is built by someone, but the builder of all things is God" (Hebrews 3:4).

God is invested in shaping His new family just like any good father would. God is the builder of all things, "For every house is built by someone, but the builder of all things is God" (Heb 3:4).

Many of us take courses in sociology but are not seriously introduced to the fundamental role that marriage and the family have on society. God is interested in building a people who are devoted to Him and share in

253

His blessings. He wants to care for them, but He expects them to be faithful to Him. Just as in a marriage, we covenant together for the other's good. It does not work for one party to gain what he or she wants and then leave.

Genesis gives us special insight into how God works with individuals to train and develop their character and faith. Peter affirms this special interest that God has in the lives of His people. "For it is time for judgment to begin with the household of God; and if it begins with us first, what will be the outcome for those who do not obey the gospel of God?" (1 Peter 4:17). Exodus is the book where we see God training leaders and a nation, but here in Genesis, we see how God provides special insight into how He works with individuals because they will soon become the heads of that nation–the people of God.

God has special life goals for each one of us and so gives us opportunities to grow in our faith. As a sovereign God, it is easy for Him to provide carefully governed circumstances to test and increase our faith. Genesis 14 shows us one instance where He highlights His dealings with Abraham and provides a way through which we can gain perspective into how God works in our lives too.

God provides insight in Genesis 14 regarding three specific steps that help us grow our faith.

Observe God's Blessing (Gen 14:1-10)

A proper understanding of God's blessings strengthens our relationship with God.

14:1 And it came about in the days of Amraphel king of Shinar, Arioch king of Ellasar, Chedorlaomer king of Elam, and Tidal king of Goiim, 2 that they made war with Bera king of Sodom, and with Birsha king of Gomorrah, Shinab king of Admah, and Shemeber king of Zeboiim, and the king of Bela (that is, Zoar). 3 All these came as allies to the valley of Siddim (that is, the Salt Sea). 4

Twelve years they had served Chedorlaomer, but the thirteenth year they rebelled.

5 And in the fourteenth year Chedorlaomer and the kings that were with him, came and defeated the Rephaim in Ashteroth-karnaim and the Zuzim in Ham and the Emim in Shaveh-kiriathaim, 6 and the Horites in their Mount Seir, as far as El-paran, which is by the wilderness.

7 Then they turned back and came to En-mishpat (that is, Kadesh), and conquered all the country of the Amalekites, and also the Amorites, who lived in Hazazon-tamar. 8 And the king of Sodom and the king of Gomorrah and the king of Admah and the king of Zeboiim and the king of Bela (that is, Zoar) came out; and they arrayed for battle against them in the valley of Siddim, 9 against Chedorlaomer king of Elam and Tidal king of Goiim and Amraphel king of Shinar and Arioch king of Ellasar--four kings against five. 10 Now the valley of Siddim was full of tar pits; and the kings of Sodom and Gomorrah fled, and they fell into them. But those who survived fled to the hill country (Gen 14:1-10).

The detailed list of names from the early section of Genesis 14 certainly can baffle us. Why spend ten verses making specific comments about these invaders from the north when it could have been summed up in one verse like so: "Four kings from the north invaded and recaptured Sodom, Gomorrah and other cities along with Lot...." and then continued with verse 11 as it is now.

There are two evident reasons for the list of names:

Historicity and Accuracy of the Text

The further we go back into history, the accuracy of the stories, reports, etc. tend to seem more unreliable. Chinese history merges into myth. Egyptian history is completely self-embellishing. The kings of historicity like to write in a fashion that promotes their name and accomplishments. As a whole, they are not interested in the accuracy of reports, like a historian might be today, but use these rare reports to polish their own image. At times they were engraved on stones or columns to create a real sense of permanence.

The details of country, city-states, personal names, and other things found in Genesis 14 and elsewhere in Genesis 10 prove that the author was not only very aware of the circumstances of that time, but that accuracy was important to him. When an author pays special attention to the facts (in details like the report that in the 13th year the city-states of the south overthrew King Chedorlaomer's dominion over them), we can be quite assured that other information included is also accurately reported. The Bible's reliability enables God's Word to be used to train His people (2 Tim 3:16-17).

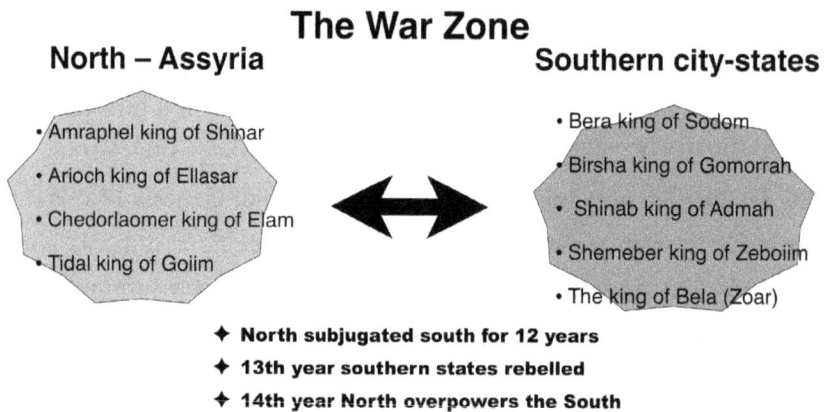

The War Zone

North – Assyria   **Southern city-states**

- Amraphel king of Shinar
- Arioch king of Ellasar
- Chedorlaomer king of Elam
- Tidal king of Goiim

- Bera king of Sodom
- Birsha king of Gomorrah
- Shinab king of Admah
- Shemeber king of Zeboiim
- The king of Bela (Zoar)

✦ **North subjugated south for 12 years**
✦ **13th year southern states rebelled**
✦ **14th year North overpowers the South**

GENESIS 14 CHART OF NORTH-SOUTH BATTLES

Over the years, unbelievers have viciously attacked the Bible by claiming that the people and places in the Bible, like these mentioned, never existed. Year by year, though, their spurious attacks are proven wrong. People doubted David's existence (though he has penned many a psalm) until they found his name on some ancient artifact.[74]

---

[74]

www.biblicalarchaeology.org/daily/biblical-artifacts/artifacts-and-the-bible/the-tel-dan-inscr iption-the-first-historical-evidence-of-the-king-david-bible-story/

Unless you are a history buff, these things probably mean nothing to you. These king's names and battles, however, are significant because they give us confidence that this is not just a made up story, but genuine historical events. If these things really happened, we can be sure the other things about Abraham also happened at some point in time, back around 2000 BC, and that God is teaching us through them.[75]

God's Protection

As careful attention is given to who fought where, it becomes very evident that these kings were fighting everywhere but where Abraham was. The kings of the north plowed through many city-states and less defendable groups on their way to regain control of the southern city-states. It is possible that the Kadesh and Seir were near Petra, south of the Dead Sea as the early Christian fathers thought in contrast to the last several hundred years.[76]

Chedorlaomer, the head of the four kings from north, was performing an all-out assault on the greater region in southern Canaan, and even defeated the Amalekites and the Amorites. On his way back

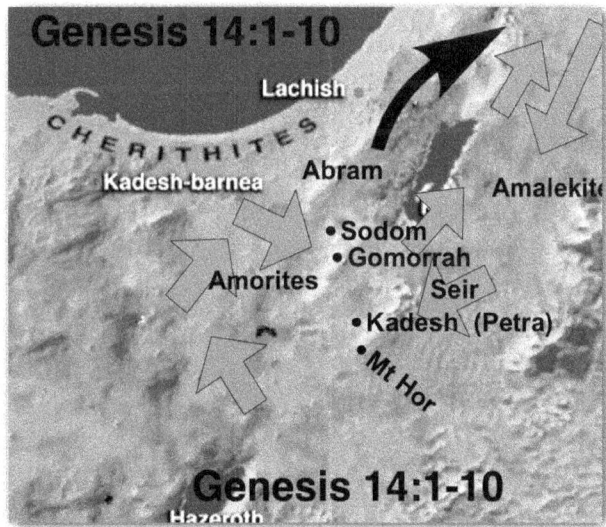

Genesis 14:1-10

through Canaan, Chedorlaomer's powerful armies defeated the

---

[75] For further reading: The Origins and Reliability of the Bible.
www.foundationsforfreedom.net/Topics/Bible/Bible_Origin.html

[76] www.bible.ca/archeology/bible-archeology-exodus-kadesh-barnea.htm

southern state alliance of five kings, which include the more familiar Sodom and Gomorrah.

Sodom was not very distant from Abraham. Remember how Lot lifted up his eyes and could see the lush valley that described the well-watered place as the garden of the Lord (13:10)?

The armies chose to go on the east of the Dead Sea rather than to fight in the place that we now know as Israel. Though they came from the south, very close to Abram, they did not invade or bother him. This is part of the unacknowledged blessing of God that we hardly ever take note of. God kept those battles out of Abram's district. Remember that he had no defense as a shepherd.

Every once in a while, I think about how much God has protected the health of my family and the ways He's taken care of us. Sometimes it takes an illness, an

Seir, the Horite

Lotan	Shobal	Zibeon	Anah
Hori	Alvan	Alah	Dishon
Heman	Manahath	Anah	Oholibamah
	Eba		His daughter
	Sheopho		
	Onam		

accident, or a problem to remind us that God has been watching over us. This is exactly the picture we should get of Abraham.

Yet it is important to be aware of God's blessings so that we can connect our heart and appreciation to the Lord. Sometimes we take things for granted. We shouldn't. Blessings in our society, economy, relationships, families, and churches are all from the Lord.

They are there because God has been working. There will be times when those blessings will not seem to be blessings. Yet He is still in control, whether He is chastising us or exposing hidden sin in our lives, God still cares for us. When we see His blessings each day, our hearts build up a solid confidence in His genuine.

Application

Go through your life. Think through the ways God has blessed you. Thank Him. Learn to be more observant each day. During our daily family devotions (i.e. family devotions), we give thanks to the Lord for various things that have occurred during the day.

A Christian once said to me that he had not seen God's blessing in his life. But when I looked at his life, things seemed to be pretty well off. I realized that this believer did not recognize that the blessings of his Christian family were blessings from God. He had harmony, love, provision, and care all around him, even though he had difficulty finding a job.

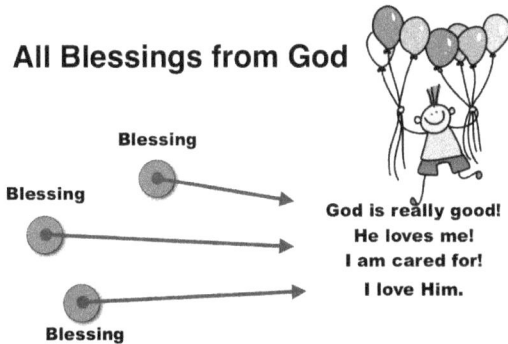

DIAGRAM: ALL BLESSINGS FROM GOD

He was not out on the street or in need of anything. Those that are brought up in Christian homes and churches can very easily take these things for granted. Be wary of doing so. God is trying to train you so that He can win your heart. By ignoring these good things, you are not reconfirming your value as stemming from Him. When this connection is not well-formed, the believer then begins to question whether what the world advocates is better, forgetting that the world honestly does not deliver on its promises.

Just look at those who have ruined relationships, confused purpose, and compromised lives–they have so much needless pain.

Application for those who grew up in Christian homes

Those who have grown up in Christian homes often get confused as to what is good and great. They reap the benefits of their parents' obedience but do not realize how they are tied to their pursuit of God. Some think that they can have both the benefits of a devout life and the lusts of the world, but they must realize that it doesn't work that way. Only trauma, pain, struggle, and bitterness come from the world.

The more we live by the truth, the more we will be blessed, and the more we will bless others. So all the harmony, love, and kindness you have is from the Lord because people live by the Word. Barrenness, strife, hatred and bitterness come when someone disobeys. This is why the young who have not seen the world in action can be so easily persuaded that a certain philosophy is right; they have not seen the long term results from that belief.

Connecting God's Truth		
All Blessings are from God (James 1:17)	Observing His ways reaps His blessings	Disregarding His truths bring pain to our lives.
Relationships	Harmony, kindness	Disharmony. arguing. fighting.
Money	Content, sharing	Discontent. greedy. selfish
Marriage	Long lasting love, genuine care	Barrenness. alienation. brokenness. phoniness.
Drive	Team welfare, God's work	Covetousness. evil plans.

CHART ON CONNECTING TRUTH WITH BLESSING

James says, "Do not be deceived, my beloved brethren. Every good thing bestowed and every perfect gift is from above, coming down from the Father of lights, with whom there is no variation, or shifting shadow" (James 1:16-17).

Utilize God's Blessing (Gen 14:11-16)

First, God trains us by pointing out how He has blessed us, so that our faith is strengthened and our hearts can affirm His goodness. Second, God trains us by giving us opportunities to serve Him.

Abram provides a powerful example here to learn from, one that might at first seem very distant from our own circumstances, but will later prove its relevancy to our circumstances. How we respond to our circumstances allows us to shape the world around us as God did through Abram.

Abram was not being attacked or provoked in any way. He was comfortable. He was blessed with God's protection. This is just the beginning of the training, however. God made sure Abraham heard the morning news through a certain escapee, who brought information about Lot's capture to Abraham. Abram's nephew had been captured, along with his family and belongings.

A Hebrew (Gen 14:11-13)

> Then they took all the goods of Sodom and Gomorrah and all their food supply, and departed. 12 And they also took Lot, Abram's nephew, and his possessions and departed, for he was living in Sodom. 13 Then a fugitive came and told Abram the Hebrew. Now he was living by the oaks of Mamre the Amorite, brother of Eshcol and brother of Aner, and these were allies with Abram (Gen 14:11-13).

Before going on, let me make note of the label 'Hebrew'. It is the first time in the Bible that it is used. The term could be interpreted as one 'from afar' or 'from beyond.' It is similar to our notion of alien or even pilgrim, as one passing through.

The scholars are pretty sure that the term is connected to Eber, one of his forefathers, making sure that the promises made to Shem, the son of Noah would follow on to Abram (Gen 10:21, 11:14-26). The term, however, was rarely used by the Hebrews to describe themselves, but as in this case was used by an outsider to describe Abram.[77] The author inserts this to remind us both of Abram's alien status, and Abram's link with the Shemite line and to God's promises.

God designs personal tests, usually triggered by some circumstances, to push us to more deeply trust Him so that we might be increasingly convinced of His glorious person, power and plans.

What is His next plan for you?

To the world, Abram was an outsider. He didn't belong anywhere, really. To God, however, Abram was precious and the chosen one through whom God would working. The parallel between Abram and God's people today remain the same. Truly we as believers in Christ are sons of Abraham. Like the disciples of old that Peter wrote to, we are but aliens scattered about (1 Peter 1:1). As pilgrims in this world, we declare this is but a temporary foreign land that we live in, and though still in God's presence, our real home is the one God has promised.

Application

Have you ever felt that you do not belong when people don't like you for your faith and decisions? Do not be tempted to side with the world, even for a moment. Rejoice in God's choice of you and thank Him for His love and work in your life. One day soon you will be with Him in the Promised Land.

---

77 Theological Wordbook of the Old Testament (TDNT), Volume 2, pg. 643.

Abram's Big Decision

Verse 13 also informs us that Abram (his name had not yet changed) lived next to some Amorites, who were allies with Abram. Notice that Abram lived out in the land as a shepherd rather than in a big city with the protection of a wall. As an outsider, new to the area, he was quite vulnerable. There were also other foreign enemies that threatened his life.

Abram's immediate response surprises us, "And when Abram heard that his relative had been taken captive, he led out his trained men, born in his house, three hundred and eighteen, and went in pursuit as far as Dan" (Gen 14:14).

Something seems odd, here, does it not? I don't mean Abram's concern for Lot, who was his nephew. We can identify with that. And if Abram had had the proper resources, we could understand that he would use those resources to help Lot out. The problem is that Abram did not have the resources. Try to picture it: these city-states were fighting each other. Finally, the allied five city-states of the south, including where Lot was, figured they were strong enough to win against the four kings from the north, yet the southern states lost the battle. They lost everything–their goods and people were killed or taken captive.

What did Abram's resources look like? Genesis 14:14 clearly tells us the exact number of men he had: 318. Fortunately, they were trained, but 318 men is nothing compared to the professional armies who were fighting numerous districts.

They were professionals and many in number. They had just defeated five kings and the armies under them. The number of Abram's men were about the same in number to a good Sunday congregation! Do you see the impracticality of it all?

Abram didn't question the logic of his decision. He knew what to do and did it. To anyone looking in, it was painfully apparent that he could do nothing. Abram mobilized his men and went after Lot, pursuing the enemy all the way to the north of Israel, even to the north of Damascus.

> And he divided his forces against them by night, he and his servants, and defeated them, and pursued them as far as Hobah, which is north of Damascus. 16 And he brought back all the goods, and also brought back his relative Lot with his possessions, and also the women, and the people (Gen 14:15-16).

The report goes on in verse 15 to describe how Abram executed his plan. Risking his nephew was a suicide mission. If he didn't come back, his whole family would be left in utter ruin. It is not like he had other family there in the land of Canaan to take care of them while he was off to war. He was an outsider!

This was not an insignificant event, and sets a wonderful picture of God's love in action, later seen in Jesus Christ being sent to earth, stepped out of His easy environment to meet hostile challenges.

A Picture of God's Love

What is it that Abram modeled so well? He left his comfortable and blessed position for the sake of others. He risked all–at crazy odds– in hope that God would perpetuate His blessing through his attempt to rescue Lot.

Christians battle on two levels. Most are aware of the struggle to refrain from doing what is wrong. We try to be good at saying no to the bad. This is part of the Christian life, but not all of it. Don't stop there.

Two ways to do good

- Refrain from evil

- Proactively do good

Abram gives us a great perspective here on the greater call upon our lives and the authority we have in Christ.

The heart of missions is to take the blessings that come from God and share it with others. To give up our comforts for the sake of others; their needs rise above our own. Through this, God's people replicate God's love and replant it in different lands and hearts.

Whenever a church or people begin to live for their own ease and comfort and do not apply the lessons of sacrificial love, that church or people begins to die.

Application

- Are there some people or situations that the Lord has set on your heart to respond to? If so, have you responded? How so? If not, why not?

- Is your church or personal life in the process of dying? Why not seek God for what you can do for others, even at a cost to your own comfort?

Secure God's Blessings (Gen 14:17-24)

Melchizedek, the King of Righteousness

Then after his return from the defeat of Chedorlaomer and the kings who were with him, the king of Sodom went out to meet him at the valley of Shaveh (that is, the King's Valley). 18 And Melchizedek king of Salem brought out bread and wine; now he was a priest of God Most High. 19 And he blessed him and said, "Blessed be Abram of God Most High, Possessor of heaven and earth; 20 And blessed be God Most High, Who has delivered your enemies into your hand." And he gave him a tenth of all. 21 And the king of Sodom said to Abram, "Give the people to me and take the goods for yourself." 22 And Abram said to the

> Do you really care for the lost?

> Do you really believe obedience is important?

> Do you love me more than these?

> Do you really love one another?

king of Sodom, "I have sworn to the LORD God Most High, possessor of heaven and earth, 23 that I will not take a thread or a sandal thong or anything that is yours, lest you should say, 'I have made Abram rich.' 24 "I will take nothing except what the young men have eaten, and the share of the men who went with me, Aner, Eshcol, and Mamre; let them take their share" (Gen 14:17-24).

Abram's Fighting Party

It was not just Abram and his men who went to fight. The scriptures, in verse 13, openly stated that three individuals, Amorite neighbors to Abram, were his allies. An ally means one who would fight with the other when they were attacking or defending. Obviously, in that day, it meant much more. Abram was not being attacked as he was just trying to help out his relative, but they still went in together.

Note in verse 24 how Abram refers to the others who went with him, Aner, Eshcol and Mamre. We should assume it was not just these three but the men of their families that went with him. Abram wanted these men to get their portion for helping him out. I think it's safe to say that it wasn't easy to convince them to pursue the nearby professional fighters.

Even still, it was remarkable that Abram went at all. Even with a few other families, probably much smaller than his, would risk all. Abram believed God would bless him in battle just as He had been recently blessed him with his sheep and other affairs. Abram made some mistakes in his life, but he certainly can't be called a coward.

A Secret Prayer

Something else is revealed here in this passage about the battle. Before we examined the battle scene by numbers of men, but there was more to the scene as seen in his conversation with the king of Sodom. Abram politely refuses to take from the goods that he returned with upon rescuing the people of Sodom, Gomorrah, etc. The King of

Sodom, evidently one that had escaped to the hills, told him to take all, "Give the people to me and take the goods for yourself" (Gen 14:21).

But Abram deferred the opportunity and explained his decision, "I have sworn to the LORD God Most High, possessor of heaven and earth, that I will not take a thread or a sandal thong or anything that is yours, lest you should say, 'I have made Abram rich'" (Gen 14:22-23).

Abram had evidently made a prayer behind the scenes about this daring expedition. It probably went something like this, "If you help me safely come back with Lot, I will not take any of the loot. Your help is sufficient for me!" It was a deal that God evidently was happy to take up. Abram had nothing to offer from his side of things except his heart. He did know, however, upon whom he was relying, 'the LORD God Most High, possessor of heaven and earth.'

Usually, our bargains, assumed or stated, are fairly equal. If you help me do this, I will help you do that. This was definitely not the case here. But what was it that God chiefly wanted? Evidently, God is happy if he can

get us to be more committed or devoted to Him. He doesn't need what we have. Even when Abram gave a tithe, it was not that God could use it. Offerings more deeply represent our devotion, appreciation, etc.

"The LORD God Most High, possessor of heaven and earth" (Genesis 14:22).

Abram was stating by his march that the power to gain victory through God was more significant than anything he had. There is no doubt that we see Abram's concern for Lot, but paralleling this concern was His brave confidence that God could and would help him.

Perhaps, Abram had seen the many ways God had been blessing him in the years past so that his faith steadily grew reaching this point where he began to see that God was really on His side. He could depend on God to not only care for him but to be concerned about what was on his heart.

A Powerful Trust

Abram got his trust from somewhere. He took his few 'fish and bread' into battle and came out victorious. He learned to trust in God's presence, which would enable him to tap into the Lord's powerful help. Psalm 46 celebrates this idea of God's presence.

> The LORD of hosts is with us; The God of Jacob is our stronghold" (Psalm 46:7). "The LORD of hosts is with us; The God of Jacob is our stronghold (Psalm 46:11).

The believer should have this same confidence. Jesus, after His resurrection, told His disciples, "I am with you to the end of the age" (Mat 28:20).

Are you getting a better picture of Abram's faith? Abram had enough favor with God to gain God's help in defeating professional armies. This is what we can learn from Abram's faith: when we take the blessings that He has already extended to us and reach out to distribute that essence of God's goodness elsewhere where there is need.

A Hidden Force–King Melchizedek (18-20)

This last point about King Melchizedek is puzzling due to its brief and surprising introduction here. Melchizedek's office, his action, and the teaching of him throughout the Bible is all so intriguing. Let's first see what two verses state about him here.

> And Melchizedek king of Salem brought out bread and wine; now he was a priest of God Most High. 19 And he blessed him and said, "Blessed be Abram of God Most High, Possessor of heaven and earth; 20 And blessed be God Most High, Who has delivered your enemies into your hand." And he gave him a tenth of all (Gen 14:18-20).

Abram returns from battle with all the loot and people. The King of Sodom even came out to offer Abram everything that he had recovered. Can you imagine how happy everyone was? Then suddenly this king out of nowhere, Melchizedek king of Salem, comes out to greet him with bread and wine.

His introduction should astonish us for several reasons. He is described as a priest of "God Most High." Salem, meaning 'peace', like Shalom, is the old name for Jerusalem. He was evidently the king of Salem, but also the high priest to the same God that made the earth and heaven. Melchizedek was priest to the same God that Abram served. Without speculating too much, we are to assume here that this paying of a tithe became a special heart response from Abram to physically express his appreciativeness of God's help.

There does not seem to be any law dictating a tithe of ten percent. The Old Testament does speak about tithes and gifts much later, but Abram's deal with God only seemed to go as far as not taking any loot from the others so that the others would know that Abram did not gain his riches from others but from God Himself. He did not do it for the reward but by God's grace for the sake of helping others. But with the high priest's visit, Abram had a way to practically show his appreciation to God via the high priest.

- God wants us to be liberal givers because He has given so much to us already.
- Do you give to your local church? Do you give ten percent? Are there other gifts that you give the Lord to celebrate your appreciation of His work in your life?

Application: The spiritual picture

How does God fit into your life? Is He contained in a small compartment that fits neatly into Sunday morning or is He a great God, the possessor and controller of all that affects each aspect of your life?

The first kind of God is not the God of the scripture. If you find that we treat God this way, know that you have formed an idol to protect your comfort.

If we try to understand all the parts of this picture, we will see that God is the almighty creator and by virtue of His authorship, He is also possessor, even of the ground upon which Abram stood. God's immense power and ability to intervene in any odd occurrence happening on earth is clearly evident. If we gain His favor, He will be the one we can go to with any need we may have.

Man, however, cannot go directly to God. God is too immense and holy. Man needs a priest to mediate between himself and God. Melchizedek was that mediator in Abram's time. He could intercede on behalf of Abram, so that when Abram brought a request to God, Melchizedek could then bring it before God.

There is no evidence at all that Abram went to Salem to gain Melchizedek's help. He had directly sworn to the "LORD God Most high' (v. 22). Abram no doubt did this where he lived through prayer. But behind the scenes, God had mobilized the high priest to bring this prayer to Him and then mobilized this king to assist him in this battle.

The Bible Connection

Whether Melchizedek had his own army or God's spiritual army of angels, we don't know. Nor are we sure that Abram understood these things. God did, however, and it is important to recognize the role the Lord played in this victory to rescue Lot.

Our understanding of Melchizedek has to partly come from our understanding of Jesus Christ, of whom Melchizedek was a type. There are only two other sections of the scriptures where he is mentioned, one in the Old and one in the New Testament.

The Psalmist writes of the Christ, the Messiah, "The LORD has sworn and will not change His mind, "Thou art a priest forever according to the order of Melchizedek" (Psalm 110:4). In verse 5 it says, very relevant to Abram's experience, "The Lord is at Your right hand; He will shatter kings in the day of His wrath."

#1 Genesis 14	Surprise visit – described as king-priest to Most High God	Reveals hidden truths
#2 Psalm 110	Messiah is of order of Melchizedek "The LORD has sworn ..., "Thou art a priest forever according to the order of Melchizedek" (Psalm 110:4).	God promises of someone greater– look for Christ
#3 Hebrews 5-8	Jesus Christ is this king-priest that we serve.	Jesus Christ is both Lord and Savior

CHART OF MELCHIZEDEK'S 3 BIBLICAL USAGES

The Book of Hebrews picks up on Melchizedek and says quite a bit about him. Starting at the end of chapter 4 where the author is speaking of Jesus both as a great high priest and as the king–the Son of God:

> Therefore, since we have a great high priest who has passed through the heavens, Jesus the Son of God, let us hold fast our confession. For we do not have a high priest who cannot sympathize with our weaknesses, but One who has been tempted in all things as we are, yet without sin. Therefore let us draw near with confidence to the throne of grace, so that we may receive mercy and find grace to help in time of need (Heb 4:14-16).

Hebrews chapter 5 to 7 give great significance to Melchizedek and to Psalm 110. Melchizedek is not only a type of the coming priest-king, Jesus the Messiah, but this new priest-king represents a new covenant. Because Psalm 110 was written after the Law (Exodus–Deuteronomy), the Old Testament itself stated that a priest great than the Mosaic one would be coming.

All of this was found in Jesus Christ who established the New Covenant. Jesus is both our priest and our king to whom we are fully obligated as servants. We give gifts to God through the way we give gifts to the local church, with a purpose similar to Abram's: to show our appreciation.

Jesus told us to pray to the Father in His Name. Jesus is the mediator. He has all authority in heaven and earth. When God puts something on our hearts, we ought to go to the Father in prayer, asking Jesus the High priest to bring it before the Mighty God, possessor of heaven and earth. In this way our prayers will be answered.

When our hearts are touched by God's intervening grace, our response should be to further devote ourselves to the almighty God.

Application

- Abraham took the opportunity to show His appreciation not only by refusing to take what was his, but by giving from what he had back to God via the High priest. What has God done for you? Have you returned a token of your appreciation?

- Jesus Christ is today's high priest and king. He challenges us to live in faith of God. When you need, ask in His Name, and He will grant it. Do you merely ask for your own comforts or ask of the Lord for the sake of others in the Name of Jesus Christ.

- The Lord expects us to follow through with our vows. "When you make a vow to God, do not be late in paying it; for he takes no delight in fools. Pay what you vow!" (Ecc 5:4)

- God's blessings are more important than earthly treasures because they help us fulfill God's greater purposes.

- Be willing to be bold for the sake of others, even if it might cost you something. Remember to do it with the Lord's help!

- If you want to help someone but find that you can't, seek God; perhaps He has some special way to solve the problem.

- As you mature in your faith, expect trials of a different kind. They might have to do with something you ought to do rather than perseverance through a hard time.

Personal Illustration

For the last ten years, each mission trip I went on could only happen if I stepped out in faith. There was no money and no way to go unless the Lord had done some dramatic things. He sometimes even waits until the last week to provide what is needed for the mission trip. But, He has always provided. Extra blessings are in store for those who wait upon Him, but we must proactively seek them by entering impossible situations. Isn't this what George Mueller clearly illustrated by the orphans that he took care of without a clear understanding where the money to take care of them was going to come from.[78]

Faith pushes us to proactively do what we should do, not because we can but because the Lord wants us to. This is His spirit of love being extended into the world. How about being patient with a child? You think you do not have sufficient patience for that day. You are easily irritated. Think about what God wants to do through you–even in your irritable days– and seek Him for the patience that comes from Him.

God places us in difficult situations to prove us, whether we will trust Him or not. The point is not whether God is powerful enough to help us. He is the possessor of heaven and earth, of course He is powerful enough to help us! The question is whether we believe it enough to do what we are supposed to accomplish and trust Him. God loves to get

---

[78] For more on this hero of faith, www.bsmi.org/mueller.htm

involved in our life affairs. He is waiting for us to seek Him and so prove His faithfulness.

God does bring a measure of blessing upon our lives. Just as God blessed Abraham, so we are blessed. He wants us to increase that blessing as we reach out to others and the world with His help.

Three Steps of Spiritual Growth

Our faith is strengthened by going over this same pattern over and over. We first observe that He is, in diverse ways, bringing blessings into our worlds. He builds up our trust in Him. We then are ready to take that blessing and bring it to the world as He leads us. This expression of faith will require more trust as it grows, but as we see Him help us, our faith is strengthened even more; it gets more personal. This is true for all of us.

(1) Observe God's Blessing (Gen 14:1-10)

- Do you regularly thank God in your heart for His blessings? Make it personal.

- Are you attracted to the world? Look at the pain of those who do not live by the truth. Get a real perspective. Affirm the Lord as the source of blessings.

(2) Utilize God's Blessings for others (Gen 14:11-16)

- Are you ready for the challenges of using your blessings to meet someone else's need? Try asking, "What's next, Lord?"

(3) Secure God's Blessing (Gen 14:17-24)

- Do you tithe to the Lord? Why?

- Build your faith: seek His help, and show appreciation to the Lord.

GENESIS

Genesis 15:7-21
The Covenant of Hope

What is it about marriage that still draws modern man and woman to bind themselves in this seemingly old-fashioned ceremony? They bind themselves financially, legally, emotionally, physically, and spiritually. Assets are combined. Lives are intertwined. Babies are born.

One of God's favorite ways to describe His people is as a bride. Christ is the bridegroom; His people are His wife. Marriage on earth helps us understand what God desires and wishes for His relationship with us, His people. The better a Christian understands this covenant, God's expectations, and displays a willingness to play his part, the greater his growth will be. Let's observe four aspects of the covenant God made with Abraham.

Abraham leads us by the model of faith. He counted God more important than his connections to the world. Let's now look at the actual covenant God made with Abraham. When God plans to do something great among man, He often pledges His faithfulness to carry it out. He does this in consideration of our weak faith. Man commonly breaks promises, but God does not. In Genesis 15, God was going to bind man to Himself via an official legal act. Although man could not establish this agreement, he was part of it. It was through this covenant that God shaped Abram's way of perceiving the world. He realized that no longer could he just go out and do as everyone else did. There was a higher call to live according to the agreement the Almighty God made with him. In Genesis 12:2, God says to Abram, "And I will make you a great nation, And I will bless you, And make your name great; And so you shall be a blessing."

How did God do it? He did it through a covenant in which God was reaching out to Abram in love, and he was affected. The more he followed the terms of the agreement, the more blessings came to his life and into the world. The genuine source of blessing is not in what Abraham did but in what God did for Abraham. And so, God's love was seen in how He took initiative to bring His own character of undeserved kindness into another's life. We don't have much room to discuss this covenant, but let me summarize.

Abram is Awake (Gen 15:8-11)

We see several things the Lord and Abraham did to get ready for the covenant.

Listening to the Lord's Directions (9)

It is so easy to forget this part. We should always try to determine if the Lord has directed us to do anything general or specific. Abraham was to gather together a bunch of animals according to God's requirement. The list contains five different animals. God says in verse 15:9, "Bring Me a three year old heifer, and a three year old female goat, and a three year old ram, and a turtledove, and a young pigeon."

It cost him his time and money. He had to prioritize his decisions to satisfy the Lord's request.

Obeying the Lord's Directions (10)

After carefully listening, we are to faithfully obey. There is no room for compromise. We cannot say, "I have a 4 year old male goat. I'll use that." No. It is not obedience. The Lord asked for a 3-year-old female goat. Abraham brought the animals and, being familiar with the preparations for making a covenant, he cut all of them, except the birds, in half.

Waiting and Watching (11)

Since the covenant would be made in the evening, Abram had to wait. But note what happened in verse 11. He also had to watch over his preparations. Genesis 15:11 says, "And the birds of prey came down upon the carcasses, and Abram drove them away." Abram protected the sacrifice; he drove the birds away. Although verse 11 seems out of place, we find that there would be things to distract Abram from obedience.

Abram is in a Deep Sleep (Gen 15:12-21)

The most significant things happened while he was in his deep sleep. We could say it is here that God takes the situation out of Abram's hand. One would normally think that if God was to bring any of us into a deep sleep, that we would have a good sleep with dreams of heaven. But it seems in his dreams, unexpected things happened.

The Terrible Vision (12)

Abraham suddenly had "...terror and great darkness fell upon him." I suppose you all have had nightmares. The only thing that we wish for during such times of terror is freedom or escape. In Abraham's case, God intervened.

The Prophecy (13-16)

And God said to Abram, "Know for certain that your descendants will be strangers in a land that is not theirs, where they will be enslaved and oppressed four hundred years. 14 But I will also judge the nation whom they will serve; and afterward they will come out with many possessions. 15 And as for you, you shall go to your fathers in peace; you shall be buried at a good old age. 16 Then in the fourth generation they shall return here, for the iniquity of the Amorite is not yet complete" (Gen 15:13-16).

God explained what would happen in the future to his descendants. The words are a prophecy that would bring direction, comfort, and help during future times of stress. Here is a summary of the main points:

- God's people would be slaves in another country for 400 years.

- God will later judge that nation.

- God will make sure they come out with many possessions. (400 years of wages, a big back pay)

- Abraham's life will end in peace at a good old age.

- After 4 generations, they will come back to the land.

God's explanation is that the sin of the Amorites was not to the point that he would completely wipe them out. But in 400 years, their sins would have piled up to such a place that they would need to be completely judged by eliminating them (16). This verse explains God's patience with sinners.

Abram Hears the Covenant (Gen 15:17-21)

This part of the covenant happened after sunset. When there was some light left, God revealed facts about the future of the land. The Lord provided special insight needed to affirm His faithfulness in the distant future. God made a covenant with Abraham. How did He do it? It might sound strange, but it was very customary to make a covenant together this way. But in the case of God and Abraham, there was one major difference, which I will share in a moment.

When everything was dark, there was an appearance of a smoking oven– think a campfire or grill of some sort. A flaming torch passed between the pieces of the carcasses that Abraham had prepared earlier in the day. God made a covenant with Abraham (15:18). It is interesting that the word for covenant actually derives from the verb 'to cut', thus, the reason for the cut animals.

We have records from back around 2000 B.C. that describe how they made agreements at the time. They would take the animals and cut them in half. Then they would each walk through them. As they walked, each would state that if they did not keep their terms and agreement, they would be cut off just as these animals were cut off (cf. 2 Tim 2:13 the faithfulness of God).

In this case, what happened? We didn't see anyone walking between the pieces. Instead we see a flaming torch go through the middle of the pieces. That torch was a representation of God. But what about Abraham? Well, evidently he was still in his deep sleep. He could see what was happening, but he himself did not take part in this covenant except as a beneficiary. We see two significant truths from this:

- God made the covenant for Abraham rather than with him. Abraham would not have a responsibility in implementing the covenant.

- God would be held solely responsible for implementing the covenant. If it didn't work out, then it would not be man's fault or Abraham's fault, it would be God's unfaithfulness.

God used a means of communication that people in that culture would understand, but purposely changed it. God knew what He was going to do. It rested with God's purpose and power, not with man's. God wanted to take full responsibility because He wanted all the praise. What was the covenant? It was as verses 18 said,

> On that day the LORD made a covenant with Abram, saying, "To your descendants I have given this land, From the river of Egypt as far as the great river, the river Euphrates ... ."

Abraham would not personally receive the land. We see it was not because of his sin, but because the sins of the pagan people were not yet great enough to judge. God would lead His people to a land where they would later become slaves. And yet, as Genesis and Exodus later tell us, God closely watches over His people and judges the nation that oppressed them, and upon their exit gave them an abundance of blessings. The Promised Land of Canaan would be given to the people of God.

In time the Israelites did go down to Egypt and became slaves. After 400 years, God led them out in an event known as the Exodus. Here God made another temporary covenant with them known as the Mosaic Covenant, and later, under the leadership of Joshua, the people defeated the enemies. Under King David, the land was united as prophesied. God was faithful.

Summary

Abraham was no longer free to do whatever he wanted with his life. God bound Abraham to himself through the covenant. You could claim it was unfair because Abraham was sleeping, but we should remember that he brought and arranged the animals. Abraham knew there was a greater way than the world offered and was willing to trust God with it.

Application

What about you and I? Has God approached you by showing you that He has a better way? Have you seen the tragic results of following the world? Have you desired the touch of God in your life? Then more than likely you also have been brought close to God by a legal action called a covenant –the New Covenant. If not, maybe today God is calling you to live by a new standard.

Abraham laid down and slept deeply. This shows that the covenant was God's responsibility. It is the same with the New Covenant. God has initiated this New Covenant with His people by the blood of Jesus Christ. Where were we? Yes, in one sense we were not there to bring the sacrificial animals; we weren't even born. However, we were part of the deep plans of God that, like Abram, He would cause us to be a blessing. Like God's covenant with Abram, God alone planned and carried out the New Covenant.

We couldn't even provide the animals for the sacrifice to 'cut' the covenant, and had we been able to provide them, they wouldn't have been sufficient. This is what God has done for us in Christ. He desired to offer us a better way, a way out by giving us the very best. He brought us out from the world and bound us to Himself. Though some of us have greatly sinned and continue to hang on to the world's ways, living as though a covenant was never made, but the sacrifice was made.

GENESIS

Genesis 18-19
Steps Down to Destruction

Sodom and Gomorrah are clear examples of how a decaying society influences those around it. Much already had to happen to these cities to arrive at the point they were at when judged.

Objectives:

- Understand the facts of why Sodom and Gomorrah were destroyed.

- Expose the tension of living in a pagan culture and learn how to resist sin.

- Deepen our discernment of our world's culture and God's hatred for those things.

- Learn to make decisions that keep us from the touch of the world.

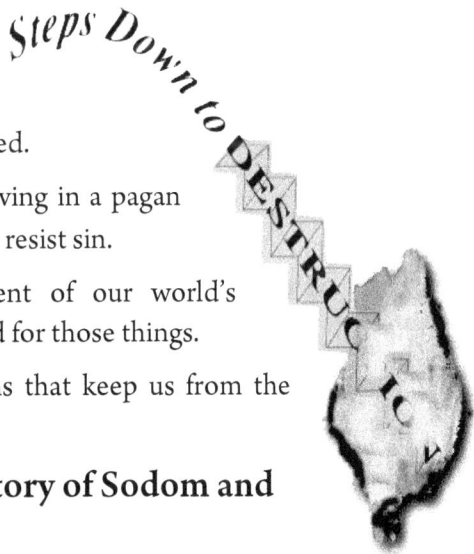

Everybody knows the story of Sodom and Gomorrah, or do they?

After all, it was God who first pointed out these cities to Abraham. We seem to only hear of God's wrath when it comes to Sodom, and never His mercy. The account in Genesis 18-19 painstakingly records both God's mercy and justice.

Actually, we have already seen one means by which God tried to reach out to Sodom and Gomorrah back in Genesis 14. There we see God reaching out to both these cities, amply displaying His love and compassion, and yet evidently they refused it–though their survival was due to Abram's compassion and God's power working on their behalf. They must have been evil already, but things were only getting worse.

People seem to step out of their secularistic spirit just so they can wave their hands at God in anger. Why did you do that? They of course still assert they don't believe in God. They do, though. Why else would they protest His ways. On the other hand, I have never heard of a naturalist who held up his hand in protest over how 'mother nature' handled its various judgments across the earth? Death is natural, they say.

Genesis 18 is given to us because God was teaching Abraham about His hatred of sin. Whenever sin is allowed to grow unrestrained, it brings about horrible destruction. Abraham had a fondness of the great cities of the world, and considering his background , it's no wonder. But this perspective kept him from sharing God's view. He simply didn't share God's hatred for sin. Nor did he value the need for righteousness. And without understanding God's justice, He couldn't understand the Lord's great mercy either.

A Study of the World's Influence

Let's take a look at an example of the intensity of the "cultural war," as it is sometimes called. Here is a Christian college that allowed a concert conducted by two homosexuals to be held in its student activity center. Compare the mission statement with a comment from a student magazine on the right. As you read this, you might ask yourself whether you would have let your grown son or daughter attend such a concert.

A Christian College: It's Mission

Calvin College... in the Reformed tradition of historic Christianity. Through our learning, we seek to be agents of renewal in the academy, church, and society. We pledge fidelity to Jesus Christ, offering our hearts and lives to do God's work in God's world. We aim to develop knowledge, understanding, and critical inquiry; encourage insightful and creative participation in society; and foster thoughtful, passionate Christian commitments....[79]

A Christian College: It's Practice

It is this struggle that makes the Indigo Girls so worthwhile. What is a faith that doesn't struggle sometimes? A questioned faith in the end is a stronger one. We, as maturing Christians, can learn from the doubts of others. Still, the best thing about this struggle is that it is put to amazingly beautiful music that will touch your mind and soul and bring you to a better understanding of what you believe. ...

The questioning of religion and God's purpose continues throughout their music. On their latest album, a hidden song with the chorus of 'The Philosophy of Loss' can be found after the last track. It starts 'welcome to why the church has died' and continues on to question the hypocrisy in the church today. One of the song's most powerful lines, 'modern scribes write in Jesus Christ,/ everyone is free, and the doors open wide to all straight men and women,/but they are not open to me,' addresses their continual battle in the area of homosexuality.[80]

Biblical concept: "This is pure and undefiled religion in the sight of our God and Father, ...and to keep oneself unstained by the world" (James 1:27).

---

[79] http://www.calvin.edu/about/

[80] The Undercurrent, pg. 5 by L. H.www.calvin.edu/sao/

Reflections on This Mentality

A worldly spirit has crept into the church so that many of its attendees do not see a big problem with sending their children to such an event. Their perspectives on exposure are melted down from relativism. Let's look at a few reasons as to why I would never allow my child or myself to attend such an event, even with a free ticket. We will first mention the popular argument and then answer it.

#1: Reject what is going on in society.

The world wants us to be one with them, but in fact the Lord wants to keep us away from the perversions of the world. This has not just to do with the homosexuals but in all places where sin is boldly taught.

> And do not participate in the unfruitful deeds of darkness, but instead even expose them; for it is disgraceful even to speak of the things which are done by them in secret (Eph 5:11-12).

Many Christians limit their activities by the first clause – "do not participate," but they fail to properly respond to the second clause which is much more demanding – "disgraceful even to speak of the things." If we are not to speak of these things, surely we are not to expose ourselves to their act. Where is the limit of this exposure? The Lord has set it for us.

#2: Strengthen our faith to rebuff the doubts of others.

The article above suggested that it is good to go through doubt. I strongly disagree. Doubt always hurts. Our last lesson spoke about the damage doubt brought. Doubt is the opposite of faith and so Satan can and does use it to inflict pain.

Think about how much faith or doubt you implant in your child. Would you rather have your child doubt the goodness of God than trust in His great sufficiency? Would you rather have your daughter wonder whether marriage was proper and so allow herself to be abused by hungry men or would you rather her wait for a godly man however long it took?

Abraham's faith accomplished much, but his doubt also caused long-lasting scars.

God can bring us through such circumstances, but it is always better to avoid them. This is why we try to disciple God's people as quickly as possible. Doubt breeds doubtful decisions bringing bad consequences.

#3: Understand the negative affects of worldly decisions

It is best if we look at concerts as a time a person passes his or her influence on another. Wherever that influencer is theologically and practically enhancing evil, we are sitting under a mouthpiece of a false prophet. We are actually using God's money to be stimulated with evil thoughts conducted by wicked sensations.

If you claim that the music can be good even though the lyrics are bad, you do not understand how music works. The spirit of the musician is passed on to the listener. If one cautiously understands and denies its influence, then perhaps we can say that we have not caught the evil message being passed on. But if you claim to be mature, then why are you using God's time and money in order to be discipled by one who openly rejects the Lord's standards?

Conclusion

Parents must protect their children from such influences. Wherever evil touches my life, I need to spend time cleansing myself. Why not instead spend an evening visiting and praying with others for God's Spirit to help those afflicted. The cultural tensions are strong even when we do not frequent such events. Like Joseph, we are to flee temptation and its influence so that we can be holy for our God.

Angels Appear to Abraham: Two Purposes (Gen 18)

To Announce a Birth (Gen 18:1-15)

We understand the announcement of the birth of Abraham's son. This relates to the many promises and hopes that God stirred up in the hearts of Abraham and Sarah. God was readying Abraham for his great leadership position.

God works through circumstances to train His children, and Abraham was no different. God was going to further purge Abraham of his love for the world. He had too much sentiment toward it. He was willing to leave Canaan for elsewhere if Lot chose Canaan. When he drifted, he often went off toward the cities (Egypt and Gerar) where more 'modern' accommodations were available.

Application

- What difference does our understanding of God's nature have to do with the way we respond to surrounding events?

- Why was it necessary for Abraham to leave the world in his heart before Isaac was born?

- When a man and woman get married, settle down and have a child, they often leave God. Sometimes they come to church but sometimes they don't even do this. They have revealed a scary love for the world. Explain your experiences and insights.

2. To Pronounce a Death (Gen 18:16-33)

- Did the LORD (Yahweh) know how many righteous were in the cities of Sodom and Gomorrah? Sure He did.

- Why did the Lord tell Abraham about the death of two cities?

- Do you think Abraham was concerned about the righteous, Lot or the survival of the city? Why?

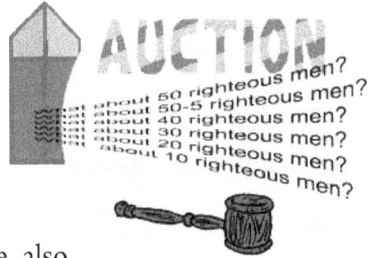

Abraham knew Lot was there, but we also acknowledge Abraham had a love for city comfort.

With the birth of Abraham's son, we see that Abraham had needed some work on his character. After all, his life would influence millions of people in the future. If any bitterness came up between Abraham and God at this stage, then this would pollute God's good work. Instead, God showed him two things about Himself.

To help Abraham appreciate God's merciful heart.

God is truly slow to anger.

Many people do not associate God's mercy with the destruction of Sodom, and yet it is very clearly found here. God is found to be slow to express His wrath. God judges only after His wrath is filled up to the top. He could theoretically judge earlier on, but He just patiently waits.

We see this in several ways. First, we see that the Lord was not looking for an occasion to bring judgment but an occasion to put off His wrath and anger.

> I will go down now, and see if they have done entirely according to its outcry, which has come to Me; and if not, I will know (Gen 18:21).

There is a pattern in the scripture. God waits to judge. He waits till His wrath has built up or been completed. In other words, the Lord waits for years until He judges a society. The Amorites in the land of Canaan would have four more generations before judgment (by Joshua). God was so patient.

> Then the LORD saw that the wickedness of man was great on the earth, and that every intent of the thoughts of his heart was only evil continually (Gen 6:5).

> Then in the fourth generation they shall return here, for the iniquity of the Amorite is not yet complete (Gen 15:16).

God was doing the same thing with Sodom. Its wrath though, had now been filled up. It was time for judgment. Even Abraham came to this conclusion as we see in the next section.

To help Abraham accept God's wrath against sin:

God must truly take revenge for rebellion.

What did Abraham's tactic of lowering the number of righteous men in Sodom reveal about the city?

Just God told Abraham about the coming destruction so that he could better grasp God's justice. Abraham never thought about it until he tried to make this bargain with God. He started his plea with the Lord at 50 righteous men. Not very confident about that, he kept reducing the number until the Lord stopped him at ten. In other words, Abraham had to come to realize that he might not want judgment hit those cities, but it fully deserved it.

In fact he was wrong not to want justice for that city. The city was evil and needed to be eliminated for the sake of others. We find the Lord wanted justice (18:21). Only there wasn't the presence of the righteous. It had to go.

Reflections on Genesis 18

Our perspective of God greatly shapes the decisions that we make. God needed to reshape Abraham's view of God. The Lord often does the same thing with us.

He takes a situation combined with the Word of God and challenges us with the purpose and works of God. We are forced to understand more of God by His works. This is essentially what Jesus was doing. He forced us to establish and think through to a new understanding of God.

One common problem is the way Christians (and non-Christians) get upset with the way God deals with some situation. A good example is the way He destroyed Sodom, babies included. When we understand more of God such as His great forbearing spirit by putting off the judgment, we should be able to accept God's final judgment. 911 was a warning for America but not a total judgment like she deserves. The droughts and falling economies are warnings but not final judgments.

We should on account of God's mercy, put off any willingness to get bitter at acts of God's judgment. We should allow the fault be our own. We don't fully understand the situation. We can fully trust God's judgment.

Lot, His Family & the Angels (Gen 19)

Angels Appear in Sodom: Two Purposes

Sodom was a huge city with big walls down along the Dead Sea. Now it is covered with a special kind of ash. They have discovered the graves of more than 100,000 so the city was big. We read about the luxurious city,

> And Lot lifted up his eyes and saw all the valley of the Jordan, that it was well watered everywhere--this was before the LORD destroyed Sodom and Gomorrah--like the garden of the LORD, like the land of Egypt as you go to Zoar (Gen 13:10).

The Lord had two reasons for sending the angels (in human form) to Sodom.

1. To Check out the Sin Level of the City (19:1-11)

As discussed earlier, God is always just. He cannot judge incorrectly. He has to judge accurately. Of course the angels' visit was not really for God's information but for Abraham and Lot. He always knows what is going on.

2. To Deliver a Righteous Man (19:12-38)

God was going to deliver the righteous people as He agreed to. Let's look at the heart of the four groups of people mentioned in Genesis 19.

A chance to escape from the world is not always desired.

Lot's son-in-laws (19:14) didn't fear the Lord. "But he appeared to his sons-in-laws to be jesting" (19:14). If you don't live the life, your warnings will not be heeded! Lot tried to get his to-be sons-in-law to come with him, but he failed. It appears that these two men just didn't respect him. He was one of the elders of the city; he sat at the gate, but in the end his testimony didn't carry sufficient weight to overcome their confidence.

Lot's wife (Gen 19:26) loved the world. "But his wife, from behind him, looked back; and she became a pillar of salt." If you look back, your heart never left!

Lot's wife just couldn't but long for being back in the city. She deserved no escape. Her body might have escaped but here soul was still there and fit to be judged with the city.

Lot eased into his comfortable living. "But he hesitated" (Gen 19:16).

> Behold this town is near ... and it is small. (19:20)
> God remembered Abraham, and sent Lot out of the midst of the overthrow (Ge 19:29).
> For he was afraid to stay in Zoar (Ge 19:29).

If you lose all, you still try to preserve some of it! Some have a problem with seeing Lot as a righteous man. They should realize that righteous did not mean completely holy but a just person. He showed this when he took the poor strangers who were going to stay in the court into his own home. He probably regularly did this, and the men of the city didn't like it. This time they protested. Lot did not abuse people but protected them.

There are documents confirming that it was one of the highest morals to protect anyone who stayed in one's home. Lot did protect their life with his. We see him outside fighting off a crowd of lusty men. He was brave but naive. He just didn't realize how unprincipled the men were.

Lot's daughters (19:31-38) loved their family name above the Lord. "

> 31 Then the first-born said to the younger, "Our father is old, and there is not a man on earth to come in to us after the manner of the earth. 32 Come, let us make our father drink wine, and let us lie with him, that we may preserve our family through our father" (19:31-32). "And the first-born bore a son, and called his name Moab" (19:37). "And as for the younger, she also bore a son, and ... he is the father of the sons of Ammon" (19:38).

If you lose your place in life, you can always improvise! These two daughters knew how to compromise! Perhaps they learned from their father. Or perhaps, they lost their respect for their father when he offered to give them to the crowd to be raped. It would have been better to die as a family then to compromise a family member like that. The result of Lot's sin was the birth of two people's that would become enemies to God's people: Moab and Ammonites.

Compare the end of two righteous men: Noah and Lot. This is a sad, sad story that continues on throughout the Old Testament. Notice that when a man gives to drunkenness, whether it be Noah or Lot, a whole lot of evil can occur in a brief period. There never is time for a little self-pity, even after a horrible judgment. For each pity party, sin leaked out and infected their descendants.

Disillusionment➡self pity➡indulgence➡sin (drunkenness & sex)➡loss

Reflection

- Which person do you most resemble? Why?

- How has the world influenced your life without you knowing it.

Why was Sodom Destroyed? (Gen 19)

Issue: Sodomites claim Sodom was not destroyed for its sodomy.

· Did they practice sodomy (homosexuality)?

Sodomy stood out in Sodom as one of their major sins:

"He urged them strongly" (Gen 19:3).
"He rescued righteous Lot, oppressed by the sensual conduct of unprincipled men" (2 Pe 2:7).
"Where are the men who came to you tonight? Bring them out to us that we may have relations with them" (Gen 19:5).

· Sodomy (homosexuality) was one of Sodom's sins.

These men were sodomites of the worse kind. They were rapists. But this extremism is exactly what occurs in our societies when sodomy is accepted. Sodomy along with other sexual sins always devalues the ones

"Or do you not know that the unrighteous shall not inherit the kingdom of God? Do not be deceived; neither fornicators, nor idolaters, nor adulterers, nor effeminate, nor homosexuals" (1 Cor 6:9).

The Greek word for homosexual

αρσενοκοιτης

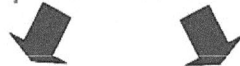

αρσενο   κοιτης

arsen (left side) = from man or male

coitus (right side)= literally bed; cohabitation; sleeping together

The meaning of homosexual is obvious and the practice clearly rejected in the scriptures.

they abuse. It is well known that some who have got a deadly disease continue to have sexual experiences, passing their sentence of death on to others. This might not be typical but it is real just as we see in Sodom's case.

They live by desires rather than by principle. Once the culture drops its sense of justice, protection is gone and leap forward in their abuse of others. Examine the present problems of sex slavery and child abuse!

If you can't speak out against a sin, then your heart is already bound. Homosexuality is a sin, but it does not survive by itself. Sodomy lives only among people with hardened hearts, and it would be foolish to think that a sin lives by itself. Note the sins listed above. We are not wrong to observe that sodomy stood out in Sodom as one of their sins. Note these two references:

1) "He urged them strongly" (Gen 19:3). This statement, combined with the following incident, demonstrated that Lot knew what the men of the city would do to anyone who camped out in the square of their walled cities. They were trapped and sexually abused. Lot could not tolerate it and risked his own life by insisting that they stay in his own home. The custom to protect a guest in one's home even with his own life if necessary. We can see this is where Lot's righteousness stood up. He liked the comforts of the city but hated the abuse. Later we see it again when he stands out in front of the crowd of lusty men protecting his guests.

2. "Where are the men who came to you tonight? Bring them out to us that we may have relations with them" (Gen 19:5). There is no doubt that these men were sodomites! They even refused Lot's daughters because they wanted the men. We should see here that we see more than sodomy with consenting adults. These men were rapists of the worse kind. They would look out for the vulnerable and take advantage of them.

"Behold, this was the guilt of your sister Sodom: she and her daughters had arrogance, abundant food, and careless ease, but she did not help the poor and needy. Thus they were haughty and committed abominations before Me. Therefore I removed them when I saw it" (Eze 16:49).

We need to be careful to think that God is only against sodomy. Homosexuality is a sin, but it does not survive by itself. Sodomy lives only among people with hardened hearts and it would be foolish to think that would be there only sin. Note the sins listed above.

> And Lot lifted up his eyes and saw all the valley of the Jordan, that it was well watered everywhere--this was before the LORD destroyed Sodom and Gomorrah--like the garden of the LORD, like the land of Egypt as you go to Zoar (Gen13:10).

What does the New Testament say about Sodomy?

Some people can argue that the word 'homosexual' is not in the King James Version of the Bible, but read the verse below. Does it not describe the homosexual as Romans 1 does (1 Cor 6:9)?

> Know ye not that the unrighteous shall not inherit the kingdom of God? Be not deceived: neither fornicators, nor idolaters, nor adulterers, nor effeminate, nor abusers of themselves with mankind (1 Cor 6:9).

Other Bible versions do translate using the word homosexuality (NASB: 1 Cor 6:9; 1 Tim 1:10). We need to be careful not to conclude that God is only against sodomy, however. Homosexuality is a sin, but it does not survive by itself. Sodomy lives only among people with hardened hearts, and it would be foolish to think that that one kind of sin would live by itself. Note the sins listed above. The Apostle Paul showed the decline of the culture in Romans 1:18-26.

The way people treat their bodies states a lot about how they think.

Summary

- Abraham's love for city comforts needed to be purged from him.

- Lot's love for the city led to spiritual decline and blindness.
- Open homosexuality is a sign of a degenerate 'culture.'
- Only revival can reverse the trend bringing God's judgment.

GENESIS

Genesis 24
Isaac.... Finding God's Will & a Bride

There are many lessons to learn from Abraham's search for a wife for his son, Isaac. Abram's search for this wife is a very clear act of faith, so different from when he listened to Sarai and went into her mistress. Abraham's whole life was dependent upon this son—including his faith. Below we will briefly address the ways people approach this passage to help them understanding how to seek for God's will.

Traditional Views

There are three traditional views of the marriage that use this model in Genesis 24 to seek God's will.

- The special guidance was beyond the moral will of God and unique for just for certain circumstances like this.

- A circumstantial 'fleece' to discover God's will in a significant decision is permissible.

- God's individual will includes the specific person a believer is to marry.

Key Factors

1. God promised Isaac a mate (15:5; 24:7) but doesn't make this promise to everyone. (Daniel evidently didn't have a wife as he was made a eunuch.) Isaac was not merely a pious man seeking a bride but an heir of the promise.

2. The servant based his request on God's character as One who is faithful (24:7,14,27). He wasn't sure the Lord would answer; he simply asked. Even when fulfilled, he was still not sure God was using it as a sign (24:2). Only when Rebekah's background was found acceptable, was the matter was settled (24:23-24). Other conditions were even more important.

3. The wife was called 'appointed' (24:14) because God promised a wife for Isaac and divinely arranged all the circumstances. (Just think of the difficulty in arranging an unmarried woman, from the right family, right faith, willing to leave her family, family's willingness to let her go, etc.!)

4. Special guidance: God promised special guidance for the servant (24:7,40) and we delightfully love to read this story!

Important factors for finding a mate

- Moral Will: Only seek a spouse who follows the Lord ("in the Lord").

- Common mission (a life-demonstrated by one's choices)

- Pursuing a good complement in a spouse – a spiritual person

- Personal counsel

- Common sense

- Personal desires

- Parents' permission

Genesis 25-35
Appreciating God's Discipline

There are two unbiblical major views of behavior. The one blames the shaping of the environment; the other the passing on of genes. It is sufficient for us to know that the world naturally comes up with 'blame' systems. They develop a thought that excuses man of his own sin. The Bible agrees to the importance of both of these shaping influences but at the same time hold man accountable for what he does. The scriptures go beyond these categories by including the spiritual aspect.

Man has insisted on excluding God's participation in the shaping of mankind. The reason is obvious. If God is involved, then man is responsible to God for what he does. The scriptures give us an astonishingly clear perspective of how God works in the life of each person. If we are not careful though, we will miss the hand and voice of our Creator.

Numerous scriptural observations of Jacob with his parents, brother Esau and his children allow us to see the effect of sin in a life, family and society. When skimming over these chapters, one is forced into concluding that God is showing us people's weaknesses on purpose!

Genesis 25	Genesis 27	Genesis 28	Genesis 29	Genesis 30	Genesis 31	Genesis 32	Genesis 33	Genesis 34	Genesis 35
Birth; Esau trades birthright	Jacob steals blessing	Jacob is sent away; promise of God	Love at first sight; Jacob is tricked by Laban	Jacob's wives struggle; Laban cheats Jacob	Jacob escapes Laban; God blesses Jacob	Jacob fears Esau; Humbled by God	Jacob restored to Esau at great cost	Jacob's daughter raped; vengeance	Jacob's new name is Israel

When God gets His holy hand on a man's life, God is determined to bring him through 'purging' incidents so that he will no longer tolerate sin's presence in his life. Of course, we must look beyond the actual discipline to its end result. God is making us holy like Himself so that we can enjoy fellowship with Him and that He can more mightily exert His power through our lives (1 Peter 1:16).

Influence in the Family

Exodus 20:5
"... Visiting the iniquity of the fathers on the children, on the third and the fourth generations of those who hate Me..."

Parent

Bad ➔ Bad

Good ➔ Good

"But showing lovingkindness to thousands, to those who love Me and keep My commandments."
Exodus 20:6

"Who will render to each man according to his deeds."
(Romans 2:6)

God confronts and challenges Jacob throughout his life. By carefully looking at Jacob's life and seeing the effect of sin and God's grace upon his life, we too will be better able to discern and appreciate how God gets involved in our own lives as His children.

We tend to be more familiar with societal degeneration than societal reformation. Having a family is the means by which we reproduce ourselves. We are not just multiplying our presence, but also our passions and beliefs.

Ready for Marriage?

The most important question in seeking a marriage mate is not whether, "I like him or her." Far more important is whether you have matured and will pass on godly passions, values, perspectives and problems to your children.

God and Man's Sin

God catches all of our moral weaknesses. Not one innocently passes by. Even if we are God's people, God judges our sins. Unfortunately some believers have reasoned that since they are a believer and are forgiven, that the Lord will not judge their sins. Sin always brings bad consequences, even if one finds salvation and eternal life. When God's people are ignorant of this, they will make costly mistakes bringing harm to their Christian walk.

Perhaps you have met such a Christian or you yourself have such false notions. God deals quite differently with His people from those who are not His people.

> By no means let any of you suffer as a murderer, or thief, or evildoer, or a troublesome meddler; 16 but if anyone suffers as a Christian, let him not feel ashamed, but i.n that name let him glorify God. 17 For it is time for judgment to begin with the household of God; and if it begins with us first, what will be the outcome for those who do not obey the gospel of God? (1 Peter 4:15-17)

God, Judgment and the Unbeliever

Unbelievers will perish in their sin. They will be fully judged for all their wrong doings. Esau serves as a case example for this (Gen 36 Esau ends). Let's look at the increasing act of divorce which God says He hates.

Get Away with Divorce?

Divorce among anyone is tragic, but divorce among Christians is even worse. Some have suggested that they even get away with marrying the person they wanted by divorcing. The Lord, however, carefully traces the lustful eye, the bitter words, and selfish deeds. Divorce reveals the couples frustration, loneliness, bitterness, and hatred. People never escape divorce nor its evil consequences for divorce, in contrast to reconciliation, only perpetuates their pain.

God, Judgment and the Believer

Believers, however, are a different case. Yahweh deals with them quite differently. God "begins with us first." Judgment begins with the household of God (cf. 1 Peter 4:17). Jacob serves as a clear example of this (Gen 37 starts).

A Christian is not judged in the sense if he is accepted or not by God. Justification by faith teaches us His children are saved by faith in Christ. Every believer is on the path of sanctification. God says that He scourges every child of His. This is a mark of belonging that we might be holy like our Father (cf. Hey 12:6). In Deuteronomy 28 we see a whole list of things that God will bring upon His people if they don't do all that He says. Although we are not under the Old Covenant, we are more closely bound through the New Covenant also requiring a certain state of behavior.

God showed His love for Jacob by working closely with him in his life. In the previous lesson we have seen how God brought special experiences of grace into Jacob's life. That goodness was nothing but grace. Jacob never deserved any special appearances of God except as Judge. In these lessons we will begin to trace the Lord's steps how He cleverly blends those spiritual experiences with life difficulties to awaken His people to His true nature.

Inherited Sin Nature

Jacob was a conniver from the start. His name meant 'supplanter' because at birth he held his twin brother's foot. Esau was the first born, but Jacob was right behind holding his heel. We all are born sinners. Our sinful natures are inherited through Adam ultimately though immediately passed through our fathers. Mankind has a natural bent toward selfishness which apart from God's grace ultimately destroys every one of them.

Only by being born again (Jacob was born second) is a new spiritual nature imparted. God's choice of the second born is what Jesus expected Nicodemus to know as a Teacher (John 3:1-10). "How can these things be?" Jesus answered and said to him, "Are you the teacher of Israel, and do not understand these things?" (John 3:9-10)

The Sinful Nature: Two Lost Treasures

The two brothers' sinful nature is clearly revealed in their lives. Esau's problem was rooted in the way he despised his godly inheritance and Isaac's refusal to do what was proper. Jacob sinned both against his father and brother from which he would pay good and long. "Is he not rightly named Jacob, for he has supplanted me these two times? He took away my birthright, and behold, now he has taken away my blessing." And he said, "Have you not reserved a blessing for me?" (Gen 27:36)

Esau was tricked two times, or at least he says so. We don't notice him, however, saying that he despised his birthright by trading it for a bowl of lentils. He showed his preference of earthly over heavenly. The birthright was the right of a double portion of the inheritance. If there were two sons, the property would be divided into thirds and the eldest would get 2 portions, the younger one portion (De 21:15-17).

> That there be no immoral or godless person likeEsau, who sold his own birthright for a single meal (Heb 12:16).

The blessing accompanied the actual property. The father's blessing is the pronouncement of goodness upon his sons near his death. It seems that the father would gain a certain amount of God's promises, and he could then bestow them upon his sons as he saw fit.

> And Esau said to his father, "Do you have only one blessing, my father? Bless me, even me also, O my father." So Esau lifted his voice and wept (Gen 27:38).

Determining Responsibility

Esau fell against hard times. This does not mean that God's curse caused him to be this way but that he had shown his fleshly heart by his worldly decisions. Esau displays what happens when a man gets what he deserves. Jacob also uncovers what happens when he didn't get the judgment that he deserved. God is under no compulsion to show grace. Giving grace is solely God's choice.

- Bad decision: Sold his birthright for porridge (25:32)

- Bad decision: Married Hittite women (26:34-35)

- Bad decision: Married an Ishmaelite to spite his Dad (28:8-9).

Bad decisions are not influenced by previous lives. Karma is an Indian religious term that describes the bad things one gets from the result of a former life. This is an unscriptural perspective. Even though Esau was influenced by Isaac, he got what he deserved from the bad decisions he made in his one life, regretfully suffering its bitter eternal consequences.

Understanding Election

> And not only this, but there was Rebekah also, when she had conceived twins by one man, our father Isaac; for though the twins were not yet born, and had not done

anything good or bad, in order that God's purpose according to His choice might stand, not because of works, but because of Him who calls, it was said to her, "The older will save the younger." Just as it is written, "Jacob I loved, but Esau I hated." What shall we say then? There is no injustice with God, is there? May it never be! For He says to Moses, "I WILL HAVE MERCY ON WHOM I HAVE MERCY, AND I WILL HAVE COMPASSION ON WHOM I HAVE COMPASSION." So then it does not depend on the man who wills or the man who runs, but on God who has mercy (Rom 9:10-16).

And when Esau was forty years old he married Judith the daughter of Beeri the Hittite, and Basemath the daughter of Elon the Hittite; and they brought grief to Isaac and Rebekah (Gen 26:34-35).

So Esau saw that the daughters of Canaan displeased his father Isaac; and Esau went to Ishmael, and married (Gen 28:8).

Passing on Sins in the Family

The parents' sins greatly affect their children's lives. The worse situation occurs when a seed of a sin in a parent is joined with a child's predominant moral weakness. This is what happened with Isaac. Note on the chart to the right that this area of deceit grew out of control in Jacob.

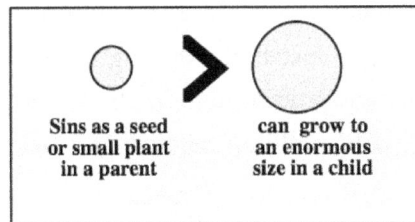

Sins as a seed or small plant in a parent can grow to an enormous size in a child

(Because of Laban and Abram's relationship, it is very possible that their forefather also worked deceitfully in some matters.)

Deceitful Scheming

Disrespect, scheming, and deceit go hand in hand. It ultimately is a sign of a person trying to get what they need by their own self-designed tactics. How should Jacob have responded to his mother's suggestion?

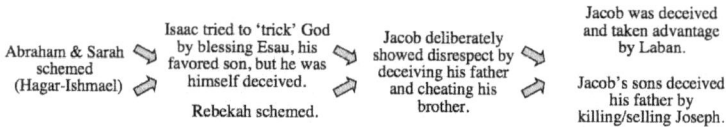

Abraham & Sarah schemed (Hagar-Ishmael)	Isaac tried to 'trick' God by blessing Esau, his favored son, but he was himself deceived. Rebekah schemed.	Jacob deliberately showed disrespect by deceiving his father and cheating his brother.	Jacob was deceived and taken advantage by Laban. Jacob's sons deceived his father by killing/selling Joseph.

CHART ON HOW DECEITFUL SCHEMING IS PASSED ON

Divided Devotions

A person's love for God cannot go beyond his love for his spouse. Marriage problems reveal more than spouse-spouse friction; they also have 'God' problem.

Weak Marriages

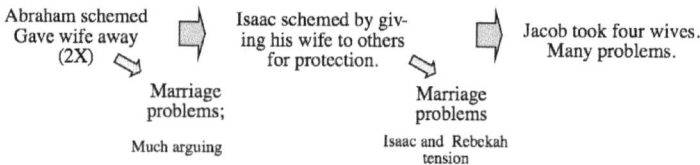

Abraham schemed Gave wife away (2X)	Isaac schemed by giving his wife to others for protection.	Jacob took four wives. Many problems.
Marriage problems; Much arguing	Marriage problems Isaac and Rebekah tension	

CHART DEPICTING PASSING ON OF MARRIAGE PROBLEMS

Anytime a husband is willing to pawn off his wife for protection, the wife is unloved and gets very insecure. We can see this marriage instability starting with Abraham and passed on to Isaac and later trouble Jacob. A chart on the names and mothers of Jacob's children can be found on the web.[81]

Spiritual principle: One can only love God as much as he truly loves his wife.

---

81 www.biblestudy101.org/Lists/12tribes.html

Impure Devotion

Isaac had a love for earthly things (food). Isaac liked the earthy. Although he knew that he should have blessed Jacob (25:23), he was willing to violate God's revelation. He was willing to mix spiritual blessing with earthly desires.

- His son Esau was lost to the world.
- His son Jacob was lost but rescued by God's grace.

Application

- Map out the sins of your parents and detect which sins you struggle with.
- Explain one sin that has been passed on down to your life because of your parents. Have you eliminated this sin from your life and family?
- How do you respond when God disciplines you? How should a Christian respond? Why?

GENESIS

Genesis 25:1-34
Making Right Decisions

Our decisions are always important. Decisions have immense effects on our lives, yet we often minimize the impact of some of our lesser decisions, and we end up making them carelessly, without thought of our priorities, or what should be our priorities. Making the decision to go to bed early or to eat noodles for dinner might seem trivial, but every decisions that we make, and the reason for every decision, shows who we're living our lives for. Once we see the importance of our decisions and what they convey, we can begin to evaluate and prioritize them in light of what God wants us to do. We grasp God's will for our lives, and implement it through our decisions.

In this section we will examine decisions that Abraham, Ishmael, Isaac, Jacob, and Esau made. We will notice how what seemed to be an insignificant decision at one point, had a great impact on each of these individuals later on.

An Overview of Genesis 25

After the prologue Gen 1:1-2:3, where we find the true beginning of all things, we discover ten genealogical records, each introduced by the same Hebrew word meaning generation, account or record

(Hebrew-toledot; see Genesis 25:12, 19). Genesis 25 captures parts of three of the ten genealogies comprising Genesis.

1. Terah: End of 6th genealogy

2. Ishmael: Whole 7th genealogy

3. Isaac: Start of 8th genealogy

There are some interesting observations to be made regarding each of these sections. Why, for example, does Abraham not qualify for a section of genealogy? Or why is Ishmael's record so short, even though he had many more sons than Isaac?

These genealogies provide the outline for this chapter.

The Last Records

11:27-25:11 #6) The generations of Terah
Now these are the records of the generations of Terah. .... (Gen 11:27).
25:12-18 #7) The generations of Ishmael
Now these are the records of the generations of Ishmael, Abraham's son, whom Hagar the Egyptian, Sarah's maid, bore to Abraham; (Gen 25:12).
25:19-35:29 #8) The generations of Isaac
Now these are the records of the generations of Isaac, Abraham's son: ... (Gen 25:19).
36:1-37:1 #9) The generations of Esau
Now these are the records of the generations of Esau (that is, Edom). (Gen 36:1).
37:2-50:26   #10) The generations of Jacob
These are the records of the generations of Jacob. Joseph, ... (Gen 37:2).

Abraham (Terah's record) (Gen 25:1-11)

What are some decisions that Abraham made in Genesis 25:1-11? What impact did they have on those around him? How did they relate to the promises that God made to Abraham?

Sarah died before Abraham (see Genesis 23). He then chose to marry Keturah (lit. concubine did not share in the inheritance). This marriage produced a number of children, including one whose name we will see again and again later in the scriptures–Midian (Gen 37:28; Exo 2:16; Num 22:4; 25:14; 31:2-3; Jud 6:2).

What did Abraham do with these sons through Keturah? He chose to do the same thing he did earlier with Ishmael: he sent them away. But perhaps he learned from the mistake he made with Hagar and Ishmael, who were sent out with nothing. Ishmael seemed bitter to the end (though he did attend his dad's funeral). Abraham gave these later sons substantial gifts to accompany them on their move to the east.

> But God said to Abraham, "Do not be distressed because of the lad (Ishmael) and your maid (Hagar); whatever Sarah tells you, listen to her, for through Isaac your descendants shall be named. "And of the son of the maid I will make a nation also, because he is your descendant" (Gen 21:12-13).

The Lord did not have to tell Abraham what he should do with his sons from Keturah as He did with Hagar. Abraham now had confidence that God's promise would be worked through Isaac. From the world's perspective, it did not make sense to give all the inheritance to just one son when he had so many others, especially when he was promised by God to have many descendants. In the case of Abraham's earthly inheritance, the promise of God helped him properly shape his priorities, and so he made choices that the world would not understand (we will read later that many of these other sons would become opponents to God's special plan through Isaac and his descendants). Many of the tribes that formed through Abraham's descendants by Keturah would later become part of the larger Arabic people that would oppose the Israelites. Study the chart below on how to see how God protected His godly seed.

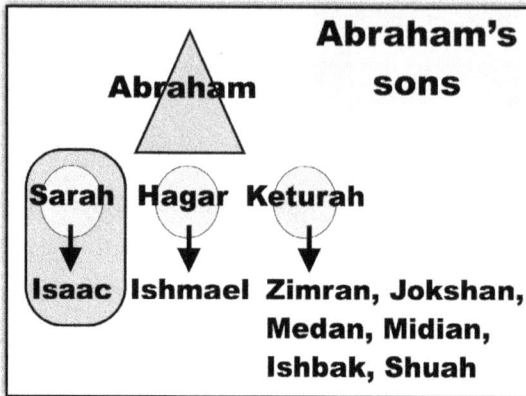

DIAGRAM OF ABRAHAM'S SONS

Ishmael's Genealogical Record (Gen 25:12-18)

It was only fitting that a summary of Ishmael's life should be presented here at the end of Abraham's life. Ishmael played a key role in the fulfillment of God's promises to him, also mentioned in 1 Chronicles 1:27-33. There are three things to note.

God's Promise

Ishmael's record was preserved to show how God fulfilled His promise that he would lead twelve nations, "And as for Ishmael, I have heard you; behold, I will bless him, and will make him fruitful, and will multiply him exceedingly. He shall become the father of twelve princes, and I will make him a great nation" (Gen 17:20). His genealogy is recorded both in Genesis 25:13-15 and in 1 Chronicles 1:29-31. Count them!

> These are their genealogies: the first-born of Ishmael was Nebaioth, then Kedar, Adbeel, Mibsam, Mishma, Dumah, Massa, Hadad, Tema, Jetur, Naphish and Kedemah; these were the sons of Ishmael (1 Chron 1:29-31).

Existence of Ishmael's Records

Genesis is composed of ten genealogical records, and Ishmael, very interestingly, had a biblical genealogical record of his own. This is amazing when we think about the several thousand years that Genesis spans, as well as the fact that Abraham did not receive his own records, but was included in his father's record.[82] Again, this seems to be because God had promised he would make Ishmael a great nation, which in turn also proved God's faithfulness to Abraham.

This is even more amazing when you think about how Ishmael's origins. Ishmael was, unfortunately, born from a lack of faith–failure on the part of his parents. He gained his blessing solely because of his association with Abraham. God, however, made him a significant part of the history of mankind. Perhaps, this memory of Ishmael is also included because of the important role these tribes (maybe also Keturah's sons together) would have in the history of God's people. Although these regions now are largely Muslim, strongly opposing God's people, many are also becoming part of God's people as believers in Christ.

Briefness of Ishmael's Records

Although Ishmael had twelve sons like Jacob, there is something markedly different when you compare the two genealogical record. One

---

[82] Abraham did not have his own genealogical record for it was lodged within Terah's. Why is this so? Perhaps this is because Abraham would initiate a new spiritual heritage through faith. "In hope against hope he believed, in order that he might become a father of many nations, according to that which had been spoken, "SO SHALL YOUR DESCENDANTS BE" (Romans 4:18). A heavenly record for those who would join this spiritual roster.

difference is the brevity of Ishmael's records. The seven verses to acknowledge Ishmael and his descendants are nothing compared to Isaac's record, with ten chapters, or Jacob's, with 13 chapters.

In the history of man he was significant, but not in the annals of God, which is a sign of judgment. In Psalm 1:6, the psalmist says, "For the LORD knows the way of the righteous, But the way of the wicked will perish." Ishmael might have gained a lot during his time on earth, but he had no eternal inheritance. He could not take it with him. He perished, but the godly seed endured.

Notice the words that close Ishmael's record, "He settled in defiance of all his relatives" (Gen 25:18). There was a great hostility lodged in his heart. Ishmael's decision to settle into defiance was key in displaying his obstinance.[83]

The Significance of Hagar and Ishmael

Hagar presents a puzzle to us. Why does God speak about her and her son Ishmael, again and again? God rescues her two times and assures her that all will be well. The Lord could have rescued her without telling us. There are a number of reasons Hagar's story is repeatedly exposed as one reads through Genesis and the whole of the scriptures.

1. Abraham's weaknesses and undersized faith are exposed each time Hagar is mentioned, thus revealing God's amazing grace upon Abraham, who will later be known as a man of great faith.

2. The tension between Abraham and his wife Sarah comes alive most vividly at intersections where we see them wrestling about not having a son with Hagar, though in the end they both compromised.

3. God makes sure that the abundant blessings that come to Ishmael are not because of obedience but because of His promises to Hagar, which stem from God's promises to Abraham's seed. The scriptures always

---

[83] The KJV does not mention this hostility, but the NASB and NIV seem a much better translation.

provides a clear picture of responsibility and liability. This includes the two scenes where Hagar's arrogance gets so heady that Sarah can't tolerate her anymore. Sarah had an attachment to Ishmael and their whole life's significance at that time depended on Abram's presence.

4. The Lord uses this whole scene to paint an allegorical picture of the law in contrast to faith. Paul in Galatians 4 describes Hagar and her son as a representation of those condemned to bondage and the law. Isaac, however, is a son of promise. Abraham's desperation to get what he wanted through Hagar shows the foolishness of the Law, while Isaac's existence came from promise and belief.

5. Lastly, the inclusion of Ishmael's descendants throughout the scriptures reveal that disobedience is never rewarded. The Jews, sons of Isaac, would be persecuted and oppressed for thousands of years by Ishmael's descendants (along with a mix of others). God will finally judge those who live outside the promises given to Abraham in Jesus Christ the Messiah (Romans 4), and that includes all of Ishmael's descendants, and yet the descendants of Ishmael will constantly oppress Israel until the very end when Jesus comes to judge.

Application

1. How did Ishmael become great?

2. Why is it that some people, like Ishmael, can experience all sorts of blessings originating from God but do not love Him?

Isaac's Genealogy (Gen 25:19-34)

Genesis 25:19 starts like the other genealogical records throughout Genesis. It begins with the traditional, "Now these are the records of the generations of…" In this case, it continues with Isaac. Interestingly, it first describes his wife Rebekah's ancestry.

Rebekah's Ancestry

Abraham sought to preserve a wholesome devotion to God by isolating his family from the surrounding Canaanite culture. The mention of Rebekah being from Syria doesn't seem consistent with this until we remember Abraham's directions to his servant when he went looking for a bride for Isaac:

> I will make you swear by the LORD, the God of heaven and the God of earth, that you shall not take a wife for my son from the daughters of the Canaanites, among whom I live, but you shall go to my country and to my relatives, and take a wife for my son Isaac (Gen 24:3-4).

Notice in Genesis 24:10 that he went to Nahor in Mesoptamia. "Now these are the records of the generations of Terah. Terah became the father of Abram, Nahor and Haran; and Haran became the father of Lot" (Gen 11:27). He found a bride from the godly seed who recognized God as creator. She was from the same place and family of his Isaac's grandfather Terah.

Isaac's sons

The first thing we note is that the sons of Isaac are obtained through prayer. Rebekah herself was barren. Isaac was forty when married (Gen 25:20) and sixty when they had children (Gen 25:26). How difficult it must have been for her! Twenty years without children! There was so much pressure (even if unspoken) from Abraham (now 160!), from God's promise, personal barrenness, and the society's expectations.

God did answer Isaac's prayer for Rebekah. This is interesting especially in light of his father's struggles to have a son.

Isaac seems a bit spiritually unresponsive here and elsewhere. The passage seems to infer that he spent twenty years failing to seek God for a child. When he does pray, the child comes. "And Isaac prayed to the LORD on behalf of his wife, because she was barren; and the LORD answered him and Rebekah his wife conceived" (Gen 25:21). Isaac seems to typify our spoiled modern generation, in that because he had so many things that he liked, he did not spend much time thinking about God. However, God was patient and through the sensitivity of his wife, Isaac finally sought God.

Application

1. Why did God wait for Isaac's prayer before He granted them children? God could have given them children earlier on without the prayer. And, Isaac could have prayed earlier on.

> **God induced a problem**
>
> ⬇
>
> **To better communicate**

2. Do we respect the Lord's desire to participate in the birth process or has secular 'family planning' issues wholly shaped our understandings and decisions? What is normal?

Significance of Twins (Esau & Jacob)

Isaac and Rebekah were driven back to God through their crisis of not having children (25:21). God obviously pressed them through this barrenness to call upon the Lord for children.

1. God induced a problem.

2. God used these problems to communicate to open hearts and make it an answer to their prayers.

Rebekah felt a struggle in her womb, a struggle so intense that she inquired of the Lord. The Lord actually used her prayer to answer her, though through a word or dream we do not know, and reveal the struggle was due to twins in her womb.

> And the LORD said to her, "Two nations are in your womb; And two peoples shall be separated from your body; And one people shall be stronger than the other; And the older shall serve the younger" (Gen 25:23).

The birth and passing of time proved this prophecy to be correct. Let's first think about what God was indicating in verse 23. Each child would become a nation (that is very significant). Imagine if God said this of one of your children, let alone two! But that's not all. God also tells Rebekah that one will be stronger (Esau stronger than Jacob), but that the older (Esau again) would serve the younger (Jacob). Esau, the red hairy hunter, was firstborn and stronger than the heel-grabber stay-around-home Jacob.

Being Responsible for our Decisions (Gen 25:27-34)

People seem to have a perpetual battle with understanding to what degree God is involved in their lives. We can understand how those who aren't believers struggle with, or outright disbelieve in, God's involvement, but when it comes to those who do know God's Word, we should not dismiss this struggle with faith. God reveals Himself to encourage us to detect His will and confidently choose it.

This prophecy to Rebekah showed God's plan for both of her sons even before they were born. Throughout the scriptures, God claims to have authority over all factors of our lives. Many significant decisions about our lives–not just with Esau and Jacob–are made even before our arrival! A grasp of God's plan for our lives should significantly enhance our confidence in His plan for us.

Esau and Jacob were both greatly blessed by God; they would each become a nation! This was foreordained by God. It is only through the prophecy that we know this (and we know that God wanted us to know this because His words to Rebekah were recorded in scripture).

The key question we need to ask about Esau and Jacob, and with all of us, is what will we choose to do with the blessings that God has given to us? This is the part that we often forget. God has greatly blessed us with life and good things. How do we respond to Him? Thankfully? Obediently? Or do we make life decisions that suit our own desires without giving Him or His will for our lives much thought?

The fact that Esau was strong and Jacob weak was God's decision. God made them. It was fine for Esau to be a hunter and Jacob to manage tents at home with the herds. But what happened when Esau was hungry? How did his decision in a moment of weakness reveal his heart?

> Our lives are largely shaped for us by God.
>
> physical features — status — culture — personalities — sex — families — skills — weaknesses

> And when Jacob had cooked stew, Esau came in from the field and he was famished; and Esau said to Jacob, "Please let me have a swallow of that red stuff there, for I am famished." Therefore his name was called Edom. But Jacob said, "First sell me your birthright." And Esau said, "Behold, I am about to die; so of what use then is the birthright to me?" And Jacob said, "First swear to me"; so he swore to him, and sold his birthright to Jacob. Then Jacob gave Esau bread and lentil stew; and he ate and drank, and rose and went on his way. Thus Esau despised his birthright (Gen 25:29-34).

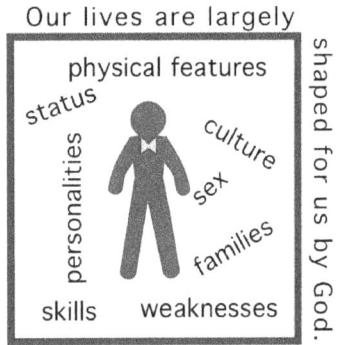

Esau did not care about his spiritual rights. God caused him to be the first-born, but Esau rejected this role, along with the special responsibilities that came with it. We can see what was more important to him; to satisfy his immediate hunger, rather than value his position and responsibility. Notice the clincher statement in 25:34, "Thus Esau despised his birthright." This event is summarized in the New Testament,

> See to it that no one comes short of the grace of God; that no root of bitterness springing up causes trouble, and by it many be defiled; that there be no immoral or godless person like Esau, who sold his own birthright for a single meal (Heb 12:15-16).

We each need to examine our lives so that the chief desire to please ourselves does not overtake us. Esau had a much better start than Jacob, but he left God out of his life, and evidence of this is seen in how he went against his parents and married local women and brought idolatrous customs into their home (Gen 26:34-35). Later, he added to his father's grief by marrying another Canaanite woman, "So Esau saw that the daughters of Canaan displeased his father Isaac; and Esau went to Ishmael, and married, besides the wives that he had" (Gen 28:8-9).

A Perspective on Our Lives

Each of us is placed in a certain context, which includes our families, culture, status, physical features, weaknesses, skill sets, and personalities. God does not judge us on these matters, and we must refuse to resent God because of what He has assigned us in life. Instead we should be thankful for what we do have, and further, we should look to see how He wants to use these things in our lives.

We should be asking, "What have we done with the multitude of blessings that He has given us?" "Have we thanked Him from the bottom of our hearts?" "Have we seized opportunities to use what we possess to please Him?"

Application

1. Why is it that people do not want to obey God and make proper choices? How do we see this rebellion in Esau's life?

2. What are you seeking for in life? A life that conforms to God's good plan or a life that fills your with temporal pleasure?

3. Are you content with the way God made and placed you in this world? Have you thought about why He made you your unique self?

Election of God's People (Gen 25:22-23)

The teaching of election bothers some (God choosing who and how He would bless). This is, however, a clear Biblical teaching not only pointed out here, but in many other places in the scriptures. This question of election is not very unlike the question on the degree God is involved in our lives. God is involved; there is no doubt about that.

There are different reasons for the unwillingness of some to accept God's sovereign hand in our lives as humans. Part of it is simply that people are taught by others that it is not right. It is more than this, though. People are innately averse to God's divine intervention. Perhaps this is because it intrudes on the modern day concept of freedom, "I can do anything I want." They do not like the idea of being boxed into God's plan, as if they have a right to decide whether or not they live or the lives they are born into.

In Jacob and Esau's case, both were greatly blessed. Each was to become a nation. Each was blessed by God. God was working in both their lives.

A Selection, a Choice

This issue of election is boldly spoken of in other parts of the scriptures.

> I have loved you," says the LORD. But you say, "How hast Thou loved us?" "Was not Esau Jacob's brother?" declares the LORD. "Yet I have loved Jacob; but I have hated Esau, and I have made his mountains a desolation, and appointed his inheritance for the jackals of the wilderness" (Malachi 1:2, 3).

It might help us to remember that God, in a sense, set up more blessings for Esau. He gave him advantages. But Esau proved by his earthly decisions that he did not desire the things of God. He got lost in what he could do on his own as a strong, wealthy man. We can understand why God summarizes Esau's life by saying that He did not love Esau. Esau never chose to use what God had given him to please God. This kind of secular living is typified by Esau and stands as a portrait of flesh-focused living.

> But there was Rebekah also, when she had conceived twins by one man, our father Isaac; for though the twins were not yet born, and had not done anything good or bad, in order that God's purpose according to His choice might stand, not because of works, but because of Him who calls, it was said to her, "THE OLDER WILL SERVE THE YOUNGER." Just as it is written, "JACOB I LOVED, BUT ESAU I HATED." What shall we say then? There

is no injustice with God, is there? May it never be! For He says to Moses, " I will have mercy on whom I have mercy, and I will have compassion on whom I have compassion." So then it does not depend on the man who wills or the man who runs, but on God who has mercy (Romans 9:10-16).

God holds it as His own prerogative to choose. "In order that God's purpose according to His choice might stand" (Romans 9:11). God's predetermined shaping of our lives happens long before we are born. In Romans, Paul is aware that some consider this predetermination to be 'unjust' (25:14), and he rebuts with, "May it never be!"

Our biggest problem with election seems to be that we think God has to be gracious. Actually God states, "I will have mercy on whom I have mercy, and I will have compassion on whom I have compassion" (Rom 9:15). Proper judgment, however, is the only thing He must impart on us. Judgment is based on not what we have but on what we do with what He has given us.

God, however, goes out of His way, in love, to reach out to us, and to offer us redemption. In contrast, the fallen angels only have judgment to face, whereas we experience God's grace. He does not have to save anyone. Whenever He extends our life by a day or brings the sun to shine on us, that is more than we deserve. The same is true about spiritual blessings, such as salvation which is totally undeserved. We dare not demand that God save this person or that one. These are things that God does as Roman 9 clearly affirms.

Many things are predetermined. Our family and home are chosen for us. Our existence is chosen for us, but it is within this context we need to responsibly carry out our decisions.

It is our choices that best characterize our lives. What do you do with the life that God has given to you? Both Esau and Jacob inherited a great spiritual and physical inheritance. We have all received from God's good hand, but the question is, are we acting like Esau who despised his inheritance or Jacob who, though in a wrongful manner sought it, did desire the best things that God would give him? The key, then, is to strategically live within the context He appointed for us.

Application

1. If you think God is committing injustice by exercising His compassion on some rather than all, then you should repent. You are dead wrong. God cannot be unjust, nor does He need to exercise mercy.

2. If you experience God's mercy, then you should be overwhelmed with joy and thankfulness. Are you? Why or why not?

One life, one path.
Will it be an earthly or spiritual one?

Understanding Choice– A Chart

	Arminianism	Calvinism	Verses
Free will vs. Total Depravity	Though morally hurt by sin in Eden, man still has a free will to choose to obey God. Sin has not corrupted his ability or desire to cooperate with God. God graciously enables every sinner to repent and believe.	Man's nature is corrupt due to his sin in Eden. He lost his ability and desire to choose good. By his own nature he will not and cannot please God. He must be given a new nature by God to choose righteousness.	Gen 2:17; Rom 5:12; I Cor 2:14; Eph 2:1-3; Rom 3:10-12; 8:7-8; Jer 13:23; John 8:47.
Election	God chose those He foresaw would believe for eternal life. Election is based on man's free choice. It was left to man as to who would believe and therefore those who would be elected to salvation.	God chose some men to eternal life by His own will. When He considered mankind, God saw only sin and no faith or good works. It is God's choice and not the sinner's that is the basis of salvation.	Ps 14:1-3; I Peter 1:2; Rom 8:28-33; 9:11,22; Ac 13:48; II The 2:13; John 17:2; Rom 11:7
Atonement	Christ died for all men. His death did not save any for certain, but only made salvation possible for all who would believe. He paid for all the sins of all men, but they must believe to realize the benefits of His death.	Christ died for those the Father chose to salvation. He died in substitution for them only. He secured all spiritual blessings for the elect, and they shall never perish or even one be lost.	Mat 1:21; John 10:11; I Pet 1:2; Ro 8:32-33; Eph 5:25; John 6:39; Heb 9:15; Rom 5:10.

Grace	The Spirit convicts all men, but only some believe unto salvation. Sinners may resist this operation of God's grace. Until they cooperate, God cannot and will not regenerate them against their free will.	The Spirit powerfully works to bring the elect to conversion. Faith and repentance are God's gifts. They cannot resist the Spirit's work. All of the elect will believe and obey the gospel.	Eph 1:19; 2:1-5; John 3:8; 5:21, 25-29; I Peter 1:2; Titus 3:5; Jas 5:19-20; Lu 22:32.
Perseverance of the Saints	In order to be finally saved, a sinner must continue in faith and good works. Some hold that once saved there is no chance of falling away, but others argue that one can lose God's grace due to their sin.	All who were chosen by God, bought by Christ, and given faith by the Spirit shall be eternally saved. They are kept in faith and holiness by the power of God and persevere in their faith to the end.	I The 5:23-24; Ga 1:6; 3:1; 4:19; 5:4; Heb 6:17-20; Rom 8:28-39; II Pet 2:7-8; II Ti 4:18

A MODIFIED ARMINIANISM VERSES CALVINISM CHART

Above chart is modified from www.letgodbetrue.com. Reference books: "The Five Points of Calvinism" by Steele and Thomas. A larger work is Boettner's "The Reformed Doctrine of Predestination."

GENESIS

Genesis 28:10-19
Surprising Encounters with God

A person's greatest good always starts with meeting God.[84] Most people today do not think this way, and in Genesis, neither did Jacob. But as we take a look at his life, we will find that a meeting with God is not only necessary, but also the best thing for his life and those around him because He is the source of all goodness. Let's explore three aspects to these encounters with God by looking at Jacob's meeting of God in his dream.

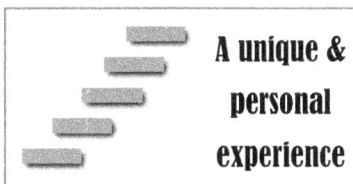

A unique & personal experience

An Unexpected Encounter

Genesis 28 stands as another one of those powerful examples in the holy scriptures that define how God unexpectedly and uniquely works in the lives of unworthy individuals. Jacob did not expect or search for his encounter with God, nor were his parents, Isaac and Rebekah, thinking about spiritual matters. This story occurs at a time when everyone was at a spiritual low. A fierce storm was brewing at home, and God was not on their minds.

---

84 This is true only on this side of life. Once judgment comes, those apart from Christ will suffer from that meeting with God. Meet God now in this life when His mercy is great and grace can be found in Christ Jesus.

The Need for an Encounter with God (28:10-12)

10 Then Jacob departed from Beersheba and went toward Haran. 11 And he came to a certain place and spent the night there, because the sun had set; and he took one of the stones of the place and put it under his head, and lay down in that place. 12 And he had a dream, and behold, a ladder was set on the earth with its top reaching to heaven; and behold, the angels of God were ascending and descending on it (Gen 28:10-12).

Our Need for an Encounter

Jacob's encounter with God must not be isolated from the context, otherwise one of the most powerful aspects of this message will be missed. Although this is a powerful and significant encounter with God, Jacob was not one of those spiritual men looking for God. Nor did Jacob do anything good to deserve God's promised blessings. In fact, the opposite is true, which is why Jacob's experiences more often than not encapsulates our life experiences, being those who are caught in the materialistic pull of the world. Jacob deserved something bad to happen to him. That was his karma–his lot in life. After all, he went along with his mother's plan to deceive his father and steal the blessing. Now his father was upset with him and his brother was out to kill him.

Some might consider Jacob not as "bad" as Moses, who killed someone and ran away, but in the sight of God, deception of one's father and stealing from a loved one reveals an evil heart that even Esau could perceive.

God's repeated intervention in the affairs of the human race is one of the key insights provided by the Book of Genesis. As in the case of Adam, Eve, Noah, Abraham, and here, Jacob, unless God intervenes in our lives, we will continue in a state of unbelief. This is still true today.

Understanding our Unbelief

Unbelief takes on several forms. We might come from a country or home with a system of beliefs quite different from those outlined in the

Bible. Our minds might be convinced that our modernistic belief is right. Or perhaps, we might not be convinced one way or the other. Many are rather apathetic to questions regarding the spiritual world. Some might even hold to a perspective of atheism, which is the denial of God's existence. They all, however, share a common problem of unbelief.

Did Jacob have a biblical perspective of God? One might conclude he did because his grandfather and father were strong monotheists. They firmly believed that this one God, the LORD, was the maker of heaven and earth. Evidence of this household faith can be seen in the approach of Abraham's servant in the way he sought after a wife for his Abraham's son. Abraham said, "I will make you swear by the LORD, the God of heaven and the God of earth, that you shall not take a wife... (Gen 24:3). Then we see this servant pray to God, "And he said, "O LORD, the God of my master Abraham, please grant me success today..." (Gen 24:12).

In one sense, Jacob and Esau both believed, and yet, by observing their life decisions we see that each had his share of unbelief. Whatever their concepts of the Lord God might have been, their choices and lives were not deeply influenced in consideration of God and His will for their lives. They did things on their own and had no fear of God. So we see Esau taking wives that displeased Isaac (Gen 28:8-9), while Jacob was cunning and deceitful. Each pursued life as though God did not exist.

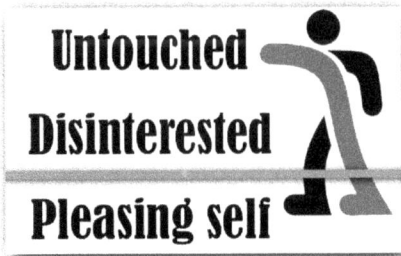

It is crucial that we understanding our belief. For example, there are many who call themselves Christians, but remain unaffected deep down in their hearts by God's presence. They would say they believe, and perhaps are even baptized, but they do not allow God to shape their lives. They are like Esau and Jacob, cutting out their path in this world, regardless of the God who made them. These people will call themselves Christians, but their approach to life testifies that they don't really know God. They know intellectually about God perhaps, but without personally encountering God, their lives closely reflect religious unbelievers.

These religious people, no matter what religion to which they belong, think they deserve God's best. In Jacob's case, his mother figured that the special word at his birth made Jacob more deserving of the spiritual inheritance (Gen 25:22-23).[85] Isn't it interesting how people ignore their weaknesses while demanding that God favor them. They deserve exactly the opposite of what they hope. Insight into the workings of a corrupt and self-seeking heart is part of the package of grace that God grants to those He reveals Himself to.

Undeserving and Unworthy

The key lesson from this incident is that Jacob did not at all deserve God's favor. He did not leave on a spiritual journey from Beersheba; he was running away to save his life, much like Moses did.

Our circumstances may be quite different from Jacob's, but God is dramatically communicating how radical His work is! Just compare Jacob's names: Jacob, meaning twisted, with the name given by the Angel later in Genesis, Israel, meaning "prevailed with God" (Gen 32:28). Religion does not save, even biblical religion. Religion does more deceiving than saving because it is built on pride. In the world's eyes we might be on a path of success, but spiritually speaking, our path will be littered with the effects of ruinous decisions.

---

[85] They should have trusted God to work out a godly way of implementing this blessing rather than pursuing it through devious ways. Though God works through our bad choices, it doesn't necessarily please Him.

God Touched Me

Only an encounter with the Lord will help us see through such devious practices. I remember when God saved me. I was quite content in my youthful pursuit of the good life. I disdained church, and yet was confident that all was well with my soul. But God popped that bubble when, at a meeting, He spoke to my heart through a vision. God revived my memories to expose the evil in my heart and my need for Him to save me.

The ladder from heaven to earth reveals God's interest in mankind. He is involved in the affairs on earth not just to exercise justice but to pour out acts of mercy and grace upon unworthy sinners. None of us should try to sleep on a rock, hoping God would somehow speak to us in a dream. It is good, however, to want to meet God; this desire shows that we are spiritually alert.[86]

Jacob's Ladder

A startling attack upon secularism.

Without experiencing God, we will run through our lives until our breath peters out. We desperately need God to stop us in our vain pursuits. Otherwise, like Esau, we will find that our end has come and that what we gained on earth is lost first through old age and then death. We cannot take these things with us. We might covet titles, wealth, deeds, etc., but age and death overtake them all. How many aging people live in exquisite places but cannot go out and enjoy life! Something greater exists and this is the One that we must pursue.

---

86 Unless we do it out of pride wanting a spiritual experience to boast of.

The Pursuer

Jacob pursued the things that are prized. This was the good side of him, though his willingness to use improper means to gain those things revealed his wickedness. More significantly though, is that God the Giver of all blessings, showed Jacob that something much greater existed than the material things that he pursued. God was putting a welcome mat out, showing Jacob that great blessings came by knowing the person of God. The ladder stood for communication between heaven and earth, and the angels represented the good things God was bringing down to the earth. This intrigued Jacob, and he thought that if that was real, and that God could make it happen in his life, then he would go for it.

Summary

We all can experience a stupor of unbelief in the great almighty God. We might sense His existence or even be brought up in a home teaching about God from the Bible, but we do not become spiritually alive until there is a special and unique encounter with God.

> There is none who understand, there is none who seeks for God; All have turned aside, together they have become useless; There is none who does good, there is not even one (Rom 3:11-12).

UNBELIEF
UNDESERVING
UNINTERESTED

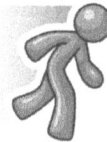

Application

Have you discovered that God is a greater good than anything you might find on earth? We might be religious, and yet not really believe it. After all, we hear so much about God not really even existing. But God does exist, and all that you can gain on earth is nothing compared to the abounding riches that can be found in Jesus Christ. If you don't really believe it, acknowledge your unbelief. But in the same breath, cry out, "God help me believe what is true, best, and awesome."

Knowing God (Gen 28:13-15)

Many want direction for their lives, but this only comes after they know God.

> 13 And behold, the LORD stood above it and said, "I am the LORD, the God of your father Abraham and the God of Isaac; the land on which you lie, I will give it to you and to your descendants. 14 "Your descendants shall also be like the dust of the earth, and you shall spread out to the west and to the east and to the north and to the south; and in you and in your descendants shall all the families of the earth be blessed. 15 "And behold, I am with you, and will keep you wherever you go, and will bring you back to this land; for I will not leave you until I have done what I have promised you" (Gen 28:13-15).

The powerful image seen in Jacob's dream should convince us that God's favor was upon Jacob. Notice how this set of promises is not conditional. It is blended together with what was in earlier years promised to Abraham and Isaac.

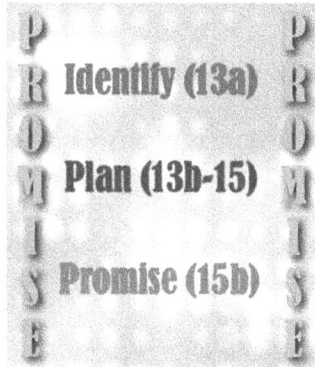

P R O M I S E

Identify (13a)

Plan (13b-15)

Promise (15b)

P R O M I S E

Identifies Himself (13a)

The Lord starts by graciously introducing who He is as "the LORD, the God of your father Abraham and the God of Isaac." Jacob was very familiar with this introduction. After all, it was all about Abraham, his grandfather, and Isaac his father who just bid him to go far away to Paddan-aram.

Peter in Acts 3:13 says the same thing, "The God of Abraham, Isaac, and Jacob, the God of our fathers, has glorified His servant Jesus, the one whom you delivered up...." Jacob's new name was Israel, which became the name of the same country that we still call Israel. It is through Jesus that this worldwide blessing came. Every day, people from all the nations give praise to God. As they worship Him, they are blessed.

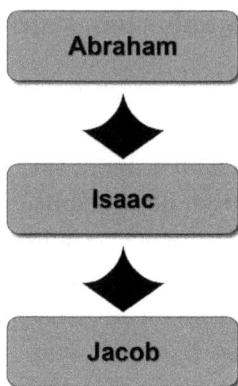

This understanding of God was wholly different from what Jacob had formerly thought or believed. Up to now the Lord Yahweh was just a God that others spoke about. Now He recognized God on his own when the Lord spoke directly to him.

The title LORD (all capitals) refers to God's own Name, Yahweh. With each new revelation, the LORD's character and plan becomes clearer. His Name (*hwhy*) is used 5194 times in the Old Testament. God's person, however, is not learned through books but experiences. Jesus' own "I am" phrases further reveal God's glorious person through Jesus Christ.[87]

Reveals His Plan (13b-15)

With great purpose, the Lord highlighted what He would be doing. He does not ask Jacob what he wants but instead reveals His plan:

- The Lord will give the land to Jacob and his descendants.
- Jacob's descendants will be in great number.
- Jacob's descendants will spread out in every direction.
- Through Jacob and his descendants all the families on the earth will be blessed.

87

www.foundationsforfreedom.net/References/NT/Gospels/John/John00_I_Am-Power.html

These are awesome promises. Jacob didn't know what he was pursuing when he obtained Esau's spiritual blessings. In John 1:31, we find that Jesus alluded himself to be of the same circumstances as Jacob–extremely blessed.

> Jesus answered and said to him, "Because I said to you that I saw you under the fig tree, do you believe? You shall see greater things than these. And He said to him, "Truly, truly, I say to you, you shall see the heavens opened, and the angels of God ascending and descending on the Son of Man (John 1:50-51).

What a startling contrast! God pours out His promise of blessing to Jacob, a liar and cheat, who is running to save his life because his brother is seeking revenge for his evil. What will God do in Jesus' case? Will not God pour out many more of His great blessings upon Jesus Christ, the Son of Man, who faithfully carried out God's work despite the pain and sacrifice? Absolutely.

God's Blessings and Christians

Genesis' message remains the same: God is good precisely because He breaks into our lives to release us from our stubborn unbelief. While secularism attempts to keep God out of this cursed world, God regularly steps in with His plans and promises, usually realizing them through Jesus Christ.

> You shall see greater things than these. And He said to him, "Truly, truly, I say to you, you shall see the heavens opened, and the angels of God ascending and descending on the Son of Man" (John 1:50-51).

What about Christian believers? How do these promises relate to our lives? God, in Christ, will pour out His blessings upon our lives. Note Paul's reflections in Galatians 3, "Christ redeemed us from the curse of

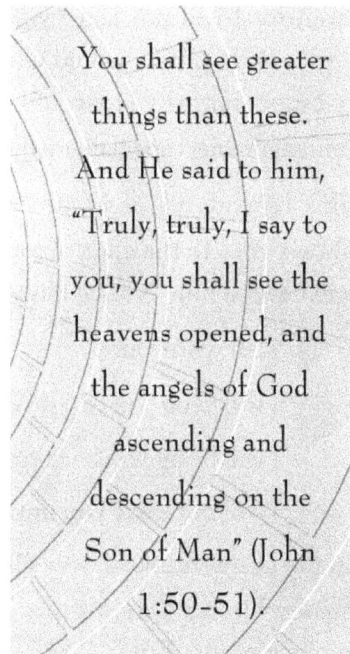

the Law, having become a curse for us... in order that in Christ Jesus the blessing of Abraham might come to the Gentiles (non-Jews; literally 'nations'), so that we might receive the promise of the Spirit through faith" (Gal. 3:13-14).

God desires us to gain His blessings. Just as He made a great creation for our delight, so He wants to bless us with the best. As we believe in Jesus Christ, all of Christ's blessings also become ours. This is the way believers genuinely are able to share in the blessings of God.

Reaffirms His Promise (15b)

God made an incredible promise to Jacob. "And behold, I am with you, and will keep you wherever you go, and will bring you back to this land; for I will not leave you until I have done what I have promised you" (28:15). Why would God make a promise to anyone is our first big question, but why He would make these incredible promises to Jacob is unimaginable, especially with the way he deceived his father.

This reminds us of Matthew 28:20, "And lo, I (Jesus) am with you always even to the ends of the earth." God pledges to a runaway that He will be with him. Notice His words:

- I am with you.
- I will keep you wherever you go.
- I will bring you back to this land.
- I will not leave you until I have done what I have promised.

In the chapters ahead, we will read about how God goes with Jacob and greatly blesses him and his descendants. The remaining books of the Bible reveals how God accomplishes these great blessings and distributes them. These redemptive promises are part of the plan God has to bring redemption to mankind across the face of the earth.

Application

What blessings do we desire and which does God desire to bless us with? We might find that we are not seeking His blessing because we do not believe it is the best. Or, due to deceitful thoughts about God's inferiority, we consider ways to gain blessings for our own lives rather than gaining them for the sake of others. Many of us need a love for God and for others.

Responding to God (Gen 28:16-22)

Hearing from God is common, but the challenge is to let Him change us when we hear from Him.

> 16 Then Jacob awoke from his sleep and said, "Surely the LORD is in this place, and I did not know it." 17 And he was afraid and said, "How awesome is this place! This is none other than the house of God, and this is the gate of heaven. 18 So Jacob rose early in the morning, and took the stone that he had put under his head and set it up as a pillar, and poured oil on its top. 19 And he called the name of that place Bethel; however, previously the name of the city had been Luz. 20 Then Jacob made a vow, saying, "If God will be with me and will keep me on this journey that I take, and will give me food to eat and garments to wear, 21 and I return to my father's house in safety, then the LORD will be my God. 22 "And this stone, which I have set up as a pillar, will be God's house; and of all that Thou dost give me I will surely give a tenth to Thee" (Gen 28:16-22).

Detecting our Response

The Lord spends extra time in the scriptures here allowing us to see a detailed account of Jacob's response to what God said in the dream. This gives us an example by which we can compare and reflect on our own responses to His words. In order to better understand Jacob's response, let us drop back to Genesis 4 where Cain encountered God. Cain was extremely angry, and the Lord stepped into Cain's life and warned him not to proceed with his angry feelings. God was again trying to break into Cain's stubborn and unbelieving heart.

God reveals Himself to us much more than we realize. Although His contact with Cain and Jacob were more dramatic, oftentimes God is using our circumstances to make us aware of better ways, of His ways. God uses the warnings of others, our consciences, or even hardship to more clearly reveal His will to us. God points out a sure path, but we often harden ourselves to His counsel. When Cain hardened his heart to God's words, his circumstances got worse and were accompanied by horrific consequences. The same thing happens in our lives. When we doubt the goodness of God's helpful words, which are often embodied in a quiet but convicting conscience, we harden our hearts and set ourselves up for failure. If faith in God's goodwill is not exercised, then we will persist in our own ways with terrible consequences.

Jacob's Pillar

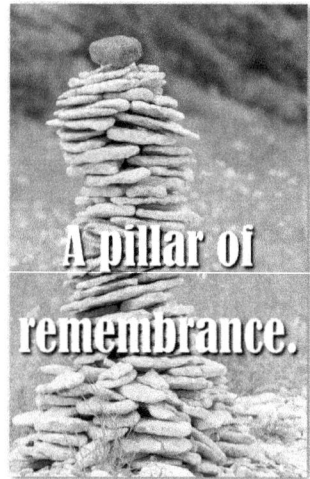

A pillar of remembrance.

Jacob, however, responded positively. He treasured God's Words. He let their surprise shake up his life. He took what God said and made it a significant stepping stone in his new-found faith to know more about God. This was no doubt the moment of Jacob's spiritual rebirth. Jesus was probably referring to these things when speaking to Nicodemus in John 3.

> 6 That which is born of the flesh is flesh, and that which is born of the Spirit is spirit. 7 "Do not marvel that I said to you, 'You must be born again.' 8 "The wind blows where it wishes and you hear the sound of it, but do not know where it comes from and where it is going; so is everyone who is born of the Spirit." 9 Nicodemus answered and said to Him, "How can these things be?" 10 Jesus answered

and said to him, "Are you the teacher of Israel, and do not understand these things?" (John 3:6-10)

Something significant happened in Jacob's life and after reflecting on God's greatness, he built a pillar by hand. This pillar was quite different from the altars that Abraham had set up when God met him. Altars require sacrifice. Jacob, though, built a pillar rather than an altar to mark this significant time and place. Pillars are a tall column of rocks. They might not be very high, but they stand out as manmade constructions. The stone he used as a pillow became the most significant stone of the monument. After building it, he placed the rock used as his pillow at the top and dedicated the whole thing by pouring oil upon it.

After this, he named the nearby city of Luz, meaning almond tree, Bethel.[88] Jacob did not stay in the city at night. As a guest going into the strange city of Canaanites, he would face unknown dangers (cf. example of angels visiting Sodom in Genesis 19). Bethel means 'house of God' (i.e. El standing for Elohim, the word for God). Jacob was thinking of greater things regarding this city. Even this name revealed Jacob's new authority. The land belonged to him and so he renamed a city. This awesome dream suddenly became a central part of his life, and yet, he held off from fully committing himself to God.

> Jacob rose early in the morning, and took the stone that he had put under his head and set it up as a pillar, and poured oil on its top. 19 And he called the name of that place Bethel; however, previously the name of the city had been Luz. 20 Then Jacob made a vow.

---

[88] Bethel is first used in Genesis 12:8 and 13:3. Keil and Delitzsch state that Joshua 16:2 distinguishes Bethel a larger area "to the southern range of mountains belonging to Bethel, from which the boundary ran out tot the town of Luz" from the town Luz, "And it went from Bethel to Luz." Commentary on the Old Testament, Volume 2, p. 176 (on Joshua 16).

Jacob's Bargain (Gen 28:20-21)

There are several parts of this bargain. Jacob again proves his bargaining nature even with God. He does make a vow but starts with four conditional 'ifs.' Let's note the four conditions:

- If God will be with me
- If God will keep me on this journey that I take
- If God will give me food to eat and garments to wear
- If God makes it so I return to my father's house in safety

At this time, Jacob had nothing. He was running away, probably with nothing more than a kind of knapsack. If he had a camel, he would have possessed more bundles, but he was poor runaway. He had nothing to sacrifice. Perhaps this is the reason he built a pillar instead of an altar.

Jacob's Part

Jacob did make a pledge. If he would come back in safety and blessing, he would properly worship and sacrifice to the Lord.[89] Jacob did not ask for special treatment but for safety and basic provisions. This shows how much he feared going far away. Jacob on his part would make God his God and transform that pillar of stones into a house of worship.

Then the LORD will be my God.

This stone... pillar, will be God's house.

All that Thou dost give me I will surely give a tenth to Thee.

The last thing he mentions is the tithing. Although Jacob didn't ask to become wealthy, his ten percent offering would reflect God's prosperity. The more he comes back with, the more he will give.

---

89 God describes Himself as the God of Bethel (Gen 31:13; 35:1) and calls Jacob to return there to complete his vow. In Genesis 35:3 he makes his decision public about leaving and returning and in fact, upon his safe return, Jacob returned to Bethel to fulfill his vow, "So Jacob came to... Bethel...he and all the people who were with him. He built an altar there...because there God had revealed Himself... (Gen 35:6-7).

Jacob's request does seem rather materialistic, but this is exactly where God met him–in his material and spiritual poverty. From the way God honors this request, we should realize that God's spiritual nature is not anti-materialism. God Himself made us with real needs that can only be met by other things that He made. The Lord does, however, demand for Himself to be our chief focus, not His gifts. If we make a vow and gain God's good gifts but disregard Him, then this becomes a great evil. Or if we despise his offer, then this too becomes evil. Let us follow Jacob's example, then, and respond in faith.

Application

More specifically to our lives, what is it that we need? What does God want of us? Have we made a vow, "If God... then I will....?" Have you been faithful in fulfilling your vows to Him? God rebuked King Hezekiah for finding healing but not properly responding back to his Healer (cf. Isaiah 38-39).

Conclusion

God interrupts our lives, whether they be boring or exciting, and uniquely speaks into them in order to significantly reshape how we think of Him so that we might pursue Him. It is helpful to identify where our unbelief has moved into belief, doubts into faith. At some point, like Jacob, we should move beyond disinterest to knowing and pursuing God, because otherwise we will end up like Esau.

The Lord interrupted Jacob's life by dropping the ladder right by his head. He has done the same for our lives by lifting the cross high on Golgotha. Whereas the dream only spoke to Jacob and his descendants, the Lord, through Christ's work on the cross, has made the door open to all. Jesus stated, "I am the door of the sheep" (John 10:7). Like a ladder, window, bridge, or door, the Lord is breaking into each of our lives. You have heard the Gospel message and the blessings are there for you and I.

Where are you right now?

Untouched ● **Believing**

Disinterested **Eager**

Pleasing self **Pleasing God**

"I am the door of the sheep." Jesus

Don't hide your unbelief! Remember that God gives hope to those without belief. We start small when God, through some unique way, catches our heart's affection and mind's interest.

Jacob's Two Wives (Genesis 29)

We can gain a tremendous amount of insight the process of training through the example of Jacob's various relationships. God was determined to shape Jacob's life. "Pursue peace with all men, and the sanctification without which no one will see the Lord" (Hebrews 12:14).

Laban: a master discipler

If we think we can take a shortcut to gain God's blessings, we are mistaken. God's training is personally suited to our personal quirks, stubbornness, and moral flaws. God uses Jacob's devious uncle, Laban, to beat Jacob at his deceitful ways so to instill moral and spiritual values in Jacob.

Rachel: an attractive hook

What kept Jacob in the training arena? Do you think he liked being tricked? No. He stayed because of his situation back home and because of his love for Rachel. God arranged the perfect circumstances in order to effectively teach Jacob.

Leah: a lesson for insensitive people

Why did God give Leah children and Rachel none? The only way Jacob would pay attention to Leah was through the bearing of children because he had no love for her. If he had children through Rachel right away, he most likely would have left Leah neglected and uncared for.

Application

- Is God training you?

- How is He working on your life right now?

- Are you working with Him or going counter to Him?

> ### What about election and holy living?
>
> Jacob didn't seem like he was elected by looking at his life, but in time, God worked with and through him. It is God's election of him that made it all work together for good.

GENESIS

Genesis 31-32
The Making of a Man of God

Stories about a long lost child who finally makes his or her way home are always moving. The story of Jacob is one of those. God brought His wayward sheep named Jacob back home, just as He promised.

We might find ourselves often surprised by whom God chooses to call. The schemer named Jacob, evil and deceitful through and through, was still chosen, despite his flaws. Jacob, though having a religious background, was very typical of the world: deceiving and deceived, greedy and hardened. God, however, worked on Him through many years, planting and slowly cultivating a seed of faith, starting at Bethel twenty years prior to the events in these chapters.

Our main focus here is to observe the process by which God works in a person's life to bring him home, that is, where he or she should be, in a spiritual sense. Perhaps when we search our own lives, we will also see how God has worked!

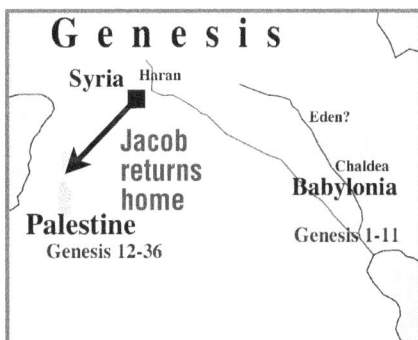

Jacob's Changing World (Gen 31)

We will first take an overview of what God was doing in Jacob's life in these two chapters.

- Observation: Signs of Change (31:1-5)

Jacob found distressing changes in his circumstances that prodded him to make a move. Laban and his son's turned hostile, and the things that Jacob worked doubly hard for were threatened. He became insecure.

- Evaluation: Evidence of God's Grace (31:6-16)

Jacob reveals his plan to his wives. He wants to make an immediate move back to his homeland where God had spoken to him. They had never been there before, and Jacob himself hadn't been home for twenty years. He recourses how God has blessed him and requests that his wives be ready to leave their home.

> **The Payback (Gen 31:38-41)**
>
> - Twenty years service
>   - 14 years for two daughters
>   - 6 years for flock
> - No animal miscarried
> - Did not eat Laban's food
> - Bore loss of lost sheep
> - Bore loss of stolen sheep
> - Changed wages ten times
> - Overpowering heat by dayFrost at night

- Evacuation: Taking Desperate Action (31:17-21)

Jacob secretly packed up all that he had and runs off in the direction of his homeland. Although Jacob might have heard God speak to him, he was still scared of losing everything.

- Confrontation: Facing the Consequences (31:22-42)

Laban and his kinsmen confronted Jacob. The previous night, God spoke to Laban telling him not to harm Jacob. Laban then rebukes Jacob for running off, but focuses on getting his house idols back. The great amount of discussion on this topic reveals all the wonderful ways that God blessed Jacob, despite the many ways that Laban greatly deceived him. All these things indeed did belong to Jacob. The hidden idols would later become a snare.

- Reconciliation: Forging a New Future (31:43-55)

Laban, interestingly, claimed that Jacob's wives and sheep were his, "The daughters are my daughters, and the children are my children, and the flocks are my flocks, and all that you see is mine" (31:42). Maybe this idea was planted by Laban's sons, "Jacob has taken away all that was our father's..." (Gen 31:2). This surely could have led to an all out fight between Laban and Jacob. Jacob claimed Laban had deceived him about wages ten times, including the quick change from Rachel to Leah on the wedding night. God, however, knew of this tension and spoke the night before in a dream to constrain Laban's actions. Though Laban still asserts that everything is his, he decides against his evil plan and initiates a peace treaty.

In summary, we should see that the Lord sometimes allows His people to suffer in order to obtain the greater goal of improved character. Laban was an unjust employer, tricking his worker, Jacob. There are many others who are trapped in an abusive work situation, and like Jacob, could say they were given unjust wages. In the end, there was no full confession. Jacob is, by God's grace, free from Laban's control, but could he get beyond this emotionally-charged twenty years? God had more tests to shape Jacob's character and attitude toward life.

Jacob's Humbled & Changed Life (Gen 32)

- The Welcome: Angels greet Jacob (32:1-2)

Are they the same angels that sent him off at Bethel? Whether they were or were not, the point is that God was doing very special things in the life of Jacob.

- Jacob humbly faces the past (32:3-12)

Jacob sent a message to Esau telling him of God's blessing, and he became alarmed when he heard that Esau and 400 men were on their way to meet him. Jacob is greatly humbled and turns to pray to Yahweh. This is a significant turn around in his life. His own resources have failed him. He knew he needed God.

- Jacob's Gift for his Brother (32:13-23)

Jacob did pray, but he still felt like he needed to send a gift to Esau. This was not just a gift. We can see this by the way he sent the gift, herd after herd. He was properly repaying Esau for his deceit. He was scared. In the end, he still took his wives and children back over the brook for an extra security measure.

- Jacob's Meeting with God - Peniel (32:24-32)

Jacob, for the first time, showed manhood. He stood between his wives and his brother Esau. He realized that all that he had could be gone in a flash. Esau could take it all, including his life. Yet he didn't flee, but stayed between Esau his family. It was here that the angel of the Lord wrestled with Jacob. Jacob endured in the battle with God, and there he received the name Israel because he successfully contended with God. This new name and the crippling of his body both show the beginnings of a new spiritual life (i.e., repentance).

Jacob's aggressiveness: a problem or asset?

This 'contending' or aggressive spirit seemed to be Jacob's problem, but it was not. God liked Jacob's enduring spirit. When it operates from the flesh, then it is sneaky and deceitful, but when the aggressiveness has to do with pursuing God and His ways, it is an asset.

God's Life Interruptions (Gen 31-32)

There is no doubt that God had made a remarkable impact on Jacob's life. This is noticeable in the way that the Lord is repeatedly referred to in Genesis 31-32. References to the Lord at work: Genesis 31:3. 5, 7, 9, 11, 13, 16, 24, 29 (Laban), 42, 49, 53; 32: 1, 9-12, 24-30.

Spiritual life and growth is a process. Spiritual birth often happens at a point, but its preparation takes place over time. Here are some observations of this process that can be seen in many people coming to new life in Christ.

- An intense struggle (Gen 31:1-21)
- Realization of God's grace (Gen 31: 22-42)
- Willing to make peace (Gen 31:43-55)
- New spiritual insight (Gen 32:1-2)
- Faces deeper conviction (Gen 32:3-12)
- Makes restitution for wrongs (Gen 32:13-23)
- A humble meeting with God (Gen 32:24-32)

Application

- What do you find surprising in Genesis 31-32? Why?
- What are some of the difficult experiences that Jacob suffered? If God was blessing Jacob, why did the Lord allow these oppressive years to happen?
- Name the steps through which God brought good spiritual change in Jacob's life?
- How is worldly aggressiveness different from biblical aggressiveness? Give specific examples.

Genesis 36
Esau and His Descendants

Esau and His Descendants (Genesis 36)

Adah (daughter of a Hittite)   Oholibamah (daughter of Anah)   Basemath (Ishmael's daughter)

Eliphaz

Timna a
concubine

Jeush Jalam Korah

Reul

Teman
Omar   Amalek
Zepho
Gatam
Kenaz

Although Oholibamah is
named second in 36:2, she is
named third later on. No
children of these 3
mentioned.

Nahath
Zerah
Shammah
Mizzah

All became chiefs in Esau's land.

DIAGRAM OF ESAU AND HIS DESCENDANTS

Kings of Edom (Genesis 36:31-39)

#1 King Bela, son of Beor, reigned in Dinhabah.

#2 King Jobab, son of Zerah, reigned.

#3 King Husham, a Temanite reigned.

#4 King Hadad, son of Bedad, reeigned in Avith.

#5 King Samlah & Shaul on Euphrates reigned.

#6 KingBaal-hanan, son of Achbor, reigned.

#7 King Hadar reigned in Pau.

LIST OF KINGS OF EDOM (GENESIS 36)

GENESIS

Genesis 39:1-23
Pursuing Integrity

The starting point

Each of us are born with a unique package determining not only our genes, but also our specific life circumstances that will radically shape our lives and desires. God determines what goes in and what stays out of that specialized package. It includes things relating to our physical bodies but also our heritage, such as our parents, culture, and basic views of life. He plants us; we grow.

Joseph had his own package: Jacob and Rachel, his parents, along with his three aunty-moms, and lots of brothers. He didn't choose his heritage of a great grandfather who had a Yahweh-God experience, but it became part of his life as he heard it repeated again and again. His relationship with his father probably meant much more when his mother died at his younger brother's birth.[90]

Our Life-long Journey

Our lives, like Joseph's, can be looked at as a journey. At the beginning, we have our original possessions, but then with those resources we are responsible to detect and complete God's plan for our lives. Most of us,

---

[90] It is not crystal clear whether Joseph's mother gave birth to Benjamin before or after Joseph's betrayal by his brothers. His mother died at his birth (Gen 35:19).

however, focus more on just getting by. The things that help us along are welcomed, but the things that frustrate us are avoided.

Joseph experienced many challenging events early and later in his life, but he overcame them. He would have been defeated had he focused on his hopes. Instead, he resolutely fixed himself on living a life of integrity before God and man.

It is best that we set our goals according to the purposes that God has for us. The better we integrate our goals and decisions with God and His grand plan for our lives, the more we will discover His glorious blessings.

Integrity speaks of the sincere intention to seek out and live consistently with God's purpose and design for life. Those who do not seek God's purpose for their lives live in darkness and deny their true identity and calling. They resist and suppress the light in their conscience to attain ulterior purposes. Those with great faith, however, not only grasp God's purpose for their lives, but embrace it.

As we study Joseph's life, we will see a great saga of sorrow and tragedy mixed with fortune. No one volunteers for such a life. Again, it is a journey that unfolds by a series of good, or bad, life decisions.

From this example in the Old Testament, we again find that God desires to break into this sin-saturated world to interact with us and open our hearts to His good ways. Genuine life blessings only stem from Him, and those blessings are largely dependent on how we pursue the Lord. Pursuing integrity is another way to describe living consistently in God's presence to experience His blessings, love, and help. In Christian terms, we might say it is living a godly life, living in the fear of God, a holy life, but do note that it implies a devotedness on our part to live consistently with the principles and goals

How does God interact with you in this world?

Do you believe God's way is best?

Can we trust God with life's difficulties?

He has set.

We usually associate Joseph with integrity due to how he resisted being seduced by Potiphar's wife, but we should think of it from a broader perspective. In Genesis 39, we discover the three basic understandings of life that Joseph adopted as the foundation for a life of integrity before God. These understandings develop the trust we need to persist through rigorous forms of opposition.

Similarly, we must not think of our lives only as a battle with temptations, though that be important; we need to look higher and remember to seek to fulfill God's purposes for each of our lives.

God Oversees our Life Affairs (Gen 39:1-6)

Trust God with the life situations He brings you.

> 39:1 Now Joseph had been taken down to Egypt; and Potiphar, an Egyptian officer of Pharaoh, the captain of the bodyguard, bought him from the Ishmaelites, who had taken him down there. 2 And the LORD was with Joseph, so he became a successful man. And he was in the house of his master, the Egyptian. 3 Now his master saw that the LORD was with him and how the LORD caused all that he did to prosper in his hand. 4 So Joseph found favor in his sight, and became his personal servant; and he made him overseer over his house, and all that he owned he put in his charge. 5 And it came about that from the time he made him overseer in his house, and over all that he owned, the LORD blessed the Egyptian's house on account of Joseph; thus the LORD'S blessing was upon all that he owned, in the house and in the field. 6 So he left everything he owned in Joseph's charge; and with him there he did not concern himself with anything except the food which he ate. Now Joseph was handsome in form and appearance (Gen 39:1-6)

Remembering our Losses (Gen 39:1)

Note some of the things that Joseph had to go through in the first verses of Genesis 39. The prelude to these events was recorded in Genesis 37. Genesis 38 serves as an additional affirmation that Joseph's brothers were not seeking God. Judah proved himself rotten to the core, and his brothers acted just like the world. We wish these tragedies, broken relationships, jealousies, and immoralities would surprise us, but they are too commonly seen.

Joseph is betrayed by his brothers and is left for dead. Behind this series of life-shaping events is a God who is in control of everyday events, and a young man, victimized by those who should have loved him. (This definitely alludes to God's Son Jesus Christ, who though did no wrong, was betrayed by His brethren.)[91] Here are three significant events overseen by God.

- Joseph was sold as a slave, rather than killed.
- The Ishmaelites took him to Egypt to be sold.
- Potiphar, an Egyptian officer of Pharaoh, the captain of the bodyguard, bought him from the Ishmaelites.

Joseph was left for dead, but instead of letting that happen, a few greedy brothers sold him as a slave for 20 shekels of silver (which was the current market price of a slave; again a type of Jesus Christ who was sold for the price of a slave, Mat 26:15). Joseph was taken by the Ishmaelites only because they came by at the precise time the brothers were battling in their conscience whether they should really kill their brother. God was overseeing this scene and delivered Joseph by the Ishmaelites. He knew who they were and where they were going. (Ishmaelites were

---

[91] Genesis 37 becomes a type on how his jealous Jewish brethren would reject and betray the Messiah, "He came to His own, and those who were His own did not receive Him" (John 1:11).

descendants of Abraham's Ishmael.) God was completing His plan, despite the evil intentions of His people

Joseph was not asked what he wanted. No one checked and confirmed whether he was a free man or not. They treated him as a slave. Figuring they could make some money off the trade, the Ishmaelites took him to Egypt. As this plot unfolds, we see how strategic this event actually became. In the eyes of Joseph's brothers, he was as good as dead (now they get his inheritance). They never expected to see him again and were already busy figuring out a way to explain his absence to Jacob (Gen 37:31-36). Also, the Ishmaelites were not thinking about God's grand purposes. They were just making a little profit; they cared little for God and less for Joseph.

Finally, we see Joseph was purchased by Potiphar. Again, chance seemed to rule the day. Potiphar happened to be an officer of Pharaoh who oversaw Pharaoh's bodyguards. Did Potiphar

- Lost love -rejected
- Lost possessions
- Lost freedom
- Lost family
- Lost father
- Lost home culture

know what happened to Joseph? Did he really care? No. Who cared that Joseph couldn't speak the Egyptian language? That was Joseph's problem. He had to learn. And who cared that he couldn't see his family? No one cares for slaves.

Joseph had to internalize his personal problems and make most of the situation he was thrust into. He lost his family, love, familiarity, freedom, his father, his homeland, his language, his possessions, and found himself a slave of strangers speaking a foreign tongue. God was gone; pagan idols now surrounded him. Joseph had to battle with the bitterness of his betrayal along with the purpose of God during these many lonely years.

Application

How important is it for us to have God significantly shape and bless our lives?

God really wants us to see how He interacts with us in this world. More often than not, we are blind to God's activity and greater work because we are so focused on our desires and decisions. What must happen in our lives that we can be made aware of God and His purposes? Only when we know that Lord is involved in the affairs of our lives, do we begin to understand life. This is the reason it says, "The fear of the Lord is the beginning of wisdom" (Pro 1:7). How tragic it is that the crowds go through life without ever understanding this! Or perhaps, we need to ask, "What will it take for God to wake me up to the reality of His presence and purpose?"

The Surprise (Gen 39:2)

Verse 2 starts off with a surprising statement, "And the LORD was with Joseph, so he became a successful man." When the average reader sees what Joseph went through, one would hardly consider Joseph blessed. Joseph received horrible treatment from his brothers, which landed him as a slave in Egypt.

But God's hand was on Joseph even in Egypt as a slave. We are being provoked to ask the obvious question, "Why would God be with Joseph in Egypt, but not in Israel?"

We are forced to wonder about God's purpose and power. If God favored Joseph, then why didn't God watch over him before he was sold as a slave? Yet, remember, God was watching over Joseph.

Although the Lord was in control, He was not responsible for the evil done to Joseph. Clearly, it was his brothers crime, not God's. As we look at the whole story, we are forced to conclude that God was in control here and even used the evil of Joseph's brothers to accomplish a greater good. The seeds of triumph were planted during this tragedy. Now, we merely read on to see the greater purpose, but for Joseph and everyone else around him, no one had a clue as to what God's greater plan might be. How could He incorporate all the evil being done to work out a greater good?

Betrayed - **personal rejection**
Bought - **lost freedom**
Beneficial - **valued**
Blessed - **successful**
What?

Application

- Was God's way of working here special for Joseph, or does God treat His other children this way?

- Does God always have a greater plan for our lives than what we can presently see or understand?

- Will God's desire for my ultimate success always be behind His plans for my life? How can I know?

God's handling of Joseph stretches us to probe into our experiences and knowledge to find answers for these key questions, especially in identifying His work in our lives. If we can allow God to be working in our lives too, then we can certainly learn a lot about the way God works in the lives of His people at large.

In any case, we should not conclude that God ever lost control or that He does not care, or that His care is intermittent. It requires faith to believe God is still kindly watching over the lives of his beloved, even when tragic things happen, and I challenge you to engage that faith.

Before his betrayal, Joseph received a seed of hope from God through his dreams. God also strengthened Joseph's faith by giving him unusual success so that he knew the Lord was still with him. Perhaps it was through this means that God renewed Joseph's faith and trust in Him. "God couldn't have left me if He is so present with me now. He has a greater plan for my life."

Joseph's Success (Gen 39:3-6)

Joseph at first was a general slave in the household. Like the others, he had to take care of the worst jobs. (Newer workers always get the worst jobs, right?) Somehow, God so blessed Joseph that what he did, he did well. He became a successful man. Most of us are not aware of how a slave can be successful, until perhaps he no longer is a slave. But Joseph was successful while a slave!

Whatever Joseph did, he did well. That is a given, but no doubt he had a spirit about him that pleased the person he was serving. He prioritized the needs of others and was not slothful in carrying out his duties. There were, no doubt, other aspects, but none are specifically mentioned. I only say this because blessing speaks to the special aurora of goodness that make things work better, more efficiently, and with increased pleasure.

Manage all affairs (39:4)

Oversee his house (39:4)

Personal servant (39:4)

General house slave (39:2)

His master, Potiphar, recognized a special something about Joseph and the tasks he was involved in. As a result, he reappointed Joseph from a general house slave to a slave in his personal care (39:4). This, however, was temporary too. From personal servant Joseph went to be in charge of Potiphar's house affairs, then to overseeing everything Potiphar had. "So Joseph found favor in his sight, and became his personal servant; and he made him overseer over his house, and all that he owned he put in his charge" (39:4). This leap of responsibility was significant. The scriptures recognize this and reinforce the fact that it was God's presence that made him so successful.

We are not allowed to mistake this fact. Even Potiphar stated it. "So he left everything he owned in Joseph's charge; and with him there he did not concern himself with anything except the food which he ate" (Gen 39:6). Let's look at the actual statements that declare God's presence.

- And the LORD was with Joseph (2)
- Now his master saw that the LORD was with him (3) and
- How the LORD caused all that he did to prosper in his hand (3)
- The LORD blessed the Egyptian's house on account of Joseph (5)
- Thus the LORD'S blessing was upon all that he owned, in the house and in the field (5)

The term 'God' is not used here but LORD: Jehovah Yahweh. Moses, the writer, did not want us to doubt that it was Yahweh bringing the blessing. Potiphar didn't care what god brought the blessing; like the Ishmaelites, he only sought a better life.

So what was the Lord doing? Why would He allow so much tragedy to occur in what seems like a good young man's life and then cause him to be blessed? This hidden plot stirs great interest. Again, remember this did not happen all at once. It was gradual. Not only was Potiphar recognizing it, but Joseph was too (39:9).

Joseph was being forced to take his ruined life in one hand and hold it up to the other hand, which showed him his life as filled with God's incredible blessings.

Summary

Within years, this young slave went from being a general slave to a successful man managing the affairs and finances of one of the most influential men in Egypt. Behind the promotion was Potiphar's increasing trust in Joseph, which enabled him to entrust everything to him. Joseph did well and therefore could be entrusted with more. Luck is not this way; it is haphazard.

We are being forced to go beyond the simple task of asking what makes a person successful, though this is an interesting discussion, as it deals with the right job, right connections, amount of wealth or education. Success is something greater, though: success, as exemplified in the Bible, is completing our God-assigned tasks through His grace in faith for His glory. Success has everything to do with our confidence in God, who has a hand in the general affairs of our lives.

As in Joseph's case, we must step beyond the tragedies of our lives so that we can see God's love working through our lives. The Lord frames the incidents in our lives in a way that allows us to see glimpses of His purpose, and as a result, that we might better know and trust Him, and bring blessings to others.

God wants to bless all of His people but will especially bless those, like David, Joseph, and Daniel, who, because they resolved any issues of bitterness, were willing to trust and obey the Lord. God is a good steward looking to promote all those who dare to live by faith.

Application

- Has the perspective of my status, success, or distress become secularized? Do I act as though God is not present?

- Am I at peace with the life God has given me?

- Each of us are on a journey. We start out outfitted by God, and then move on. What interruptions are you now facing?

- Perhaps most important, we need to evaluate our lives and see if we have locked God out by refusing to step out of our losses earlier rather than later? Are we living barren lives alone with our suspicions and criticisms, along with a measure of spite towards what God hasn't give to us?

Joseph opened his life to God, accepted the pain, and moved on to regain His trust in God so he could faithfully serve Him and others; he did not allow himself to become preoccupied with his own problems.

God's Standards (Gen 39:7-20)

We need to be willing to live by God's standards. Trust the Lord that His way is always best.

The second requirement to developing integrity is to adopt God's standards. Those who carry out their duties in spite of inconveniences and challenges are making a bold statement about what they believe and the strength of their belief.

7 And it came about after these events that his master's wife looked with desire at Joseph, and she said, "Lie with me." 8 But he refused and said to his master's wife, "Behold, with me here, my master does not concern himself with anything in the house, and he has put all that he owns in my charge. 9 "There is no one greater in this house than I, and he has withheld nothing from me except you, because you are his wife. How then could I do this great evil, and sin against God?" 10 And it came about as she spoke to Joseph day after day, that he did not listen to her to lie beside her, or be with her. 11 Now it happened one day that he went into the house to do his work, and none of the men of the household was there inside. 12 And she caught him by his garment, saying, "Lie with me!" And he left his garment in her hand and fled, and went outside.

13 When she saw that he had left his garment in her hand, and had fled outside, 14 she called to the men of her household, and said to them, "See, he has brought in a Hebrew to us to make sport of us; he came in to me to lie with me, and I screamed. 15 "And it came about when he heard that I raised my voice and screamed, that he left his garment beside me and fled, and went outside."

16 So she left his garment beside her until his master came home. 17 Then she spoke to him with these words, "The Hebrew slave,

whom you brought to us, came in to me to make sport of me; 18 and it happened as I raised my voice and screamed, that he left his garment beside me and fled outside." 19 Now it came about when his master heard the words of his wife, which she spoke to him, saying, "This is what your slave did to me," that his anger burned. 20 So Joseph's master took him and put him into the jail, the place where the king's prisoners were confined; and he was there in the jail (Gen 39:7-20).

The Dangerous Circumstances (Gen 39:7-23)

Verse six serves as a special transition that moves us from focusing on Joseph's success to his temptation, "Now Joseph was handsome in form and appearance." Joseph not only had wit and charm, but physique and looks.

Many people wish they could be like someone else–taller, stronger, more handsome, cleverer, etc. Behind discontentment and greed lie specific dangers associated with enhanced gifting like beauty, wealth, and power. Success in a person's life is the opportunity that temptation looks to seize.

The Temptation (Gen 39:7)

• "After these events" (39:7)

Joseph didn't look attractive until he gained the trust of everyone, or did he? Before, he was just a handyman, but now he was a top manager (though still a slave). People are willing to break moral boundaries and cross castes with those they think are rich, clever, charming, etc. Something connected to Joseph's high position made Potiphar's wife rethink her relationship with him. Regular interaction and meetings compounded the problem. The timing was strategic for the evil one. God had a plan, but so did the evil one.

The most dangerous temptations lurch at us when we are doing our best. It is much more difficult to remain stable on a pinnacle, as opposed to a broad plateau. Joseph was lifted high up in responsibility in a fairly short time. This was a ripe time for the luring touch of glory, vanity, beauty, giftedness, authority, etc. to become reasons to justify special privilege.

- "His master's wife looked with desire at Joseph, and she said, 'Lie with me'" (39:7).

Although Joseph's temptation was associated with his position, etc., its underbelly was sexual in character. Sexual temptation starts with being discontent with what God has given and defined. Here, the no-name woman, though having an important position in society, was not engaged in serving her husband. It does not matter what the reason is, right? He might no longer have interest in her, or he may be having affairs with several other women. But, at the same time, Potiphar could just as easily been fully devoted to his wife. Even when we think of the worst scenario for Potiphar's wife, none of them legitimize the unleashing of her desire for Joseph.

Her motives are hidden, but she did not shield her interest in Joseph. She said in her lustful voice, "Come lie with me," clearly indicating her sensual desires.

(1) RECOGNITION OF SUSCEPTIBILITY
(2) CLEAR IDENTIFICATION OF EVIL
(3) ADOPT GOD'S PERSPECTIVE (TRUTH)

Expressed desire is different from hidden desires. When hidden, the person subtlety plans for times to meet, etc., but when openly expressed, the person's purpose, plan, and vulnerability are open to the minds of others. She has the potential to seduce him because she has already revealed her nefarious purpose. When such things are expressed, the power of the temptation increases its pull on the heart, mind, and values.

Battling with Temptation (Gen 39:8-9)

But he refused and said to his master's wife, "Behold, with me here, my master does not concern himself with anything in the house, and he has put all that he owns in my charge. 9 "There is no one greater in this house than I, and he has withheld nothing from me except you, because you are his wife. How then could I do this great evil, and sin against God?" (Gen 39:8-9)

Joseph verbally refused his master's wife and importantly established the proper protocol. He does this in several lines of reasoning, which he probably had to again and again work through to protect his fleshly inclination to consider her offer.

> **Do we believe God's way is best?**
>
> **All the time?**

These reasons would become his wall of sanity against her unfailing sensual calls to his flesh.

#1 Under ownership

"My master" indicates that he kept his position in mind. He has a master that controls his life. Not all of us can use this excuse, but Joseph did, and it helped define lines. These words pronounced his identity as a mere slave so that she might be less inclined to pursue him as a slave.

#2 Matter of loyalty

Joseph places a lot of emphasis on the trust his master had in him. We gain a lot of insight here into what made Joseph so successful–it was his commitment to faithfully serve others. This potential affair was off limits because of his loyalty to the husband. He clearly sets the reasons out before her to hinder her pursuit and give him clear reason to steer clear of embracing this potential affair.

#3 Identifying the evil of immorality

The phrase, "This great evil," clearly declares the evil of taking another's wife as his own, as well as the potential breaking of trust with his master. Even in that society, marriage was held as a binding commitment– "Because you are his wife."

#4 Bringing in God's perspective

"Sin against God" defines the inherent definition of evil by bringing it into the view of his Maker's purpose and design. A successful fight against temptation must recognize adultery as a sin against God. The word sin comes from 'missing the mark' and thus incurs guilt.

He used the general word for God (Elohim) though it is not sure what concept the Egyptian culture understood this term to mean. Were they aware of God as Creator? In any case, Joseph believed it, and his words clearly articulated his viewpoint so she could recognize it. He was unafraid to identify what made him the way he was. Again, he was hoping these words would turn her desires aside. Unfortunately, they did not.

Summary

Joseph highlights the process of gaining integrity. Though we be severely tried even through godly reasoning, we must wholly pursue God's way. This pursuit will involve discerning God's will, rejecting what God rejects, and affirming God's pleasure with our decisions. Integrity cannot be evaluated within oneself because we are made in God's image. We must reflect the Lord, His ways, and His purpose for our lives. (Samson was an example of compromise rather than integrity–Jud 14:7.) Upholding godly standards is so important, and attests as to why failure brings guilt.

True success is built on merging our values with God's principles so that we can clearly identify evil and withstand its onslaught. Joseph displayed his integrity without ever knowing this bedroom temptation scene would be passed on for thousands of years. His reasonings became a firm wall of protection for him.

Application

When our principles are tested, we see whether the decisions we make in life are established upon biblical principles or upon our convenience or preference. Were we simply raised that way? Every person should consciously define his standards and decisions upon the Word of God before temptation comes—not afterwards! This is perhaps the problem many teens face today. They have not matured enough to think through these issues on their own apart from temptation and therefore allow their peers to make poor decisions for them. "Oh, okay. I guess it doesn't matter that much." This approach is quite different from Joseph's response, and often results in sin.

- What are your sexual standards?
- Have you had to battle with sexual temptations? What sort of reasonings went through your mind?
- Do biblical values affect your work ethic? How so?

Handling Ongoing Temptation (Gen 39:10-12)

10 And it came about as she spoke to Joseph day after day, that he did not listen to her to lie beside her, or be with her. 11 Now it happened one day that he went into the house to do his work, and none of the men of the household was there inside. 12 And she caught him by his garment, saying, "Lie with me!" (Gen 39:10-12)

Harassing Temptations

The persisting temptation created a grave problem for Joseph. The text states that she persisted, "day after day." We might not think that God would allow him or us into such a challenging situation, but obviously He does. Though the Lord sometimes does not remove the temptation right away, He will always provide the wherewithal to stand against sin.

By being in her house, she could make the temptation unbearable by suggestive behavior and words. In Joseph's situation, he could not escape it due to his job responsibilities (maybe his desk was located near her) and limitations (as a slave he was told what to do and where to be).

(1) PERSISTENCE (LUST VS. INTEGRITY)
(2) CRISIS: THE **STRONG** INVITATION
(3) FLED OUTSIDE (NO GARMENT)

Ongoing temptation is hard to beat. This scene depicts the earnestness of Joseph in not obliging this woman of her evil plans. The frequency and regularity of the temptation made the seduction more intensive (sexual desires can be very intense!) so that we can more deeply understand Joseph's integrity. Perhaps he said to himself, "She wants me, but I am a faithful steward of all my master's affairs. Adultery is evil. God wants me to wait for His provision of my own wife."

The Overpowering Invitation

She caught him by his garment, saying, "Lie with me!" Some suggest that Joseph got a little too close to her, perhaps even allowed the tempter's breath and kisses to touch him. It is possible, but not at all a necessary conclusion from an examination of the biblical texts.

He certainly was tempted when she grabbed his robes with her hand, but to say that he got too close to her body on his own seems to go against the meaning of the passage. She was the seductress. She could easily catch his flowing garments by going up to him, holding his garment and drawing his body next to hers.

> The question is not if we will be tempted
> but when, how, and the ongoing nature
> of the temptation.

Saying No to Sin (Gen 39:12-19)

And he left his garment in her hand and fled, and went outside. 13 When she saw that he had left his garment in her hand, and had fled outside, 14 she called to the men of her household, and said to them, "See, he has brought in a Hebrew to us to make sport of us; he came in to me to lie with me, and I screamed. 15 "And it came about when he heard that I raised my voice and screamed, that he left his garment beside me and fled, and went outside." So she left his garment beside her until his master came home.

17 Then she spoke to him with these words, "The Hebrew slave, whom you brought to us, came in to me to make sport of me; 18 and it happened as I raised my voice and screamed, that he left his garment beside me and fled outside." 19 Now it came about when his master heard the words of his wife, which she spoke to him, saying, "This is what your slave did to me," that his anger burned (Gen 39:12-19).

In today's world, we find people are willing to use other people's money and connections, and sexual encounters to gain something 'better'. Surely the temptation was not only of being sexually attracted, but the promises that were attached to such a relationship. He vehemently rejected these desires.

"Run for your life" (39:12)

And he left his garment in her hand and fled, and went outside." Evidently, the only way out of her grip and touch was to allow her to hold onto his outer clothes while he wiggled out of his robe. It makes perfect sense. I remember getting out of certain wrestling holds as a boy by slipping my arm out of my sleeve. The technique worked for Joseph, but it brought serious consequences. In the end he ran and got out of the house.

It seems that this incident shaped the Apostle Paul's words, "No temptation has overtaken you but such as is common to man; and God is faithful, who will not allow you to be tempted beyond what you are able, but with the temptation will provide the way of escape also, that you may be able to endure it" (1 Cor 10:13). It is great to know that by God's grace we can persevere. Even when things look bad and get increasingly worse, God will provide a way out. He assuringly promises to give grace to withstand temptation

At a certain point, the form of temptation might break out into another form, which can overpower one's mind, like in Joseph's case. We need to resist, but that might mean that a more physical break away is important in order to remove us from that context. It just might be that God answered Joseph's prayer to remove him from temptation by allowing this false accusation to rise up.

Her Unconvincing Story (39:13-16)

"And it came about when he heard that I raised my voice and screamed, that he left his garment beside me and fled, and went outside."

She changed the story. Did he not flee before she screamed? She lied. Evidently, after he ran off, she came up with this plot and screamed, causing the servants to come. But he was long gone. Her pride and anger rose higher than her desire to have him. She spited his resilience.

The accusation, though untrue and not very probable, was enough to get him in trouble. Remember, a slave would never approach a free woman. Furthermore, why did she scream after he had taken off his robe? Should she not have screamed beforehand? She admitted to allowing him to be too close to her.

The evidence was not substantial, but when it comes to defending one's wife against a slave, surely the slave must go. Joseph had to face the consequence of his integrity. The consequences for Joseph were not good, at least in the temporary sense.

Unresolved Questions (39:19)

Something doesn't match.

> "That his anger burned. So Joseph's master took him and put him into the jail, the place where the king's prisoners were confined" (39:19-20).

It seems that if Potiphar was angry with Joseph, he would have had him tortured and killed. That penalty is fitting for a slave attempting to rape the master's wife.

A more likely scenario is that Potiphar was angry with his wife for messing up his arrangement with a faithful servant. The text does not clarify who Potiphar's anger was against. Note how Joseph was put in a special jail for the king's prisoners rather than one for slaves. Potiphar was probably close to the one in charge of this royal prison. As we examine the charges and the final punishment, it seems that Potiphar trusted Joseph more than his wife.

God's Way is Best

The temptation scene was so elaborately drawn for us so that we could see that it was God, not man, who helped Joseph through this situation. There was something more, though, and that was his faith. Joseph was known for godliness, but this was an outcome of his faith in God rather than a natural trait. He wanted God's blessing more than anything in life. Joseph treasured what the Lord prized.

When we are convinced that God's blessing is what we want, then we will recklessly pursue it without a concern for what the world counts as important. Joseph was punished because he refrained from compromise, but it was much better than being caught in bed as an adulterer. Certainly giving in to her desires would have been horrible, not only with respect to what would happen when he was finally caught, but in light of missing out on God's special plan through Joseph that unfolds as Genesis continues.

The world would describe this opportunity at fulfillment as love and good. Some would assert that Joseph deserved it. He worked hard. These manipulative thoughts are straight from the devil's. God's blessings are always better, so we should never take short-cuts. Instead as we trust God with what He gives us, we will find contentment. He does not give us that which belongs to others. Remember the tenth commandment? This is a command we often forget, "Do not desire that which belongs to others..." (Exodus 20:17).

Pursuing integrity is the way we pursue God. Compromising on our values is a sure way of stepping further and further into unbelief.

In the short term, it looked like faithfulness brought worse results. He got wrongly accused and lost all that God had given. This is not the end, though. We must remind ourselves that what we have at any given instance is not the whole picture. When time provides, we shall see how God remains with Joseph. This adjustment of Joseph's situation is a means to move him closer to the royal staff.

Summary

Joseph encountered many things that he had no control over, not only in his early life but later on. But his sexual desires were something that he did control. They were his, and he chose to use the few things he had, his desires and attitudes, to please God and his master.

Application

- Never try to displace the responsibility of your actions by saying, "I couldn't help it!" Instead, like Joseph, stay firm in prizing faithful service to the Lord.

- There is no doubt that immorality has risen in our society, especially now when women are just as common in the work force as men. We might dismiss the frequency of contact as a factor, but it remains to be a condition that the evil one regularly uses to foster temptation. We often can and should change the frequency we meet up with a certain person by changing friends, classes, transport, chatrooms, or even our home. Do you need to move the place you watch the web because of immorality? Would you mind showing the public what you watch in private?

- What kind of reasoning enables you to withstand lust's power? Are you willing to run? Even if there are consequences to pursuing integrity?

- When temptation came, Joseph hid behind his wall of reasoning each time. What works once can keep working (though it had a point of breakdown when he was brought too close!). The problem is that we do not consistently allow the truth to fully affect us each time. Do you sense your resistance breaking down?

- If one goes by sight rather than clear reasoning, the sight dominates. Once a person looks at a seductive picture, great forces come out in droves, enticing him to look more until reasoning loses its footing.

- Is our behavior predictable because of our character?

- Do we believe God's way is best? All the time?

God's Plan (Gen 39:20-23)

Trust God with life's ups and downs

The third level of trust to live a life of integrity is found in these last verses of Genesis 39, though the same theme continues on into the next chapters. One must come to trust God through all the ups and downs of life if He is to accomplish His purposes through your life. If our trust in His plan fails, then we will not be able to live strong virtuous lives. We will compromise.

> So Joseph's master took him and put him into the jail, the place where the king's prisoners were confined; and he was there in the jail. 21 But the LORD was with Joseph and extended kindness to him, and gave him favor in the sight of the chief jailer. 22 And the chief jailer committed to Joseph's charge all the prisoners who

were in the jail; so that whatever was done there, he was responsible for it. 23 The chief jailer did not supervise anything under Joseph's charge because the LORD was with him; and whatever he did, the LORD made to prosper (Gen 39:20-23).

Several observations from this passage help us affirm God's trustworthiness.

The Prison Sentence (Gen 39:20)

"He was there in the jail." This prison sentence at first sight seems similar to his betrayal and being sold into slavery. He lost everything. He didn't 'deserve it.' In this case, Joseph kept himself pure but ended up being burdened with a prison sentence. Notice that though the Lord had raised Joseph up by allowing his power and status to rise within Potiphar's estate, He then allowed Joseph to lose all that he had gained. Sometimes people suffer for doing the right thing, as in Joseph's case. (Peter differentiates these two kinds of sufferings in 1 Peter 3:16-18.)

Joseph no doubt had a tough time trying to figure out God's plans. On the positive side, Joseph had been removed from temptation and had been placed in a royal jail rather than those other jail houses where he would probably rot to death. God was incorporating this unjust situation into yet a greater plan. Joseph couldn't see it but had to trust God with it. Satan would have us question God's faithfulness by pointing to some isolated difficult circumstance, but the Lord is over all things and wonderfully watches over all our circumstances.

Rediscovering God's Extraordinary Favor

"But the LORD was with Joseph and extended kindness to him, and gave him favor in the sight of the chief jailer" (Gen 39:21). Yahweh was still with Joseph. This is the irony about the whole situation. Just when Joseph might have given up serving God, we find that the Lord begins to turn the situation around again. The worst becomes the best. It is possible that God prompted Potiphar to share with the chief jailer how much God blessed him, but in the end it would again be Joseph's cleverness, attitude, helpfulness, etc. that made everyone rightfully conclude that God was with him.

Trust God with life's ups and downs

Betrayed

w/Pharaoh

Potiphar's

Royal jail

Slave

Forgot him

Falsely accused

DIAGRAM OF JOSEPH'S UPS AND DOWNS

The Lord was With Joseph (Gen 39:23)

"The chief jailer did not supervise anything under Joseph's charge because the LORD was with him; and whatever he did, the LORD made to prosper" (39:23). The pattern is clear. God is doing the same thing He did with Joseph in Potiphar's household (39:5-6). Joseph increasingly gains authority over the king's prisoners. The comments observed here are similar to that above and will not be repeated.

The repetition that "the Lord was with him" and "the Lord made to prosper" are too clear to be avoided. This is the main thrust of the passage. That though Joseph was accused and treated wrongly, he was blessed of the Lord. This blessing is a vindication of his righteousness.

Are you willing to trust God with life's difficulties?

This whole scene was a set up. Joseph could never have understood God's plan for his life by looking at his experiences. Looking back, however, it is all so evident that God used trouble to guide Joseph into the right positions and carefully develop his skills and maturity for a very important position further down the line. The problem Joseph no doubt faced was the cultivation of patience with his unjust circumstances, and keeping a good attitude and trusting God for the best.

When we step back and view Joseph's life with a wider perspective, we will see a mountain and valley pattern. There are the ups and downs of life, the good times and the bad, but when combined together we see God carrying out His creative plan.

Pursuing Integrity

Be faithful where you are!

The patterns can only be seen when we step back from life, which may not happen until we're older. But it takes that faith, especially when we are down on hard times, to live in the belief that God works all things together for good (Romans 8:28). Our trust is only as strong as our confidence that He has everything in control and is specially concerned with our lives.

Life turns from bad to good and back again, but Joseph has the same wonderful, persevering trust. Whether he struggled with feelings of shame, hopelessness, and regret is not known; we only see that he turned his eyes to the Lord, and even with the possibility of those feelings, God again shined through his dark circumstances. While good situations can teach us about God's goodness, we learn much more of His goodness through the difficult situations where we see God seeding an unimaginable amount of goodness in our lives.

Our future is unknown. As we trust our Lord with whatever comes our way, we will be able to gain His peace.

- We will never be able to fully recover what was lost. Accept it and go on in hope and trust.

- God is overseeing your life to accomplish His special plan through you. Trust Him.

- Sexual purity is a place to demonstrate your trust in God's timing and plans.

- Accept life's ups and downs. Be ready for turns and twists. Cling to God's plan not to your hopes.

Application

- What are the twists and turns in your life?

- Trust ushers us into the room of blessing.

- Do you tend to panic? Don't panic when going through difficult times, whether it be that your child is sick, you didn't make it into the school you wanted, lost your job, marriage is not working well, kids aren't adjusting well. Panic reveals unbelief. Every trial is a place for God to display more of His excellent glory and power.

Righteousness and Faith

"The righteous live by faith" (Hab 2:4; Rom 1:17). One cannot be righteous without living by that faith. Faith comes first and righteousness closely follows behind, hand in hand, so to speak. Joseph's faith is made evident by his important life decisions.

Faith comes before blessing. Faith gives us time to show our commitment, which is, in the end, what God richly rewards. Trust in God's faithful care for our lives enables us to live in light of God's special work, even when it does not seem apparent. That same faith allows us that deep-down relentless pursuit of His blessing all while experiencing the many tragic events of our lives. There is a curiosity derived by faith in how God is going to work things out.

We want good marriages, good families, good jobs, nice homes, great friends, right? We can pursue them but only with a willingness to let go of them. God knows our needs and wants. But because we do not understand His plan for us, we cannot assume that the things that others experience is what we should expect to be normal for us. Pursue God's plan and you won't go wrong (Mat 6:33). This is what leads to a life of integrity. Our trust can be maintained all the way through the troublesome times and the good times, rather than just when God is blessing us with good.

Joseph as a Type of Christ

Joseph is a type of Jesus. This is not as clearly taught as others are (such as Jonah). Many things suggest this, including, as was earlier stated in this chapter, his betrayal and sale for the price of a slave.

The pattern that we see here seems to portray the resurrection. Certainly, this pattern is seen, though in a lesser degree, in Isaiah 52:13-53 where the Servant was made to suffer and prosper, "Behold, My servant will prosper, He will be high and lifted up, and greatly exalted" (Isaiah 52:13). Note the connection of God's presence with the One who suffered, "But the LORD was pleased to crush Him, putting Him to grief; If He would render Himself as a guilt offering, He will see His offspring, He will prolong His days, And the good pleasure of the LORD will prosper in His hand" (Isaiah 53:10). This passage certainly hints at the resurrection and gathering His people to Himself. At this point in Genesis, however, the seed is too small to see events like the resurrection depicted.

GENESIS

Genesis 42-47:12
Joseph's Disillusionment

Disillusionment is not a small problem. It happens when we lose perspective. We become ignorant of or doubt the truth. We simply do not know how to interpret any given circumstance. One man, in his fight with God about the existence of suffering and racism said, "A god who can't stop it has no right to my loyalty or my belief." Another said, "God is cruel. I can't believe in Him." We at times all go through periods of confusion. A better understanding of God and this world will help us through these dark times.

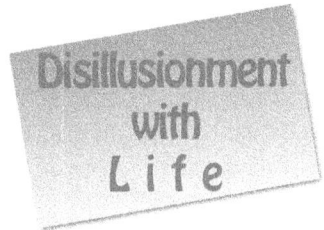

Disillusionment with Life

We need to wait upon God. In His time He will show how He is more just, righteous, and compassionate than ourselves. We can trust Him with our concerns. Meanwhile, we are called to carry out His will to do what is good and loving for this world. We do not give up what is good because we are confused. The extensive story of Joseph helps us deal with disillusionment. Real individuals: Joseph, Jacob, Judah, and the rest of Joseph's brothers all went through very difficult circumstances. It is much easier to understand big topics like suffering on an individual level rather than on a very general and global level.

Joseph's Tests

He sent a man before them, Joseph, [who] was sold as a slave. ...
Until the time that his word came to pass, The word of the LORD
tested him (Psalm 105:17,19).

The psalmist tells us that the "word of the Lord tested him." This is
exactly what we see here in Genesis. Let us note the three tests:

Test of Trust–Betrayal & Abandonment (37)

**Situation: How did Joseph bear the fact that his brothers sold him
and almost killed him?**

Joseph had a few great dreams, but they were dashed to the ground
when his brothers manifested their hatred and jealousy towards him and
sold him off as a slave. God hinted, early in Joseph's life, at the things He
wanted to do, but would Joseph hold onto these words from his dreams
as the seeds of hope that they were?

When going through difficult times in life, are you able to trust God to
fulfill what He wants to accomplish through your life? This is the test.
Would Joseph trust God? There are two options: either a person will
become discouraged and self-focused so that he will get bitter at God
and depressed (and maybe violent). Or, through faith in God's
promises, he will trust God that somehow He will grow that seed of faith
in time.

Joseph did not see his dreams come true until late in life, but when it
came, he was ready. Joseph knew it was his special calling to help the
world and God's people through his wise and kind food program. Do
you trust your life with the Lord? Even in the difficult times? Do you
believe that God can and will use you?

Test of Pride–Extreme Ups and Downs (39-41)

Situation: How does the 'blessed' Joseph deal with successive successes and imprisonments?

Joseph's life had extreme ups and downs. God spoke with him. His father adored him. Then he is almost killed and sold off as a slave. Great blessings were followed by disaster, time after time. He does his best serving Potiphar as a slave, but in the end, in order to preserve his moral purity, he turns his back on sin and is cast into jail. While there, he interprets the cup bearer's dream, but then is forgotten.

In each test he was able to humble himself to his new position, rely on God, and faithfully serve Him. He chose to live in fear of the Almighty God in his given circumstance rather than indulge himself with his master's wife, or party in self-pity. The changing circumstances were painful, but he kept focused on serving God wherever he was cast. Do you think you deserve to be treated nicely but find yourself being treated rudely or unjustly? Joseph found himself in this situation several times.

Test of Compassion– Opportunity for Revenge (42-50)

Situation: How does the powerful Joseph treat his brothers before and after his father dies?

The third test Joseph faces is privilege and power. It is perhaps the most dangerous. To be in a place of privilege and power means you can do what you want in life and few, if any, can hold you back.

What a person does when he is under constraint can be quite different from what he does when he has power and wealth. Power corrupts. Even with all the opportunities for revenge, Joseph stuck firm to his plan. He forgave his evil brothers and was gracious to them. He could have tried to eliminate the painful memories of the past by ridding himself of his brothers and their kin but instead chose to exude God's tender compassion to his needy brothers. Joseph shows great levels of grace, before and after his father's death.

• Forgiving and feeding his brothers before his father died(Gen 42-47)

• Forgiving and blessing his brothers after his father died (Gen 48-50)

This section focuses on the first level of forgiveness seen in Genesis 42-47:12.

The Big Picture (Gen 42-47:12)

Genesis chapters 42-47 sketches out for us the way Joseph revealed himself to his brothers and the guilt they carried for their treacherous act against him many years prior. Through Joseph's careful treatment of his brothers, his gracious and forgiving spirit becomes increasingly apparent with each journey to Egypt, right up to the end of the book. These difficult situations went on and on without any tangible resolution. Years and years went by without any sign of answers. So it is with our lives, which often run into similar confusing situations. When we step back and take a wider look, we will discover that our problems are networked with many other people's problems.

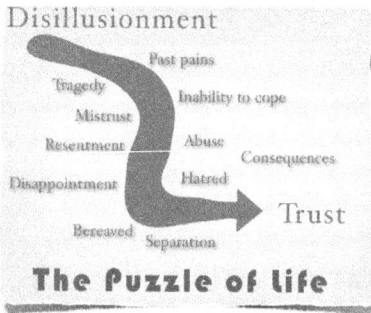

Disillusionment
Past pains
Tragedy   Inability to cope
Mistrust
Resentment   Abuse
Consequences
Disappointment   Hatred
Trust
Bereaved   Separation
The Puzzle of life

These individual problems or crises are like the pieces to a puzzle. Until we know how the piece fits into the whole puzzle, we remain confused. With time we probably find answers, but what about before then? Should we despair? No. If we trust God, He will give us faith that it will work out, and the faith to uphold us until it does so.

And we know that God causes all things to work together for good to those who love God, to those who are called according to His purpose (Romans 8:28).

Our faith enables us to entrust the situation into His hands rather than insist on an explanation before the time is right. Many life lessons can be observed in Genesis 42-47. We will highlight some of the most significant ones, and while we do so, think about your own life. Let's look more carefully at these confusing 'puzzle pieces' and see how in the end they all worked out into a beautiful puzzle of grace.

Fearing Loss (Genesis 42:4)

> But Jacob did not send Joseph's brother Benjamin with his brothers, for he said, "I am afraid that harm may befall him" (Gen 42:4).

An old tragedy engenders thoughts of another possible loss. Jacob was still jittery over Joseph's implied death. Benjamin was all he had left of his beloved wife Rachel, and Jacob still seemed to be oblivious to the special needs of his other sons. He was willing to send his other sons to Egypt, but not Benjamin. Jacob only really loved Rachel. Now that she was gone[92], Benjamin was the only one to console him. Losing him would be tragic. His other sons and God's presence did not comfort him.

Application

What is it that 'makes' your life? What if God takes your friend, spouse, wealth, fame, health, etc. away? When we place our security in things that perish, God will knock them out of position so that we can learn to place our trust in Him, rather than in those idols.

Special Insight (Gen 42:9)

> And Joseph remembered the dreams which he had about them, and said to them, "You are spies; you have come to look at the undefended parts of our land" (Gen 42:9).

---

[92] Rachel died when giving birth to Benjamin soon after Jacob met God at Bethel where he had received the new name of Israel and God's promises. This all happened soon after arriving in Canaan (Gen 35). It seems that this challenge shook Jacob's confidence and brought him into a stage of despair.

When Joseph saw his brothers bow before him, the dreams of his youth returned to his mind. Joseph's new position enabled him to rethink the past bitter treatment that he had received. He no doubt first thought of the dream of the sheaves bowing down to him. His brothers once despised Joseph for telling them about the dreams. It is interesting that Joseph thought about the dreams rather than the old hateful memories.

> And he said to them, "Please listen to this dream which I have had; for behold, we were binding sheaves in the field, and lo, my sheaf rose up and also stood erect; and behold, your sheaves gathered around and bowed down to my sheaf." Then his brothers said to him, "Are you actually going to reign over us? Or are you really going to rule over us?" So they hated him even more for his dreams and for his words (Gen 37:6-8).

Is it possible that Joseph also thought about the other dream too, where even his father and mother would bow down to him, along with his brothers? He might have surmised from this that his parents (only his dad was living) would come and visit him. Joseph perhaps at first did not reveal himself so that he could get to see his brother and father.

Or perhaps with his new authority, Joseph was still deliberating over what he would do with his brothers. Had he by this time forgiven them? If so, why not reveal himself then? Why would he at first put his brothers in jail? We are not sure but recognize that both these things, his longing to see his beloved dad and brother and his ability to bring revenge upon his brothers, were impacting his life.

Application

We are not often sure of God's full will for our lives. What is it that He wants to do through our lives? Sometimes he gives us dreams to shape our own dreams and hopes, but more often than not, He doesn't. But the Lord always reveals enough for us to understand what He has designed us to do. Are you seeking His will? What you have found?

Past Haunting Sins (Gen 42:21)

> Then they said to one another, "Truly we are guilty concerning our brother, because we saw the distress of his soul when he pleaded with us, yet we would not listen; therefore this distress has come upon us (Gen 42:21).

Joseph rightly calculated that his brothers would learn the lesson better if he hid himself from them and manipulated the circumstances a bit. At first, Joseph put all his brothers in jail for three days (Gen 42:17). Later, he changed his mind and had only one imprisoned until they returned with his brother Benjamin to prove their honesty. It is unclear whether he changed his mind upon thinking about his father's concern or further forgave his brothers for their evil to him. In the following verses, Joseph gives his brothers several occasions to think back upon their sins of their past not the least by secretly having the purchase money placed back into their sacks.

Application

We certainly do not understand why some things happen to us, but we would be wise, like Jacob's sons, to reflect on whether what is happening now is because of some sin in the past. Is it possible that God is disciplining you through a difficult situation?

Being Desperate (Gen 43:14)

> And may God Almighty grant you compassion in the sight of the man, that he may release to you your other brother and Benjamin. And as for me, if I am bereaved of my children, I am bereaved (Gen 43:14).

Jacob was quite old. He hated the situation here where he was to give up his self-confidence and wait for what comes. As we think back through the lessons that he has learned in his life, we are forced with Jacob to consider what God is like. Why does the Lord allow these situations to develop in this way? Jacob evidently had not rejected his faith, yet we can see through the loss of his beloved Rachel and Joseph, and now

Simeon who was held in Egypt's prison, that he was battling with depression. But through it all, he had a faint hope that El Shaddai would go on ahead of them in restoring what was left of his family.

Application

Jacob was again brought to his inability to cope with things. Are you the type where you try to avoid the pressures of life just so you can protect the few things you have left? God sometimes tests our hearts to give us opportunities to freely love Him.

Tragic Circumstances (Gen 43:27)

> Then he [Joseph] asked them about their welfare, and said, "Is your old father well, of whom you spoke? Is he still alive?" (43:27).

When we think of Joseph, we often think about the way he overcame all sorts of difficulties, and less rarely meditate upon what he suffered. His brothers rejected him. They plotted to kill him. He was now living only by the grace of some caravan passing by in the desert. Not only was his relationship with his brothers broken, but he was separated from his beloved father. His mother had already died.

It is difficult for those who have not suffered to identify with those who have gone without. There are long times of struggling, where we try to understand why things had to be a certain way. He no doubt questioned, "Why he couldn't grow up with his dad like others?" Instead he was confronted with a brutally evil world. Joseph, now that he knew he father was alive, is now forced to pondering what it means. Will he actually be able to see him again after all these years?

Application

Healing takes place in lots of ways, but especially through our careful reflection upon what we had lost due to our careless and foolish decisions. Have you had a good relationship with your father, or was it cut off because of situations beyond your control? What childhood traumas continue to ensnare your soul?

Genesis 43:30– Tragic separation of two close brothers

> And Joseph hurried out for he was deeply stirred over his brother, and he sought a place to weep; and he entered his chamber and wept there (Gen 43:30).

Benjamin was Joseph's only full brother. The others were half brothers. He had a special affection for Benjamin. Joseph was 17 years old when he was taken as a slave to the Ishmaelites (or Midianites) (Gen 37:2). His brother must have been at least a couple of years behind him (some suggest ten years-old) because he was born as they went into the land of Canaan (Gen 35:16).

Joseph treated Benjamin so much better than his other brothers, serving him five times the portion of food (see also Gen 45:14, 22). Benjamin probably was not part of the group of brothers that betrayed him, but this is not clearly stated.

Application

Sure, Joseph was in charge of the world, but it seems his little brother's presence meant more to him than his position or power. Relationships are precious. Do you treat your siblings well? Do you value those around you or do you tend to take them for granted? What steps do you need to take to restore any broken sibling relationships?

Handling Mistrust (Gen 44:33-34)

> Now, therefore, please let your servant (Judah) remain instead of the lad a slave to my lord, and let the lad go up with his brothers. "For how shall I go up to my father if the lad is not with me, lest I see the evil that would overtake my father?" (Gen 44:33-34)

Note that Jacob trusted Judah but not Reuben, his oldest son. Reuben offered his pledge, but Jacob did not take him up on it (Gen 42:37-38). Perhaps it was because Reuben slept with his father's concubine (Gen

35:22), or because Jacob blamed Reuben for Joseph's death. If we carefully read the account of Genesis 37, we will find that Reuben sought to deliver Joseph out of his brothers' evil plot. He was devastated when he found Joseph missing. Did his brothers ever tell him what happened to him? We do not know. In any case, Jacob might have wrongly assumed Reuben's carelessness when he actually was trying to save Joseph.

> Reuben further said to them, "Shed no blood. Throw him into this pit that is in the wilderness, but do not lay hands on him"--that he might rescue him out of their hands, to restore him to his father (Gen 37:22).

> Now Reuben returned to the pit, and behold, Joseph was not in the pit; so he tore his garments (Gen 37:29).

Jacob trusted Judah a bit more and accepted his offer (Gen 43:8). Judah felt very responsible. This is all the more true after he also had not protected Joseph, even though he saved him from being killed and instead sold him as a slave (Gen 37:26).

Application

It can be hard if we are no longer trusted because of a past failure. Reuben, the oldest in the family, no doubt had the chance to show a change of heart, but let his devotion to his father remain at a low ebb. Perhaps his own guilt over Joseph kept him from facing his father. Do you have any guilt toward your father? Confess it now and clear it up so that your days might be well (Exodus 20:12).

Handling Hatred and Abuse (Gen 45:4-5)

> Then Joseph said to his brothers, "Please come closer to me." And they came closer. And he said, "I am your brother Joseph, whom you sold into Egypt. And now do not be grieved or angry with yourselves, because you sold me here; for God sent me before you to preserve life (Gen 45:4-5).

Joseph could no longer hold back his compassion and love. The lessons that his brothers learned at this point would be on a whole different level. They now had to face the fact that their brother was alive and their deceit revealed for what it was. Joseph, however, noticeably jumps in and halts any grieving or arguing that might start up among his brothers. Instead he tells his brothers how he has seen God's hand at work, *because* of their betrayal.

His statement is remarkable, "God sent me before you to preserve life." By explaining that he was looking at the larger situation, his brothers could begin to find hope that they would not immediately be killed. He had every option to drag this thing out and keep his brothers in suspense and terror, but Joseph had a greater vision for his people. He did not allow personal hatred to take over his heart, but instead he focused on the mission that God had sent him on. Joseph forgave his brothers of their treacherous treatment.

Application

Most people never have the chance at revenge. Joseph did, but he did not consider paying his brothers back for their evil. Upon mentioning who he was, he immediately told them how God used the situation for a greater purpose. He cleared the hidden threats that could have stood behind the scenes. Are your revengeful? Do you desire to get back at another person? Put it aside. Forgive. Fix your heart on doing God's glorious will. Share your new way of handling the situation to those who fear your revenge.

Learning God's Lessons (Gen 45:26-27)

> And they told him, saying, "Joseph is still alive, and indeed he is ruler over all the land of Egypt." But he was stunned, for he did not believe them. When they told him all the words of Joseph that he had spoken to them, and when he saw the wagons that Joseph had sent to carry him, the spirit of their father Jacob revived (Gen 45:26-27).

Jacob was shocked. Joseph's brothers were astonished and terrified. Jacob simply did not believe. He couldn't believe that Joseph was just alive, much less that he was ruler over all Egypt. All the anguish in Jacob's soul refused to come out until he saw the wagons that Joseph had sent from Egypt. His spirit was then revived.

Jacob had once deceived his father Isaac, and was bereft of him. Now it is Jacob's turn to learn the bitterness of losing one's son. Before, he allowed his greed to separate him from his father. Now, Jacob learned how terrible his greed was. It devastated his father-son relationship and in the end his whole family. Now, after many years, the bitter lesson has ended.

Application

Many people forget the tough things that happen in life, but some hardships are never forgotten. God does not forget them either. According to His wise ways, He disciplines us, and uses hard times to shape us. We can, however, trust God to care for these deeply painful memories. We cannot change the events, but we can change how we perceive them and our response to them by trusting Him and enduring the consequences. Is there something deeply troubling you? Turn it over to God to handle. Seek what lessons might be learned. Perhaps the duration of the discipline will be shortened.

Disappointment and Disillusionment (Gen 46:1-4)

So Israel set out with all that he had, and came to Beersheba, and offered sacrifices to the God of his father Isaac. And God spoke to Israel in visions of the night and said, "Jacob, Jacob." And he said, "Here I am." And He said, "I am God, the God of your father; do not be afraid to go down to Egypt, for I will make you a great nation there. "I will go down with you to Egypt, and I will also surely bring you up again; and Joseph will close your eyes" (Gen 46:1-4).

Israel (i.e. Jacob) returned to God. He deliberately went back to Beersheba. Beersheba was where he had originally sinned against Isaac his father (Gen 28:10). Beersheba was the center of most of Abraham's activities (Gen 26:23). Not only was Beersheba the place God spoke to Abraham, but the place he lived, made reconciliation with God, and offered sacrifices to God.

An additional life lesson can be learned here. The question is, "Why does it take so long for us to return to God?" "Why do we have to go through difficult situations before we wake up?" The answer is short, "We simply do not trust Him." Trust would have enabled us to believe that He had a larger mission that was only able to be accomplished on the back of small troubles (pieces of the puzzle) that shape us in life.

If wrestling with the angel was Jacob's salvation, hearing about Joseph led to his revival. God was real. God had not utterly forsaken him. Jacob trotted back to Beersheba where God had formerly spoken to him.

Application

God is always there, close to us, but sometimes we shut ourselves out from His love and comfort. Jacob faced many life struggles, but he did not turn to God until his son was returned to him, in his old age. Have you grown bitter toward God, or have you withheld your trust of Him with some part of your life? Now is the time to return. And then, like Jacob, you will again hear God speak to you.

Accepting God's Timing (Gen 46:27)

> And the sons of Joseph, who were born to him in Egypt were two; all the persons of the house of Jacob, who came to Egypt, were seventy (Gen 46:27).

Jacob now had a full household. With Simeon and Joseph back in the picture, he suddenly could see how God had greatly blessed him. He had been wounded along the way, but his family (direct descendants, not including those through marriage) was a full seventy in number.

Jacob could finally see how God miraculously and sovereignly was fulfilling his plan. These seventy would become a great nation (Gen 46:3). The full plan did not come into sight until much later when Jacob was 130 years old.

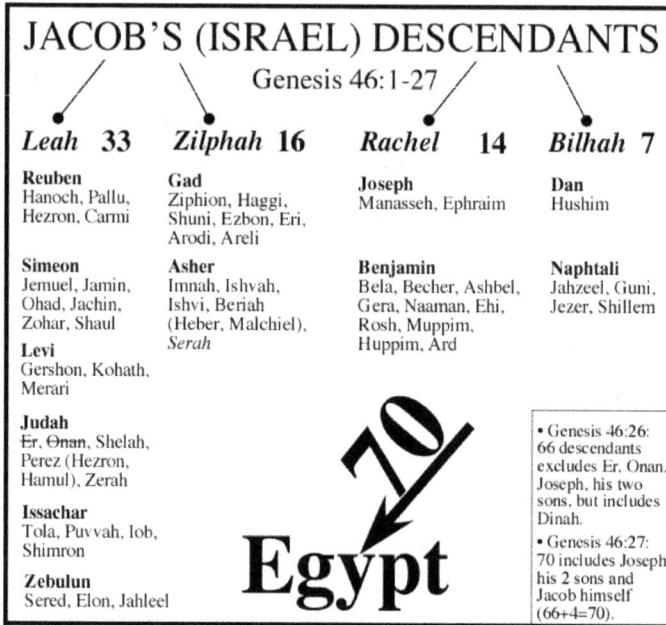

JACOB'S (ISRAEL) DESCENDANTS
Genesis 46:1-27

Leah 33

Zilphah 16

Rachel 14

Bilhah 7

Reuben
Hanoch, Pallu,
Hezron, Carmi

Simeon
Jemuel, Jamin,
Ohad, Jachin,
Zohar, Shaul

Levi
Gershon, Kohath,
Merari

Judah
Er, Onan, Shelah,
Perez (Hezron,
Hamul), Zerah

Issachar
Tola, Puvvah, Iob,
Shimron

Zebulun
Sered, Elon, Jahleel

Gad
Ziphion, Haggi,
Shuni, Ezbon, Eri,
Arodi, Areli

Asher
Imnah, Ishvah,
Ishvi, Beriah
(Heber, Malchiel),
Serah

Joseph
Manasseh, Ephraim

Benjamin
Bela, Becher, Ashbel,
Gera, Naaman, Ehi,
Rosh, Muppim,
Huppim, Ard

Dan
Hushim

Naphtali
Jahzeel, Guni,
Jezer, Shillem

70

Egypt

• Genesis 46:26:
66 descendants
excludes Er, Onan,
Joseph, his two
sons, but includes
Dinah.

• Genesis 46:27:
70 includes Joseph,
his 2 sons and
Jacob himself
(66+4=70).

CHART OF JACOB'S DESCENDANTS (GENESIS 46:1-27)

Application

If we are going to live a life of faith, we must trust God with His timing in the fulfillment of His intricate plans. Sometimes we do not know the end of his plans until much later like Jacob. Sometimes we do not see it fulfilled during our lifetimes. Do you make your decisions based on what God has done or what He has promised to do?

Seeking God's Best (Gen 47:10-11)

And Jacob blessed Pharaoh, and went out from his presence. So Joseph settled his father and his brothers, and gave them a possession in the land of Egypt, in the best of the land, in the land of Rameses, as Pharaoh had ordered (Gen 47:10-11).

The pinnacle of Jacob's life was when he blessed Pharaoh. Here was this little deceiver who once liked to hang around his mother at home, now in Egypt blessing the greatest man on earth. It is incredible. God raised up a sinner to be the vessel of His glorious grace to the world. This is the same story we read in the New Testament when God chooses sinful people to join Him in His great plan of righteousness throughout the world. This is a picture of God's extraordinary grace.

Application

Are you ready? God wants to bring the riches of His grace into the world through your life. Open your life and shine. God is ready to use you. Just be careful to obey so that you will not have to suffer as many difficult training sessions as Jacob.

Conclusion

Disillusioned men and women will often rail against God. They see suffering and injustice. They accuse God of powerlessness, lack of compassion and even injustice. These opponents of the Lord are desperately trying to resolve their inner problems, but these kind of 'solutions' do not bring them any closer to an answer. Only faith can strengthen our relationships with God in these trying times.

Puzzle Pieces

God alone has the answers and will reveal them in the end. The Lord prides Himself in the very things man accuses God of not having: omnipotence, sovereignty, compassion, and true justice. The solution for us is to wait for God to unwind the story.

Can we explain away the way Job was stripped of his wealth and family? Can we happily tell others how Daniel was made an orphan, eunuch, and shipped far away from all that was familiar? Can we comfort Joseph in the midst of his trials that there was a greater reason for his brothers' desire to kill him and separate him from his beloved father? These are explainable if we give them time. God will show Himself Just. The real question is not whether we fully understand what we are going through right now, but whether we can trust God to fully resolve our deep inner anguish from what we and others around us have experienced.

Give it time. Focus on your responsibility in your given situation. Clarify your mission. Trust God. You will, like Joseph, see God's glorious way of resolving the crimes of man. Disillusionment does not come from rightly perceiving things, but by questioning the truth as revealed in God's Word.

Our troubles and crises are pieces of the larger puzzle. We need to trust God according to His promise to work out all things together for good to those who love and serve Him (Romans 8:28). He is faithful, and we need to trust Him in His time to show us the whole puzzle. But even if we do not understand the whole while on earth, and sometimes God does not show us the whole puzzle here (e.g. Abraham did not see God's promises fulfilled, and yet he believed (Hebrews 11:13), we will one day see it all.

Why are these chapters of Joseph (Gen 37-50) in the Bible?

The inside story regarding Joseph and his brothers' lives should delight us. These chapters have all the power of a tremendously stirring movie: violence, seduction, victimization, greed, jealousy, pain, success.

What would we know about these things if it was not left in the Holy Scriptures? The plain and simple fact is, we wouldn't. And yet, we are forced again to ask, "Why are these chapters here?" Why did God put them in? He could have spent the time and precious space by writing more about creation at the beginning of this book where only one or two chapters are used.

There are several answers to this question. Any of them, or several of them together form an answer.

Joseph: a Picture of Jesus

Adapted from Philip Chang and Life Application Study Bible

1. Sent unto his brethren
2. Loved by his father
3. Hated and rejected by his brothers
4. Prophesied his coming glory
5. Endured unjust punishments
6. Sold for pieces of silver
7. Handed over to Gentiles
8. Went to Egypt
9. Made a servant
10. Tempted but did not sin
11. Falsely accused
12. Made no defense
13. Associated with two criminals
14. Showed compassion to others
15. Had divine wisdom
16. Glorified after humility
17. Blessed the world with bread
18. Only source of bread
19. People saved when obedient to him
20. Found favor in the sight of God and man
21. A shepherd for his father's sheep
22. Robes taken from him
23. Bound in chains
24. Placed with two other prisoners, one was saved and the other lost
25. Started public ministry at 30 years old
26. Forgave those who wronged them
27. God turned for good man's horrible evil
28. Given up for dead in order to bring life

- **Prophetical**: Joseph is a type of Jesus: betrayed by brothers, sunken down before being raised up, forgives those who hurt him, etc.

- **Historical**: In order to clearly set the stage for redemption, they had to go into the land in order to be rescued out of it. Otherwise the Book of Exodus makes no sense.

- **Grace**: To illustrate the depth and riches of God's grace and forgiveness that He is willing to give to His undeserving people through Jesus.

- **Faithfulness**: To show His faithfulness in disciplining His own and in fulfilling the dreams and covenants of old.

- **Purity**: To reveal that the blessing of God follows those with integrity and trust in God.

This extended record of Joseph's life, with all the trials and glory, stands as one of the few ancient life characters preserved for us to further set the framework of understanding God, redemption, and our redemptive relationship with God. These last chapters of Genesis beckon us to trust God with the difficulties in life by looking forward to God's way of working through evil for our good, and the good of others through our faithfulness.

Genesis 50:15-26
Essentials of Forgiveness

The opportunity to forgive people is always before us. The joy and freedom we have in life will largely depend on how we forgive.

It is easy to make excuses for not forgiving others, but Jesus clearly told us to forgive as He forgave us. One of scriptures most powerful pictures of forgiveness is found in the Book of Genesis chapters 37-50 in the life of Joseph.

Joseph's troubles are clearly depicted. Any reader might be puzzled to see how a good man faced so many problems. Even more puzzling was how God's presence with Joseph rescued him from those troubles. Many of these troubles are where people were unfaithful or unfair to Joseph, things we often face in life today.

As we study Joseph's interactions with his brothers in Genesis 50:15-26, we will discover four essential lessons about genuine forgiveness, which is essentially treating people as though they never hurt us.

Freely Forgiving (Gen 50:15-19)

You could have taken revenge.

15 When Joseph's brothers saw that their father was dead, they said, "What if Joseph should bear a grudge against us and pay us back in full for all the wrong which we did to him!" 16 So they sent a message to Joseph, saying, "Your father charged before he died, saying, 'Thus you shall say to Joseph, "Please forgive, I beg you, the transgression of your brothers and their sin, for they did you wrong."' And now, please forgive the transgression of the servants of the God of your father. "And Joseph wept when they spoke to him. 18 Then his brothers also came and fell down before him and said, "Behold, we are your servants." 19 But Joseph said to them, "Do not be afraid, for am I in God's place?" (Gen 50:15-19)

Lesson 1: God is the Avenger (Rom 12:19; I Th 5:15; I Pe 4:19)

We all know what these brothers of Joseph were thinking. Without their father alive, Joseph was liable to do anything. They were in deep trouble. Grudges are like that. "What if Joseph should bear a grudge against us and pay us back in full for all the wrong which we did to him!" Grudges and deep bitterness hide away deep in our hearts and minds, sometimes for years, until they surface unexpectedly and accomplish their spiteful work. After all, could you think up a greater evil than what they did to Joseph their own brother?

Joseph's brothers were so fearful of this possibility that they conjured up a lie telling Joseph that His father requested him to forgive them for their sin.

The guilt and blame after all these years was still there. Guilt never goes away unless it is effectively dealt with. The fear of judgment follows one's guilt. This longstanding fear (how many years?) that accompanied them throughout their lives is the reason they lied to Joseph about what their father said. The point is not whether Jacob might have made that statement, but that the brothers stated it. They knew they were guilty and deserved just treatment.

Joseph's response was simply to cry. Why?

Joseph cried because he was deeply grieved at the notion that they still carried that guilt with them, even though he had forgiven them. His brothers never did get over their guilt.

The big problem that Joseph's brothers faced was that they feared man rather than God. The feeling of guilt should cause us to face up to our spiritual responsibility. God wants us to go to Him and find grace and forgiveness in Jesus. We are to trust God for His forgiveness through Christ (1 John 1:9-2:2).

When we do not handle our guilt in a timely manner, it haunts us. Think about how Joseph's brothers could have had a different life if they never sinned against their brother (Gen 37) or, having sinned, rightly went to God to find mercy. We are blessed to find that the scriptures speak so clearly on the ability to find free forgiveness through Jesus Christ. We can be forgiven by humbly asking God to forgive us through Christ Jesus. This is the privilege of being a believer in Christ.

This doesn't mean that Joseph's brothers did not need to apologize to Joseph. If they had, they would have found that Joseph had forgiven them long ago. Joseph, for the longest time, did not have opportunity to meet up with his brothers. Even when meeting with his brothers with the kindness that he did, they were not sure he had completely forgiven them.

Joseph's Steps to Forgiveness

Joseph forgave his brothers in his heart for almost killing him and selling him as a slave even without them asking. This is our first lesson on forgiveness. Joseph freely forgave even before his brothers ever asked. (We do not know whether they asked at all.) We can see Joseph having done this when he first spotted his brothers and spared their lives. The question is how did Joseph do this. Many of us struggle with how we can forgive someone who so deeply hurt us.

The key is this: Joseph knew that God is the avenger. "Joseph said to them, 'Do not be afraid, for am I in God's place?'" (Gen 50:19)

Joseph's job was to forgive those who brought terrible evil into his life. There was no closer relationship than brothers and no greater trouble in life than to be wholly rejected and stripped from the presence of one's precious dad. This act of treachery was simply horrible. But when we recognize the truth that God will carry out the necessary vengeance, we can busy ourselves with loving. Part of this love is forgiving others as needed.

This important truth is repeated through the Old and New Testaments. Revenge is the Lord's, not ours. "Never take your own revenge, beloved, but leave room for the wrath of God, for it is written, "VENGEANCE IS MINE, I WILL REPAY," says the Lord" (Romans 12:19).

This promise for God to rightly account for things in the end brings a certain relief. We do not need to 'take care of things.' And as a result, we are free to do what God wants us to do. We forgive because God forgave us. This is what it means to freely forgive.

Freely forgiving is forgiving people even if they do not ask.

- Have you been deeply scarred by someone's actions? Who? When? What happened?

- Have you ever forgiven someone before they asked? When? How do you know?

Fully Forgiving (Gen 50:20)

You could have taken advantage of those who hurt you.

And as for you, you meant evil against me, but God meant it for good in order to bring about this present result, to preserve many people alive (50:20).

Lesson 2: God's good providence includes even man's malice (Rom 8:28)

We all need to gain a bigger picture of God. The greater the picture, the more true the understanding. We are not trying to paint a romantic or emotive notion of God, because we know that that will not hold up to time. We need an accurate picture of God.

We are thankful that the scriptures provide us this clear perspective of God, which is partly provided by this long passage in Genesis (chapters 37-50). This passage provides an important insight into the nature of God. The Lord graciously helped pull Joseph out of many difficult situations, though we also see that He allowed Joseph to get into them too.

Joseph knew his whole life was under the watch of God. When he looked at the treacherous act that brought him to be far from his father and home, Joseph still could remember that God was in control. (We assume he learned this over his father Jacob's life story and the years of trial he himself experienced.)

Joseph had developed a great faith in God's sovereignty from his own life experience. This teaching of God's full control of events might sound cold to some, but it is foundational for those facing such despicable acts in their personal lives.

As much as we might put our hope in our dreams or the goodness of man, each of us will go through evil times. It is then that we need to trust our Maker's sovereign hand over our lives. Let us closely look at what this practically meant for Joseph.

1. Joseph placed himself under God's leadership.

Power and riches often corrupt because man is not living under God's rule. Joseph had complete power to bring about revenge, but what constrained him? It was only the humbling of his soul to the Lord who was greater than himself. Joseph said, "Am I in God's place?"

> **God's sovereignty includes control over all events or He would not be sovereign.**

2. Joseph could see that all the evil and good were under God's sovereign control.

If there be but one thing that seems to elude God's control, then that one thing will bring us down in worry, fear, and evil.

Joseph saw that God used all the good and bad events to bring about the present result. Individual episodes in our own lives often are not well understood because we're only looking at a piece of the puzzle. We must not demand a full understanding. We, like Joseph, must find hope in God, who assembles the experiences of life to bring about the result that He desires.

God brought it all about, "In order to bring about this present result." Unless God is in full control, He would not be able to bring about all the pieces to His satisfaction. Our full trust comes from commandeering even the parts of life called evil or 'not fair.'

3. God Meant it for Good

Joseph said this exact thing, "God meant it for good." It is hard to understand that a greater good can come from our personal tragedies. In this case, God saw the need to deliver His people from a famine that hadn't happened yet. Joseph, even with the precious dreams from his youth, hardly understood this from the beginning. The dreams only spoke of hope, not the path to reach that glory.

God is always interweaving all things together to accomplish a greater good (Rom 8:28). Notice how God used even the evil of putting Jesus to death to accomplish the redemption of man. There could not be anything more tragic than the death of God's righteous Son, and yet it was God's most fine and precious work, and which will be remembered over and over again into eternity.

Joseph teaches us how to fully forgive. We can only do this when we step back and allow God to make and assemble the pieces the way that He desires. God will judge; we will forgive because we can trust God to care for everything else.

Application

- Can you accept how God can work through your life, even though it might include evil acts?
- If you gained an advantage over those who wrongly treated you, would you humbly forgive them or take revenge?

Friendly Forgiving (Gen 50:21)

You could have ignored them.

"So therefore, do not be afraid; I will provide for you and your little ones." So he comforted them and spoke kindly to them (50:21).

Lesson 3: We have the opportunity to show kindness, even to those who wrong us (Luke 6:7-28).

The third picture of full forgiveness is to show kindness to your enemies. Jesus said to do good to your enemies. "But I say to you who hear, love your enemies, do good to those who hate you, bless those who curse you, pray for those who mistreat you" (Luke 6:27-28).

Forgiveness is a tricky issue. It is usually very difficult to forgive someone who has deeply offended or mistreated us. This is why the Lord gave us clear commands as to what was right to do in those situations. But even after forgiving others, we might still feel a bit resentful or unhappy with others. The evil one knows how to sneak in and agitate us against them, despite the forgiveness we show. We need to break through this problem, and Joseph shows us how.

We are to friendly forgive, meaning we are to show some act of kindness to those we have forgiven. For Joseph it meant to help protect the Israelites and their families. "I will provide for you and your little ones." There is some form of kind action that needs to be done.

I encourage those going through the challenge of forgiveness to simply ask what you can do for that particular person? (Note: I did not say, 'to do for' the person but simply 'to ask to do for' the person!) It might just be to pray that God will shower them with His love and goodness. Whatever the Lord leads you to do, do it.

Joseph brought this whole event to a full climax by displaying a genuine love for his brothers. He comforted and spoke kindly to them (50:21). He did not do it just because he 'had' to.

When we forgive someone, we need to act out that forgiveness. In other words, we are treating them as if they had never needed forgiveness in the first place. We are not forgetting the event. How could Joseph forget it? All those years without his dad! But yes, we treat people as God made them, in His image. In faith we do what we need to do as God expects of us.

Friendly forgiving enables us to focus on the kindness that we need to exercise. Instead of focusing on the wrong, in compassion we must think about their needs and try in some little way to fulfill them.

Application

- Have you completely forgiven someone?
- How have you practically loved someone who has hurt or offended you? List some things you have done.

Forgetful Forgiving (Gen 50:22-26)

You could have nurtured your pain so that you couldn't trust them at all.

22 Now Joseph stayed in Egypt, he and his father's household, and Joseph lived one hundred and ten years. 23 And Joseph saw the third generation of Ephraim's sons; also the sons of Machir, the son of Manasseh, were born on Joseph's knees. 24 And Joseph said to his brothers, "I am about to die, but God will surely take care of you, and bring you up from this land to the land which He promised on oath to Abraham, to Isaac and to Jacob." 25 Then Joseph made the sons of Israel swear, saying, "God will surely take care of you, and you shall carry my bones up from here." 26 So Joseph died at the age of one hundred and ten years; and he was embalmed and placed in a coffin in Egypt (Gen 50:22-26).

Lesson 4: Entrust those who hurt you (Heb 11:22).

The fourth big step is to entrust your hopes on those who purposely hurt you. Joseph had a concern. He oversaw the family's needs, but now he needed his brothers' help. Forgetful forgiving is the fourth picture of complete forgiveness.

Joseph needed to entrust what was very important to those who had earlier offended him. This was the final test of true forgiveness; when the pain and hurt that had happened so long ago lunges at you, shouting, "You can't trust them." "You can do better without them!"

Joseph had every reason to employ the Egyptians to care for his bones, but he wanted to go with the Israelites back to the land of Israel. Because Joseph could trust his brothers, this whole act became a sort of prophecy. The Israelites one day would go back to Israel, and they would take Joseph's bones with them.

> By faith Joseph, when he was dying, made mention of the exodus of the sons of Israel, and gave orders concerning his bones (Heb 11:22).

Some people can act as if they have forgiven someone, but they really haven't. They cannot really trust them. Perhaps your spouse has disappointed you again and again. True forgiveness means that you can treat them as though they never disappointed you.

When the Israelites came out of Egypt many years later, they did bring Joseph's bones back to Israel. What a final picture of what true forgiveness means! This is such a different picture than one where bitter family members gather together at a funeral. Everyone tries to be outwardly polite, but there is deep animosity in their hearts. They can be all dressed up on the outward, but inside they are fuming.

Forgetful forgiving is the last step in giving full forgiveness. In forgetful forgiving, we entrust our hopes on those who purposely try to hurt us. This is the very spirit we see in Jesus, who, after His resurrection, then puts His whole kingdom in the hands of those who denied Him.

Application

- Have you ever forgiven someone to the point that you entrusted yourself into their hands?

Forgiveness should never be put off. Satan is the accuser and he is ever so willing to provide you reasons as to why you shouldn't fully forgive someone. Or even better, he will give you crooked eyes so that you think you have forgiven someone when you really haven't.

Take action now. Follow Joseph's example and see God's extreme grace in your lives and in the lives around you. Remember the four steps! You could have nurtured your pain, preventing yourself from trusting them at all, but instead you surprised yourself and asked them a favor. The bitterness has been fully replaced by love and trust.

Put aside all bitterness and grudges. It is time we all join Joseph's example and transform hatred into love, just as Jesus taught His disciples to do. We are, after all, Jesus' disciples.

Appendix 1: OT English Books in Chronological Order

Old Testament Books
Chronological Order

Old Testament Books
Chronological Order

The Poetical Books

(Job)
Psalms
Proverbs
Ecclesiastes
Song of Songs

Reveals man's inner and outer struggles as he seeks to serve God by observing the Law.

Isaiah
Jeremiah
Lamentations
Hosea
Joel
Amos
Obadiah
Jonah
Micah
Nahum
Habakkuk
Zephaniah

The Prophetical Books

Challenges God's people to rectify themselves according to the Law before judgment comes.

Ezekiel
Daniel

Haggai
Zechariah
Malachi

Before | During | After

Ruth | 1 Chronicles 2 Chronicles | Esther

| J O S H U A | J U D G E S | 1 S A M U E L | 2 S A M U E L | 1 K I N G S | 2 K I N G S | Exile 70 years captivity | E Z R A | N E H E M I A H |

The Historical Books

Details the spiritual growth or failure of God's people according to how they have responded to the Law.

Conquered

Saul David Solomon | **Israel** (north) ⇔ Assyria
United Kingdom | **Judah** (south) | ⇔ Babylon | Exiles Back

360 years | 460 years | 160 years

Job

| G E N E S I S | E X O D U S | L E V I T I C U S | N U M B E R S | D E U T E R O N O M Y |

THE LAW
(Torah)
(Pentateuch)

The Law legally sets up the terms on which man is to respond to the LORD.

Appendix 2: Old Testament Books in the Hebrew Bible

Jesus in
Luke 24:44

".. which were written
... concerning Me."

Old Testament Books — Arrangement in the Hebrew Bible

in the Law of Moses,   *and the Prophets,*   *and the Psalms*

The Law (Torah)	The Prophets (Nebhim)	The Writings (Kethubhim or Hagiographa)
1. Genesis	**A. Former Prophets**	**A. Poetical Books**
2. Exodus	1. Joshua	1. Psalms
3. Leviticus	2. Judges	2. Proverbs
4. Numbers	3. Samuel	3. Job
5. Deuteronomy	4. Kings	
		B. Five Rolls (Megilloth)
	B. Latter Prophets	1. Song of Songs
	1. Isaiah	2. Ruth
	2. Jeremiah	3. Lamentations
	3. Ezekiel	4. Esther
	4. The Twelve	5. Ecclesiastes
		C. Historical Books
		1. Daniel
		2. Ezra-Nehemiah
		3. Chronicles

Possibly organized by the position of the authors.

• **The Law**
  Moses, the distinguished prophet.

• **The Prophets**
  Held the office of prophet.

• **The Writings**
  Had the prophetic gift but not office.

Appendix 3: Geographical Summary of Old Testament

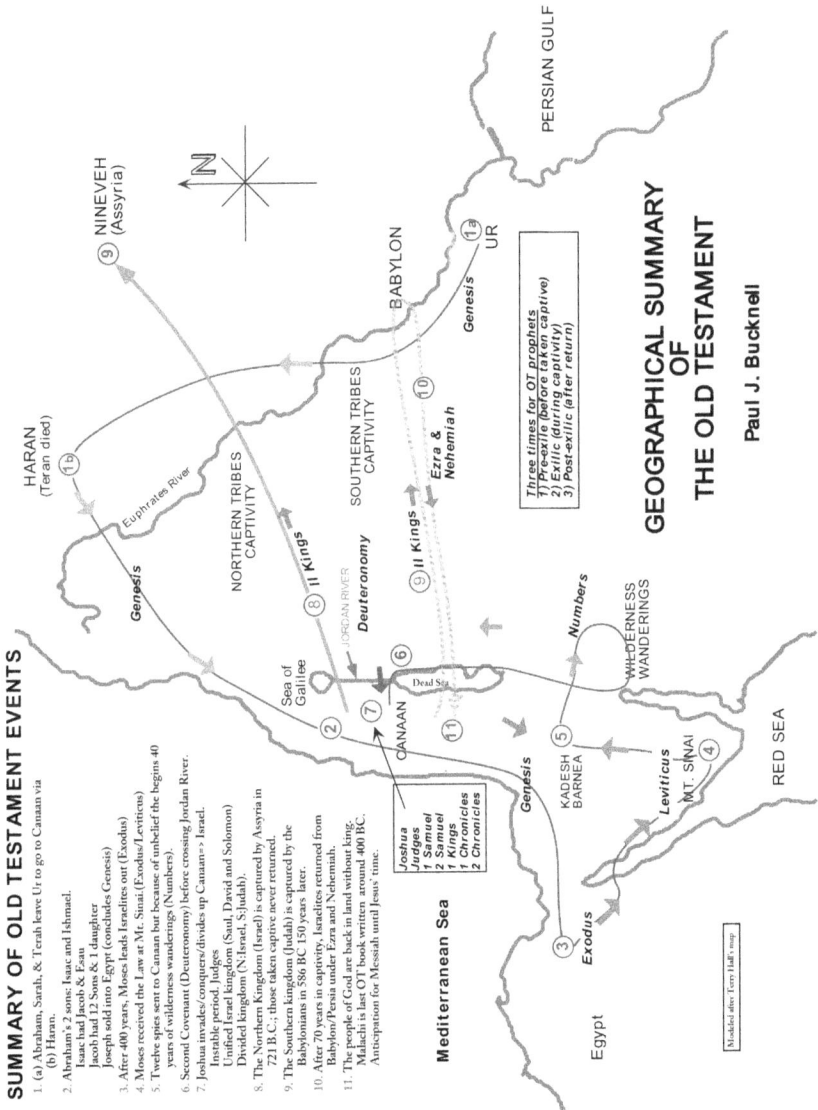

GEOGRAPHICAL SUMMARY OF THE OLD TESTAMENT

Paul J. Bucknell

Three times for OT prophets
1) *Pre-exile (before taken captive)*
2) *Exilic (during captivity)*
3) *Post-exilic (after return)*

Map labels: PERSIAN GULF, NINEVEH (Assyria) ⑨, HARAN (Terah died) ①b, BABYLON, UR ①a, *Genesis*, *Ezra & Nehemiah* ⑩, NORTHERN TRIBES CAPTIVITY, SOUTHERN TRIBES CAPTIVITY, *II Kings* ⑧, *Deuteronomy*, *II Kings* ⑨, Euphrates River, JORDAN RIVER, Sea of Galilee ②, ⑥, ⑦, CANAAN, Dead Sea, ⑪, *Numbers*, WILDERNESS WANDERINGS, KADESH BARNEA ⑤, *Genesis*, *Leviticus*, MT. SINAI ④, RED SEA, *Exodus* ③, Egypt, Mediterranean Sea

Joshua
Judges
1 Samuel
2 Samuel
1 Kings
2 Kings
1 Chronicles
2 Chronicles

Modeled after Terry Hall's map

SUMMARY OF OLD TESTAMENT EVENTS

1. (a) Abraham, Sarah, & Terah leave Ur to go to Canaan via
   (b) Haran.
2. Abraham's 2 sons: Isaac and Ishmael.
   Isaac had Jacob & Esau
   Jacob had 12 Sons & 1 daughter
   Joseph sold into Egypt (concludes Genesis)
3. After 400 years, Moses leads Israelites out (Exodus)
4. Moses received the Law at Mt. Sinai (Exodus/Leviticus).
5. Twelve spies sent to Canaan but because of unbelief the begins 40 years of wilderness wanderings (Numbers).
6. Second Covenant (Deuteronomy) before crossing Jordan River.
7. Joshua invades/conquers/divides up Canaan = Israel.
   Instable period. Judges
   Unified Israel kingdom (Saul, David and Solomon)
   Divided kingdom (N: Israel, S: Judah).
8. The Northern Kingdom (Israel) is captured by Assyria in 721 B.C.; those taken captive never returned.
9. The Southern kingdom (Judah) is captured by the Babylonians in 586 BC 150 years later.
10. After 70 years in captivity, Israelites returned from Babylon/Persia under Ezra and Nehemiah.
11. The people of God are back in land without king. Malachi is last OT book written around 400 BC. Anticipation for Messiah until Jesus' time.

Appendix 4: Genesis 11:28-32
Terah's Descendants

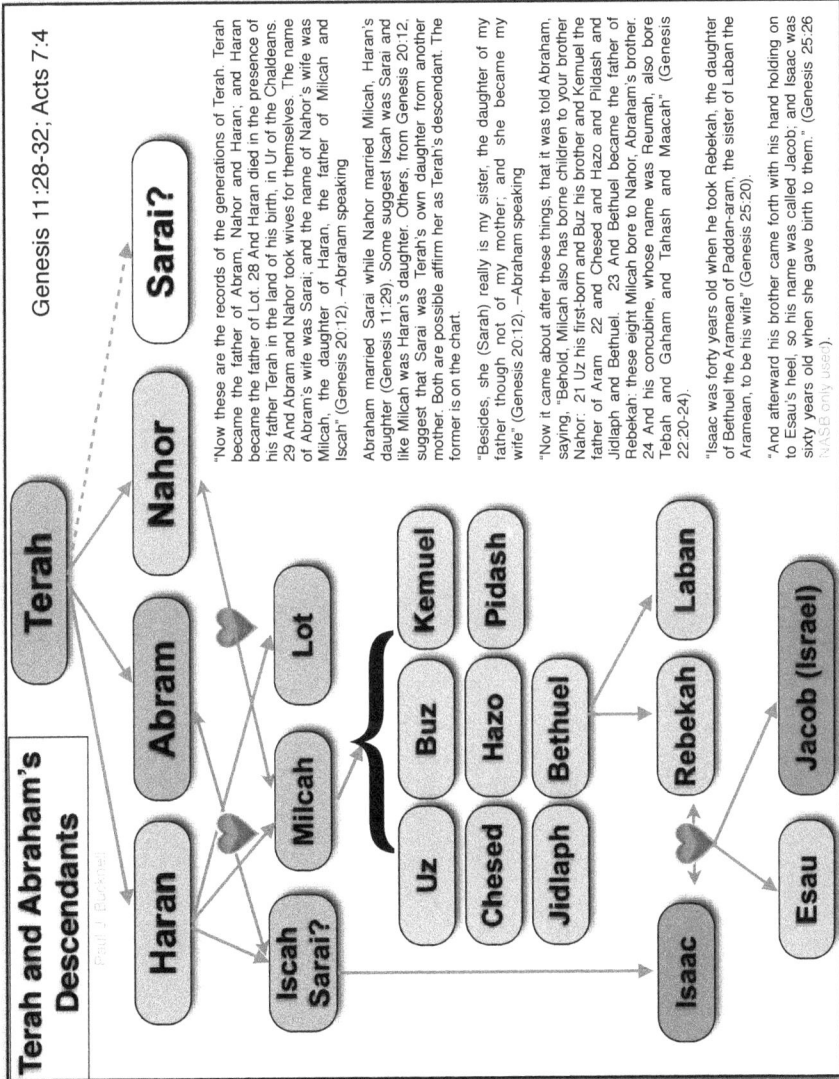

Terah and Abraham's Descendants

Genesis 11:28-32; Acts 7:4

Terah — Haran, Abram, Nahor

Haran — Iscah (Sarai?), Milcah, Lot

Nahor — Milcah

Abram — Sarai?

Milcah — Uz, Buz, Kemuel, Chesed, Hazo, Pidash, Jidlaph, Bethuel

Bethuel — Rebekah, Laban

Isaac + Rebekah — Jacob (Israel), Esau

"Now these are the records of the generations of Terah. Terah became the father of Abram, Nahor and Haran; and Haran became the father of Lot. 28 And Haran died in the presence of his father Terah in the land of his birth, in Ur of the Chaldeans. 29 And Abram and Nahor took wives for themselves. The name of Abram's wife was Sarai; and the name of Nahor's wife was Milcah, the daughter of Haran, the father of Milcah and Iscah" (Genesis 20:12). –Abraham speaking

Abraham married Sarai while Nahor married Milcah, Haran's daughter (Genesis 11:29). Some suggest Iscah was Sarai and like Milcah was Haran's daughter. Others, from Genesis 20:12, suggest that Sarai was Terah's own daughter from another mother. Both are possible affirm her as Terah's descendant. The former is on the chart.

"Besides, she (Sarah) really is my sister, the daughter of my father though not of my mother; and she became my wife" (Genesis 20:12). –Abraham speaking

"Now it came about after these things, that it was told Abraham, saying, "Behold, Milcah also has borne children to your brother Nahor: 21 Uz his first-born and Buz his brother and Kemuel the father of Aram 22 and Chesed and Hazo and Pildash and Jidlaph and Bethuel. 23 And Bethuel became the father of Rebekah; these eight Milcah bore to Nahor, Abraham's brother. 24 And his concubine, whose name was Reumah, also bore Tebah and Gaham and Tahash and Maacah" (Genesis 22:20-24).

"Isaac was forty years old when he took Rebekah, the daughter of Bethuel the Aramean of Paddan-aram, the sister of Laban the Aramean, to be his wife" (Genesis 25:20).

"And afterward his brother came forth with his hand holding on to Esau's heel, so his name was called Jacob; and Isaac was sixty years old when she gave birth to them." (Genesis 25:26 NASB only used).

Paul J. Bucknell

APPENDIX 4: GENESIS 11:28-32
TERAH AND ABRAHAM'S DESCENDANTS

Appendix 5: More on the Author

Rev. Paul J. Bucknell, an active author and international instructor, has written more than twenty books on pertinent Christian training topics. His books are written with the conviction that the more we build our lives on the truth of God's Word, the stronger and more vibrant our faith and lives will be. Paul's international training seminars takes God's Word and powerfully applies His truth to different aspects of Christian living for pastors and Christian leaders. As founder of Biblical Foundations for Freedom, Paul provides printed and digital media along with video training courses and an ongoing website ministry. Paul with his wife, Linda, are still busy raising eight children and presently delight in having four grandchildren.

For more on Paul and Linda and the BFF ministry, check online at :

www.foundationsforfreedom.net